ELECTRIC RUNWAY

ELECTRIC RUNWAY

How Emerging Technologies are Transforming the $3 Trillion Fashion Industry Around the World

AMANDA COSCO

WILEY

Published by John Wiley & Sons, Inc., Hoboken, New Jersey.
Published simultaneously in Canada.

Library of Congress Cataloging-in-Publication Data is Available:

ISBN 9781394267088 (Hardback)
ISBN 9781394267101 (ePDF)
ISBN 9781394267095 (epub)

Cover Design: Wiley
Cover Image: © Artem/stock.adobe.com
Author Photo: Courtesy of the Author

SKY10122446_072125

Contents

	Author's Note	*vii*
	Preface	*ix*
	Introduction	*xix*
Chapter 1:	**The Smartphone**	**1**
Chapter 2:	**The Internet of Things (IoT)**	**35**
Chapter 3:	**Automation**	**67**
Chapter 4:	**Spatial Computing**	**95**
Chapter 5:	**Web 3.0**	**127**
Chapter 6:	**Artificial Intelligence**	**157**
Chapter 7:	**Biotechnology**	**187**
	Conclusion	*203*
	Notes	*211*
	About the Author	*239*
	Index	*241*

Author's Note

This book incorporates **QR codes** to link to multimedia content such as images, videos, and other digital resources. As a deeply visual industry, fashion often requires more than words to capture its essence. The QR codes provide a direct gateway to runway shows, iconic garments, movie clips, and other examples that enrich the concepts discussed in the text.

While scanning the QR codes is completely optional, doing so offers a more immersive experience, allowing readers to engage with the material on a deeper level. Whether or not you choose to interact with the multimedia content, the book stands on its own, ensuring a comprehensive understanding of the topics explored.

These QR codes link to external multimedia content, which I do not own or control. As such, the availability of these links may change over time. If you encounter a broken link, please feel free to email me at amanda@electricrunway.com.

QR codes are powered by Blue Bite Connect, a tool designed for linking physical products to digital experiences. (Full disclosure: Blue Bite is a client of mine. I think their tech is cool, and I talk about them further in Chapter 2 on the Internet of Things.)

QR Code 1 Scan the QR code to make your own QR codes and learn more about Blue Bite Connect.

Preface

I know what it is like to be brought up with unconditional love. In my life, that came from my grandmother.

—André Leon Talley

1555 Dundas Street West, Mississauga, Ontario

Growing up, I spent a lot of time in a tailor shop. My parents were middle class and worked full time, so I spent many evenings after school with my Nonna (Italian for "grandmother") and Bunka (not Italian for anything, but a name we all affectionately adopted after my younger cousin couldn't pronounce "Grandpa").

My grandparents' tailor shop was in the basement of a two-story stucco building on Dundas Street West, just outside Toronto (Figure I.1). They purchased the property in the 1970s, almost two decades before I was born. The building was originally a bank, but they converted it into their small business and built an apartment on top.

Bunka was a tailor, and Nonna was a seamstress. Nonna immigrated to Canada from Italy after World War II, and my grandpa was born in a small northern Ontario town called Sioux Lookout. They met at the Tip Top Tailor Building in Toronto's fashion district in the 1950s when the city was a busy manufacturing hub. Tip Top Tailors still stands today, but the building is now luxury lofts—a sign of the city's gentrification over the years.

Figure I.1 Frank Cosco's at 1555 Dundas Street West—my grandparents' store and home.
Painting by Paul Mack.

My grandfather worked for Simpsons' flagship department store at Queen and Young, managing their made-to-measure department. Nonna worked from home making dresses for wealthier neighbors, until they'd saved enough money to open their store. My grandfather's specialty was men's suits, and he was known as a master fitter. At Simpsons, he made suits for the Toronto Maple Leafs. After opening his shop, his claim to fame was that he made hockey personality Don Cherry's suits. Mr. Cherry was known for his loud personality and even louder taste in patterns. He'd visit the tailor shop with yards of fabric he'd picked out at the upholstery store or Fabricland and commission my grandparents to create custom suits to wear on

Coach's Corner during *Hockey Night in Canada*. Everyone would see Don on TV and talk about his suits.

The tailor shop had a large green table for cutting patterns in the middle of the room. At each end of the table were large cardboard boxes for collecting fabric scraps. My cousin and I would sift through the leftover fabric and make clothes for our Barbies and stuffed animals. Around the perimeter of the tailor shop were four sewing machines and two industrial irons. All day long, the mechanical whirring of the sewing machines and the hissing of the irons created a familiar rhythm that became the soundtrack of my childhood.

Adjacent to the tailor shop was an office where my aunts worked. One had her own business, and the other handled the accounting and paperwork for the family business. Two computers could connect to the internet if you knew exactly how to work the modem and endure the sound of dial-up. I mostly used them to play with Microsoft Paint, an early computer program for making digital drawings.

The retail part of the business was on the main floor of the building. The shop had two display windows that faced the street, which my grandfather would merchandise with the latest men's fashions. Inside the store, there were five mannequins dressed in different suiting styles. They all had brown hair and features that were so lifelike they gave me nightmares. Several bookcases lined the store's perimeter, their shelves filled with thick books that contained swatches of fabric samples. There were three changing rooms with gray fabric walls for customers, and an Interac machine for accepting debit and credit card payments.

A side door led out of the store toward a garage and the upstairs entrance to my grandparents' self-contained apartment. The twenty-second walk from the store to their apartment was the only work-life separation they knew. The apartment had high ceilings, an open-concept kitchen, and a living room perfect for hosting large family gatherings. I fondly remember Christmases, Thanksgivings, and

July BBQs playing card games and Bingo with cousins, aunts and uncles, and second cousins twice removed. Everyone was welcome in Nonna and Bunka's house.

It was here at 1555 Dundas Street West where I first came to understand the world of fashion: the scrappy underworld of the tailor shop, the polished front of the store, and a life built on top of that.

My father worked for the family business until 1990, when he got a job at Harry Rosen, a Canadian luxury men's retailer where he'd work for the next thirty years. He carved out a position for himself as the National Director of Tailored Clothing, where he managed the tailor shops and implemented custom suiting into the business.

My mom sold advertising for print media, first for the local newspaper *Abbey Oaks News,* and later for a glossy publication called *West of the City Magazine*, which Metroland Media owned. Before working in media, my mom worked for Lipton's, another well-known Canadian fashion retailer for women. I still have one of her navy suit jackets from Lipton's. It has oversized gold hardware and shoulder pads, a signature of the late 1980s and early 1990s. My parents were—and still are to this day—the most stylish people I know.

You might think that a girl raised in a family like mine was destined to work in fashion, but that was never my plan. Growing up, I cared less about fashion and more about horses and books. I spent weekends and summers at an equestrian horse farm on Oakville's outskirts, teaching horseback riding and running the stable's summer camp program.

After receiving the English award at my high school graduation, I studied English literature at York University. I took several elective writing courses that I enjoyed so much that by my third year I applied—and was accepted—for an honors program in English and professional writing. At that moment, I knew I didn't just want to read stories—I also wanted to write them.

I earned my master's degree in English literature from Toronto Metropolitan University (formerly Ryerson University). In true Canadian fashion, I wrote my thesis on Margaret Atwood. Specifically, I examined the metaphor of hunger in her seminal novel *The Edible Woman*.

When I graduated from my master's program, I was trying to work in the world of ideas. I knew I wanted to write but wasn't sure what to write about. I spent countless hours attending cultural events in the city—from gallery previews to live music performances—trying to find my entry point into what was becoming a very noisy conversation. It was the 2010s, and everything about the media industry was getting confusing. Newspapers I'd dreamed of writing for were shuttering, and influencer culture was on the rise. I'd moved away from home to live with one of my best friends in Toronto.

While trying to find my path, I earned a living copywriting, designing websites, and helping brands launch on social media. By this time hotels, restaurants, and other companies were beginning to recognize the importance of having a Facebook page and a Twitter presence. (Instagram had just launched, and many companies weren't sure of how to use it yet.)

In the spring of 2014, I was working on a freelance copywriting assignment for a media company called Newsrooms when I stumbled upon a story that would lead to my first big break as a journalist and change my career trajectory forever.

A Cyborg Comes to Town

I was researching the attendees of the Mesh Conference, an upcoming tech and media event, when I first learned about a self-identified cyborg who was coming to Toronto.

Neil Harbisson is an artist and the founder of the Cyborg Institute in Barcelona, an organization that helps people become transhuman. Harbisson is a self-identified cyborg. An antenna is osseointegrated into his head (meaning it's attached to the bone) so that he can hear color. You read that right—so he can *hear* color.

Every color gives off a sound frequency, and Neil's antenna picks up that frequency and delivers this information to him via bone conduction. The antenna is permanent. He doesn't remove it to shower or sleep, and he appears with it in his passport.

QR Code 2 Scan to see a picture of Neil Harbisson, the self-identified cyborg I interviewed for *The Globe and Mail*.

Now, you may be thinking, *why would anyone want an antenna attached to their skull?* Well, it's interesting, considering that Neil was born with a rare visual condition called achromatopsia—total color blindness. He sees everything in grayscale. Imagine being an artist but not being able to see color!

I didn't know all this about Neil then, but I would eventually learn this and much more when I wrote my first national story about him for *The Globe and Mail*. I emailed the technology editor my pitch with the subject line "A cyborg is coming to town." With a subject line like that, I knew he would have to open the email. Within minutes, he got back to me to greenlight the story. It would be my first article for a major news organization.

I interviewed Neil over Zoom before his appearance in Toronto to learn more about his story. I discovered his antenna is called an Eyeborg, and it started as a wearable device he could take on and off.

An earlier iteration of the Eyeborg required him to wear headphones and a computer with a battery pack, which he carried in a backpack. This setup was not ideal, he told me, because the headphones blocked an existing sense (his hearing), and the backpack (which weighed more than ten pounds) was taxing on his body.

In 2010, Neil collaborated with a digital agency to turn the computer he carried into a chip installed in the back of his head. The chip enabled him to hear color through bone conduction. "It's a different feeling than hearing normal sound," he told me.[1]

For Neil, silence is white. A trip to the art gallery is akin to visiting a concert hall. The supermarket sounds like a nightclub. "I can listen to a Picasso and arrange my food into my favorite songs," he explains in his 2012 TED Talk, which has more than a million views.[2] Mr. Harbisson says before the Eyeborg, he would dress to please the eye, but now he dresses to please the ear: a C-major outfit is achieved with canary yellow pants, a peacock blue shirt, and a flamingo pink jacket.

Neil said a secondary effect of wearing the Eyeborg was that regular sounds started to generate color associations. For example, the telephone's ring became a green experience, and the monotone beeps of the BBC felt turquoise. While some would recognize his experience as synesthesia (a neurological phenomenon in which people experience a collision of the senses), it's important to remember that, unlike other synesthetes, Mr. Harbisson's condition is cybernetically introduced.

I became fascinated by Neil's description of the mental union between the software and his brain: "I started to hear electronic sounds in my dreams," he said. "My brain was creating the same response as the software, and I couldn't tell the difference."

For me, Neil represented our deepening relationship with digital technology: We carry our phones around all the time, we're beginning to wear our technology, and eventually we will *become* our technology.

As a part of my research for my *Globe and Mail* story, I connected with Tom Emrich, the founder of We Are Wearables, a growing meetup of wearable technology enthusiasts. The group met monthly at the MaRS Discovery District in Toronto to demo and discuss emerging technology. Emrich told me the meetups started with a few hundred people and grew into more than 120,000 members across the United States and Canada.

Through We Are Wearables, I had the opportunity to meet Steve Mann, the professor and engineer who is often referred to as the father of wearable technology. I also met many other prominent figures in this space, including Ariel Garten, the founder of InteraXon, creators of Muse, a brain-sensing headband. It became clear that Toronto was becoming a hotbed for pioneering wearable technology, experiencing a flurry of activity and curiosity in this space.

As all this was happening, technology appeared on the runway in ways never seen before. The same year I published my article on Nail Harbisson, fashion designer Diane von Furstenberg collaborated with Google and sent models down the runway wearing Google Glass, an early attempt at making smart glasses fashionable. The following year, Intel, the manufacturer of semiconductor chips, was the official sponsor of New York Fashion Week. Everywhere I looked, fashion and technology were coming together in fascinating ways.

#FashionTech Around the World

I started using the hashtag #fashiontech on Twitter to discuss how fashion and technology collided on and off the runway, and I began connecting with like-minded entrepreneurs and creatives from all over the world. I began learning about events and companies that would showcase innovation in both fashion and tech, and—as much as I could—I started showing up in these spaces: I flew to Calgary to meet a team of makers organizing a high-tech, high-fashion runway show; I went to New York to interview robotic dressmaker Anouk Wipprecht; I showed up in San Francisco for the first-ever Silicon Valley Fashion Week; and, after a kind of cosmic chain of events, I ended up at Burning Man taking in some of the most awe-inspiring light-up costumes I'd ever seen.

Eager to keep up with the speed of innovation, I started publishing my findings on my blog, electricrunway.com. Rather than pitching traditional newspapers, which often took three or four weeks from pitch to print, I found it more efficient to self-publish on Electric Runway and have editors buy articles off my blog if they wanted them. I would share my work on Facebook and Twitter, eventually building a small online following.

I remember learning about a conference the Canadian Printable Electronics Industry Association organized in my hometown of Oakville, Ontario. For those unfamiliar with printed electronics, it's a way of making electronic devices by "printing" special inks that contain conductive materials (like silver or carbon) onto flexible surfaces such as plastic, paper, or fabric. This process is similar to printing designs on a T-shirt or paper, but instead of just making something look nice, it creates functional electronic circuits.

I contacted the industry association organizer to see if anyone at the conference would be speaking about wearable technology. He told me the agenda was full, but one of the speakers had dropped out at the last minute, so he offered me the speaking spot. I took it.

Although public speaking in a room of strangers made me anxious, I knew it was essential to building my brand as a thought leader, so I forced myself on stage. After giving my presentation on wearable technology and the future of fashion, the organizer introduced me to the head of PRINSE, an annual printed intelligence industry conference in Oulu, Finland. He asked if I'd be interested in traveling to Finland later that summer to give a similar talk. I immediately said yes.

Shortly after, Lisa Lang invited me to speak at Fashion-Tech Berlin, an arm of PREMIUM exhibitions and one of the leading fashion innovation events in the world. Lang founded Elektrocouture, a pioneering fashion-tech company elevating wearable light into haute couture.

With one speaking engagement at the beginning of June and the next at the beginning of July, I decided to make an adventure of it. I traveled all around Europe to meet some of the fashion-tech entrepreneurs I'd connected with online, interviewing them to update my blog and my podcast, the *Electric Runway Podcast*.

Those talks in different parts of Europe, which I also chronicled on Electric Runway's Instagram account and YouTube channel, kicked off a series of speaking engagements and international delegations worldwide. Before I knew it, I was in Moscow covering Mercedes-Benz Fashion Week Russia and then keynoting at StyleFest PH in Manila. I delivered talks in Estonia, Hong Kong, Bangladesh, Nigeria, and Spain. It seemed that fashion tech was taking off as an intersection of interest.

Each adventure deepened my understanding of fashion tech and my appreciation for the global fashion industry. I discovered early on that fashion tech means different things to different people depending on where you are. In New York, fashion tech means shopping apps and styling tools, which makes sense considering New York is a style and shopping destination. Compare this to a place like Bangladesh, a country primarily known for its garment manufacturing. In Bangladesh, fashion tech means automation and manufacturing technologies. The colloquial definitions of fashion technology fascinated me and enabled me to tell stories that considered contexts like geography, culture, climate, and the economy. Fashion became the lens through which I could see the world of innovation around me.

A decade later, I'm still unraveling the thread I started pulling ten years ago. My curiosity has taken me to places I'd never imagined, leading me to write this book. I can't wait to see where it takes me next.

Introduction

Fashion is not about looking back, it's always about looking forward.

—Anna Wintour

Humans are the only animals that wear clothes. Although hermit crabs will occupy shells for protection, and bowerbirds may decorate their nests to attract a mate, the consistent and deliberate wearing of clothing as a cultural practice is specifically human.

When we first started fastening bear skin stuffed with dry grass to our feet, it was to protect ourselves from the elements. Animal hides provided warmth and helped us survive previously inhospitable environments.

As clothing became our second skin, it allowed us to migrate all over the world, shielding us from insects and extending the hunting season.

Beyond helping us survive, clothing has long been leveraged as a means of communication. So long as we've worn clothes, we've augmented them to signal wealth, social status, and personal identity. In ancient Egypt (3,000 BCE), royalty would wear fine linens embellished with gold thread, beads, and jewelry to symbolize wealth and divinity. In China during the Zhou dynasty (1,046–256 BCE), embroidered motifs signaled rank and position within society and were part of court protocol, and in ancient Mesopotamia (900 BCE), robes of the elite were adorned with tassels and fringes.

Today, the global fashion industry is estimated to be worth 2% of global GDP—approximately $3 trillion dollars—yet we often overlook its impact on culture, the economy, and the planet. Perhaps because fashion is closely associated with aesthetics and the feminine, it's often considered frivolous.

Despite being dismissed as unimportant, fashion touches us all, literally and figuratively. Clothing is the interface between our bodies and the world around us. Every day, we wake up and get dressed, and our clothing choices communicate. Whether we like it or not, what we wear signals our preparation for the weather, our role in society, our allegiances, status, mood, and taste.

On a macroeconomic level, fashion is a global industry, with supply chains that reach every corner of every continent on Earth. Estimates put the number of people employed by the apparel and footwear industry between 75 and 300 million. Our clothing links us to a network of suppliers who toil behind the scenes to bring what we wear into this world.

From an environmental standpoint, the fashion industry is responsible for approximately 8–10% of global carbon emissions—that's more emissions than all international flights and maritime ships combined. Additionally, the industry produces around 92 million tons of waste annually and consumes 79 trillion liters of water per year.

While we may consider fashion and technology separate spheres, they are inextricably intertwined. Binary code, for example, was inspired by the Jacquard loom, an early nineteenth-century invention that revolutionized textile manufacturing. The loom used a series of punch cards to control fabric weaving patterns. Each punched card represented a series of instructions, much like how binary code in computers represents data through a sequence of ones and zeros. Charles Babbage, known as the "father of the computer," drew on the concept of punch cards for his early computing machine, the analytical engine.

As technology develops, it impacts fashion design and pushes the limits of what's possible on and off the runway. 3D printing, for example, allows designers like Iris van Herpen to create innovative structures with lightweight materials that would otherwise be impossible.

This book looks at technological evolution through the lens of fashion. It takes place at the crossroads of two seemingly opposite industries that have evolved in tandem since the Industrial Revolution. My goal with this book is to combine my boots-on-the-ground experience with my research to synthesize a decade-long career reporting on fashion innovation around the world.

I've interviewed hundreds of makers, founders, designers, CEOs, and entrepreneurs to write this book. I've gathered stories from every stage of the fashion supply chain across fifteen countries, from garment factories in Bangladesh to the front row at New York Fashion Week. Sometimes it was glamorous—like flying first class to Manila and staying at a luxury hotel for a speaking engagement. Other times, it was the opposite of glamorous—like throwing up on the roadside in Dhaka, sick from the food, the air, and the dizzying traffic.

I have a complicated relationship with fashion. At once, it's my way of expressing myself and putting my best foot forward in the world. An outfit offers the possibility of stepping into another personhood, if just for a night. After all, it is the magic slippers that turn Cinderella into a princess.

I remember exploring my mom's closet as a young girl (and let's be honest, even as an adult) with wonder and excitement at the treasures inside—all the people she'd been, and all the people *I could be* while wearing her clothes. My dad always said if you want something in life (a job, for example), you must first dress the part. It will change how you show up in the world, how people treat you, and your self-perception. In this way, fashion is a magical gateway, like a wardrobe that leads to a Narnia of possibilities.

At the same time, clothing takes up a disproportionate amount of space in my head, in my apartment, and on my bank statements. Like many of us, I'm guilty of chasing trends, coveting labels, and purchasing fast fashion.

I've always been an early adopter of technology. I was the first kid in my high school class to have a cell phone. I saved up money from working at the grocery store and on a horse farm to buy a Motorola V2288E. I was also the first kid to bring a laptop to school. I don't remember the model, but it was a brick, and it was so distracting in tenth grade that my teacher told me to put it away. Growing up in the 1990s with an older brother who loved video games, we always had the latest Nintendo and PlayStation consoles. In the early 2000s, I looked up to Paris Hilton, who simultaneously made me want UGG boots and a flip cellphone.

I wrote this book because I'm fascinated by internet culture and modern media. I love technology and fashion but struggle with my relationship to consumerism. I'm also concerned about the future of our planet and its people.

As I write this, children in the Democratic Republic of Congo are slaving in subhuman conditions to mine for the materials used to power our smartphones. Scientists have found one in five items sold for toddlers by ultra-fast fashion companies contain elevated levels of chemicals like lead.

At the same time, it seems we could be on the precipice of something else. A UK-based startup called PACT has just developed Oval, a biomaterial made from natural collagen that's supple and flexible like leather. It's 100% traceable and free of plastics and harsh chemicals. Italian luxury house Prada is collaborating with Axiom Space to design Extravehicular Mobility Units—spacesuits—for the 2026 moon mission. Yes, *the astronauts will wear Prada*.

Fashion and technology are both challenging yet transformative industries. This book takes on the task of untangling their complexities and celebrating their possibilities, leading us toward a deeper understanding of where technology can drive us forward—and where we need radical change. With greater understanding, we gain the power to shape a better future.

Chapter 1

The Smartphone

And Its Killer App, Social Media

The future is already here—it's just not evenly distributed.

—William Gibson

From the Outside Looking in: Nigeria, November 2022

It was my first time in Africa, and the sun was hot on my skin. This was the closest I'd ever been to the equator, and I was used to a different latitude. Standing on the airport tarmac at the Murtala Muhammed International Airport in Lagos, I was already sticky from the heat. The sky was blue and relatively cloudless, and palm trees lined the streets. I had flown more than seventeen hours on two connecting flights to attend GTCO Fashion Weekend, an event hosted by Guaranty Trust Bank, one of Nigeria's most prominent multinational financial institutions.

Founded in 2016, GTCO Fashion Weekend is a consumer-focused fair and business platform designed to showcase the best of Africa's fashion to a global audience. The event includes master classes taught by international fashion industry experts. For their 2022 edition, the organizers invited me to give a talk on the key technologies transforming the future of fashion.

It was more than an hour's drive from the airport to Victoria Island and the Wheatbaker Hotel, which would be my home for the next few days. As we slowed through traffic, dozens of street vendors with portable stands weaved between the moving cars, selling everything from corn on the cob to phone cables. Nigeria was the only place I'd ever visited where you could buy almost anything in gridlock. Along the roadside, merchants cooked hot meals in large pots over open flames and sold them to pedestrian passersby for 300 naira (about thirty-four cents).

For Nigerians, selling is a way of life. Street vending accounts for over 70% of urban employment in Nigeria,[1] and there are 42 million small and medium enterprises, accounting for 90% of businesses in the region.[2] The country is still dominated by cash, but that's quickly changing. According to the McKinsey Global Payments Map, Nigeria is expected to experience significant growth in mobile payments in the coming years.

My chaperone was a young woman named Tolu Aribisala. In addition to being a part-time fashion designer and influencer, she was also the brand and communications manager for Squad, a payment solutions subsidiary of the bank. Squad offers entrepreneurs the digital tools to start and grow their businesses, like payment links and point-of-sale solutions for accepting mobile money transfers. Squad's North American counterpart would be Square, a startup founded in San Francisco in 2009 by Jack Dorsey, the co-founder of Twitter. Dorsey came up with the idea for Square when his friend, a glassblower, lost out on an art sale because he couldn't accept payment via credit card. That's when Dorsey and his co-founder, Jim McKelvey, developed a credit card reader that plugged into the audio jack of mobile devices. Square enabled merchants of every size to turn their smartphones into a point-of-sale system. Dorsey was one of the first entrepreneurs whose ventures linked real-time connection, social media, and the need for mobile payment solutions. Squad, like Square, is an enabling technology that makes digital payments reliable, secure, and affordable to sellers of all kinds.

"What the PC was for the advanced world, the mobile phone became for Africa," Adeyemi Atanda tells me.[3] He's a digital payment strategist based in Nigeria and the chief marketing officer for Squad. Ten years ago, he says, mobile payments were SMS-based and accounted for 2–5% of small-ticket transactions. Today, about 70–80% of transactions are mobile-based.

After we'd settled into the hotel, my driver took me to the venue where I would deliver my talk the following day. It was in a neighborhood called Oniru, which consists of a mix of residential and commercial buildings bordered by the Atlantic Ocean. At first I was struck by the building's size. I was accustomed to fashion conferences in Toronto or San Francisco, with fifty or a few hundred people in attendance. GTCO Fashion Weekend would host more than 250,000 visitors from 13 different countries over two days. The scale makes sense, considering Nigeria is the most populous country in Africa, and Lagos alone is home to more than 15 million people. By comparison, that's about twice the population of New York packed into a city the size of Rhode Island.

On opening day for GTCO Fashion Weekend, the buzz was palpable. There were just as many people outside the official venue as inside. Influencers posed for photos on the large lot outside the site, while vloggers spoke with attendees in street-style interviews. Women wore their Sunday best; one on-camera personality donned a bright orange asymmetric dress with a matching fascinator. A crew of young men all flaunted their own personal style; one of them wore black overalls so low they exposed his nipples, which were covered with black tape to create an X-mark over them, like homemade pasties. In contrast, one of his friends wore a three-piece suit, even though it was more than 90 degrees Fahrenheit outside. Everyone was young and full of life (in fact, 70% of the population in Nigeria is under the age of 30).

A shopper at heart, I delighted in browsing the rows of retail exhibitions. GTCO Fashion Weekend was just as much a marketplace as a business conference, with hundreds of vendors selling everything from dresses and accessories to hair and fabric. There were feathers, sequins, and neon—sometimes all on the same dress. I felt as if Nigerian clothes might be a bit flashy for my liking, but perhaps that's because I was so steeped in the normcore[4] that had taken over North American fashion. I'd soon learn that Nigerian style is a lot like Nigerian food: spicy and not at all boring.

Every vendor I spoke with told me Instagram is the number-one technology transforming their business. Although the social media application launched in Nigeria in 2010, it didn't take off until a few years later when it was rolled out on Android, which is much more widely used in West Africa.[5] While internet penetration has been slower in Nigeria compared to North America, the country has experienced hockey stick growth in the past twenty years, especially with the introduction of 5G in the latter half of 2022, which happened to be right when I was visiting.

This would explain why visiting Nigeria in 2022 was like stepping back in time and revisiting North America in the early 2010s: Influencer culture was on the rise, and social media was opening up new revenue opportunities for entrepreneurs and enterprises. Small shops were now digital storefronts, launching Nigerian businesses from marketplace setups to global e-commerce startups. It was an up-close look at the impact of an emerging technology on society, but now I was seeing it as an outsider looking in, and this time it was on a scale I'd never seen before.

Like the rest of the world, Nigeria experienced a boom in electronic payments in the wake of the COVID-19 pandemic, with online commerce growing 40% during lockdowns.[6] Now it was on the brink of something else entirely, with a new generation of socially savvy entrepreneurs coming up who were keen, confident, and more connected than ever before.

How Technologies Change Us: An Information Renaissance

The introduction of new technologies profoundly impacts a society—impacts that often can't be fully measured and accounted for until years, sometimes decades later. As American historian Elizabeth Eisenstein points out, when the printing press was first introduced in the mid-fifteenth century, the transition from script to print allowed knowledge and ideas to spread faster than ever before.[7] As a result, literacy rates increased, as did critiques of the Catholic church. The printing press enabled the publishing of maps, which fostered travel and exploration. It was responsible for the Renaissance, the European cultural movement in the fifteenth and sixteenth centuries that marked the transition from the Middle Ages to modernity. In many ways, the printing press laid the foundation for the modern information society as we know it.

Similarly, the introduction of televisions in the homes of North Americans in the 1960s changed how information was disseminated. News broadcasting, documentaries, public education programs, celebrity culture, and commercial advertising would not have been possible without the television. It became the cornerstone of popular culture, political debate, and public opinion. As educator Neil Postman highlights in his 1985 book, *Amusing Ourselves to Death: Public Discourse in the Age of Show Business*[8] television and a predominately visual culture turned everything, including politics, into entertainment. For example, Nixon lost the 1960 presidential race to John F. Kennedy largely *because the presidential debates were televised*; Kennedy appeared confident and charismatic, while Nixon was sweaty and pale. The visual contrast impacted the public perception of the potential leaders, and Kennedy won.

As Canadian media theorist Marshal McLuhan has pointed out, the medium is often the *massage*—meaning communication tools often shape (or *massage*) what's being said.

When the history books are written about my generation (I'm a millennial) and the generations that follow, the defining feature will be the smartphone and its killer app, social media. Together, they are my generation's printing press and television; together, they have informed our culture and shaped its content.

Although IBM invented the smartphone in 1992, it wasn't connected to an actual 3G network until 2000. In 2007, Apple introduced its first iPhone, a device that would radically shape the world as we know it. Today, smartphones are ubiquitous. Globally, almost 90% of cellular phones are smartphones, and as of 2016, there are more smartphone subscribers than people.

The impact of the smartphone on the fashion industry is manifold. First, there's the physicality of a device that brings the camera into what was once a closed and opaque industry, a development that forced the fashion industry to open up. At the same time, there's the trend of converting services and tools into mobile web applications, a phenomenon referred to as "appification." We'll talk about the importance of the camera's presence before delving into the impact of apps. Both have to do with the way fashion is presented and consumed.

How the Camera Broke Down Fashion's Fourth Wall

Along with the smartphone came the ubiquity and portability of the camera and the ability to capture and send images worldwide in seconds. The first commercial phone to include a camera was the Kyocera Visual Phone VP-210. Released in 1999, had a 0.11-megapixel camera and could take up to twenty pictures before its onboard storage was full. The following year, in 2000, both Samsung and Sharp released phones with cameras. It wasn't until 2007, when Apple released the first iPhone that cameras became standard on smartphones. Although the first iPhone only had a two-megapixel camera, the camera quality would improve over the years as lenses and sensors became miniaturized, more affordable, and more readily available.

How did the smartphone camera impact fashion? Consider the two images: in QR Code 3.

QR Code 3 Scan to see an image of Fashion Press Week from 1943.

This is an image of the first official Fashion Week in New York in 1943. Although there were undoubtedly fashion gatherings and even shows in Europe prior, the first official fashion week was called "Press Week," and it was created to showcase designers to fashion journalists who could not travel to Paris due to World War II. Fashion Week was once an industry-only event for editors, journalists, and buyers. The only people in attendance with cameras were the photographers, and they would sit in the designated media pit at the end of the runway to capture images for newspapers and magazines to print. Now consider a second image (QR Code 4).

QR Code 4 Scan to see an image of Gigi Hadid walking for Tommy Hilfiger in 2016.

The second image shows Gigi Hadid walking the runway for Tommy Hilfiger in 2016. The first thing you notice is all the smartphones. In the first image, everyone is watching the show. In the second image, seventy years later, everyone is watching the show *through their smartphone*, capturing the moment with their camera.

The smartphone camera has augmented the runway and extended it beyond the confines of Fashion Week. It used to take days before magazines and newspapers printed photographs from fashion events for circulation; Today, runway shows are livestreamed and images and videos captured at Fashion Weeks are shared instantly.

It wasn't just consumers who were let in via the camera's lens. Brands like Zara grew in popularity because the company was able to take inspiration from the runway and quickly manufacture similar-looking items for a fraction of the cost. The ethics of these "dupes"[9] have long been scrutinized, but Zara's growing success has been a direct result of more consumers wanting access to trendy pieces. We'll talk more about Zara in Chapter 3, but for now, it's important to note how the smartphone camera enabled (and accelerated) fast fashion.

In his final runway presentation before his suicide, legendary designer Alexander McQueen anticipated the pervasiveness of the camera's presence and its impact on fashion. McQueen's last show, Plato's Atlantis, was one of the first presentations livestreamed online in high definition for internet audiences (QR Code 5). It was an otherworldly and intergalactic presentation. Face prosthetics were used to make models look like aliens. Two robot-mounted cameras on dual tracks ran up and down the runway. Throughout the show, the cameras seemingly tracked the models and cast footage of them in real time from the runway onto a video screen. The size of the cameras dwarfed the models, and the equipment's dark, bulky presence contrasted strikingly with the ethereal dresses.

QR Code 5 Scan the QR code to watch McQueen's spring/summer 2010 runway presentation Plato's Atlantis.

At the show's close, as all the models came out for their final walk to the tune of Lady Gaga's song "Bad Romance," the cameras panned over the audience, as if gesturing to them as an integral part of the show. McQueen had broken the fourth wall and was pointing to the ever-important presence of the audience—both the physical audience in attendance and the wider audience let in via the camera lens.

With each model who walked the runway, more prosthetics were used, as if to show a transformation from recognizable people to otherworldly creatures. "It's some sort of evolution," said Peter Philips, one of the makeup artists for the show.[10] "The last fifteen girls start to transform into creatures with applications and special-effect makeup," he said in a backstage interview with FashionTV.

In a conversation with Nick Knight, McQueen talked about the decision to livestream the show. "Fashion is a very small world, especially the professional part of the world," he said.[11] McQueen goes on to say that he didn't want to pigeonhole himself, and that design as an artform can only develop when it's opened up to a larger audience.

The camera was the tool that let in a wider audience, and it broke down the barrier separating the fashion industry from its spectators, recognizing consumers not just as observers but as characters in the narrative.

The smartphone also paved the way for the appification of social networks. Facebook, which was once the dominant social network in terms of usage and popularity,[12] was originally designed for desktop and offered a less than compelling mobile app. When Instagram was released in 2010, it was designed for the small screen, prioritizing a simple user interface and touch interactions. This made it a quick rival to Facebook. Shortly after its launch, Mark Zuckerberg, the CEO of Facebook, made a bid to buy Instagram for a record-setting $1 billion. The acquisition was about combating social media rivals at the time and about boosting Facebook's strategy on mobile.[13]

Instagram was one of the first American tech giants to focus on images first. The icon for the original Instagram app was itself a version of a Polaroid, a camera traditionally used for capturing and printing a moment in time. Instagram did the same thing, only it used the smartphone camera for capturing the moment and the social feed for "printing" it.

What differentiated Instagram from other image-sharing platforms like Flickr was the robust social graph. Instagram prioritized a network of social connections on your feed, which showed images from people you were following, and a news section, which displayed interactions between those in your network.

Since the introduction of Instagram, runway shows have become increasingly aware of—and have pandered to—the social camera. Fashion Week has transformed from an industry-only event to a live entertainment extravaganza for public consumption. Brands like Tommy Hilfiger and Rebecca Minkoff lean into the theatrics of fashion shows and orchestrate moments seemingly made for social media virality. Runway shows have featured Ferris wheels, lobster rolls, temporary tattoo parlors, and celebrity musical performers. On the stranger side, catwalks have included faux baby dragons and models carrying wax replicas of their heads—I'm looking at you, Gucci. What's become apparent in the last decade is that fashion shows are no longer just for buyers and decision-makers; they're for celebrities, influencers, and their followers. As journalist and fashion critic Suzy Menkes wrote in 2016, "Fashion shows are aimed at the people, not the pros."[14]

Viral Fashion: Social Media and "the Dress"

When the capabilities of the camera combined with the reach of social media, unprecedented things started to happen, including the phenomenon of viral content. The notion of virality as we know it today was born in the social media era. Before the 1970s, the term "viral" was only used to describe infectious diseases. During the computer boom starting in the 1970s, "virality" had the connotation of a virus. The term "going viral" wasn't used in print until 1999.

With the invention of platforms with image-sharing capabilities like Facebook (launched in 2004), Tumblr (2007), and Pinterest (2009), images had a place to end up aside from your family photo album. The social feed—a stream of content including updates from friends, family, and pages that each user follows—quickly became an integral part of everyday news consumption. Platforms like Facebook encourage interaction by prompting users to like, comment, and share. If enough people share something, it "goes viral."

One dress in particular achieved virality in the early days of social media, and that was due to the controversial nature of its image. In February 2015, Cecilia Bleasdale was shopping at Cheshire Oaks Designer Outlet in Chester, England. She was looking for something to wear to her daughter's wedding and took a photo of a bodycon dress she was considering for the event and sent it to the bride-to-be (QR Code 6).

QR Code 6 Scan QR code to see the original image of "the dress."

The dress was blue with black lace, but upon receiving an image of the dress, the daughter said she perceived it as white with gold lace. The two went back and forth and were perplexed by one another's perception. They decided to post the image of the dress on Facebook to get other people's opinions. To their surprise, friends and family disagreed: some saw the dress as white with gold, while others saw it as blue and black. A few days after the wedding, a friend of the newlyweds posted the image of the dress to Tumblr asking people what color they thought it was. The post received thousands of comments and caught the attention of an editor at *BuzzFeed*, who then posted an article about the dress with a poll asking readers what color they saw. The page set a record for the online publication in terms of traffic to the site. Soon the image ended up on Twitter with celebrities including Taylor Swift weighing in. Within a week, more than ten million tweets had mentioned #TheDress, and the story had appeared on hundreds of news programs. It received so much attention that Bleasdale and her family were invited on *The Ellen Show* to share the whole story.

The appearance of the dress as blue and black or white and gold has since been accounted for by neuroscientists: Your perception of color depends on how your brain interprets the light in the image.

What's interesting for our purposes is the virality of the image of #TheDress and how it reflects the way fashion has become a hyper-social conversation. Anyone with an internet connection can weigh in with their optical opinions.

The impact of social media on fashion as a cultural conversation can especially be observed during red-carpet events like the Met Gala and the Oscars. As celebrities appear on TV screens, we also turn to platforms like X (formerly Twitter) to provide and read commentary about the event in real time, a phenomenon known as "the second screen." Public opinion—something that was once much more abstract—can now be measured. Software platforms monitoring online conversations quantify sentiments and can tell us exactly what everyone thought of Sarah Jessica Parker's hat, or how people felt about Zendaya's outfit change. This practice of real-time social listening provides brands with more insights into the customer's mindset than ever before. For example, tools like Brandwatch and Semrush help marketing teams monitor audience behavior and sentiment so they can adjust their strategies in real time as needed.

The Appification of Commerce

The smartphone also put commerce at everyone's fingertips, making it easier than ever for people to browse, research, and order items online from anywhere.

Appification represents the rapid movement of digital tools and media from web-based platforms to mobile apps.[15] Mobile commerce (m-commerce, essentially shopping from your smartphone) is on the rise, and quickly becoming the shopping channel of choice. In 2023, retail m-commerce sales in the United States hit $491 billion.[16] According to Statista, mobile commerce will account for more than 60% of all global retail e-commerce by 2028.[17]

With the launch of Apple's app store in 2008, marketplaces, starting with Amazon, eBay, and Etsy, began releasing mobile apps that enabled users to search and shop for products. The Google Play Store launched four years later, the official app store for Android users. The growing number of smartphones and 4G along with LTE (Long-Term Evolution) technology made mobile browsing fast and easy. Loyalty programs, such as the Starbucks Rewards Program, could be integrated into apps, combining personalization and payment.

Today, every major retailer from IKEA to Walmart to Sephora has their own app, making mobile shopping easier than ever before. Apps from brands like Zara, ASOS, Uniqlo, and H&M simplify browsing, purchasing, and tracking orders from anywhere, which has transformed the way consumers interact with fashion retailers. As a result, shopping experiences have become more personalized based on user's preferences, past purchases, and browsing history.

The practice of picking up your phone and ordering more socks or underwear on Amazon may seem commonplace today, but it wasn't that long ago when your only option was to go to the store and purchase items in person. The department store, once a mecca for modern retail, has been displaced by the Amazon app. After all, why go to the department store *when the department store can come to you?* The result has been a decline in physical retail and the rise of consumer expectations, a phenomenon known as the Amazon Effect.

In a world where Amazon looms large (the company has a market capitalization of $2.30 trillion), same-day or next-day shipping has become the standard for many people in and around large cities.

Recent reports into Amazon's labor practices have revealed there's a human cost to achieving lightning-fast delivery speeds.[18]

Because of Amazon, consumers also expect to be able to return items for free. Returns from Amazon generate 6 billion pounds of landfill waste per year, and 16 million metric tons of carbon dioxide emissions, according to Tobin Moore, CEO of returns solution provider Optoro.[19] A 2021 investigation found that Amazon destroys millions of unsold items every year—products that are often new and unused.[20]

More recently, apps like Chinese-owned Temu have dominated the mobile commerce space and opened shoppers up to a global market. On Temu, you can buy anything from electric scooters to lingerie to miniature furniture for dollhouses. The app is an endless virtual aisle of affordable necessities (a five-pack of seamless underwear for $10.63) to novelties (a 70-inch pepperoni pizza blanket for $5.99). According to reporting from *Business Insider*, Temu was the most downloaded app in the first ten months of 2024. Temu's parent company, PDD Holdings, reported $13.4 billion in revenue for Q2 of that year.[21]

Apps have created mini-ecosystems where brands connect directly with consumers, which makes them a valuable asset for blending commerce, community, and convenience. For example, Nike's SNKRS app is a gateway to exploring and purchasing Nike sneakers, especially when it comes to limited-edition items and exclusive releases. Launched in 2015, the SNKRS app is a go-to place for shoe enthusiasts (known as sneakerheads). In addition to featuring items for sale, the app also showcases photos of Nike customers wearing their kicks. Nike leverages data from the app to better understand and cater to its customers. For example, the brand looked at its most engaged app users in New York. When they discovered that many were from Dominican neighborhoods, the company went to speak with them. Based on these learnings, Nike created a campaign and a shoe, the De Lo Mio Air Force 1. The brand worked with Dominican photographers to shoot Dominicans wearing the shoe. When the sneaker finally launched, it quickly sold out.[22] Nike's SNKRS app is just one example of how apps become ecosystems for commerce, content, and community.

Social Commerce, Peer-to-Peer Marketplaces, and Digital Thrifting

Another notable result of the convergence of cameras with social media and app ecosystems is the rise of social commerce—the practice of using social media platforms to market and sell products or services.[23] Social commerce bridges the gap between social interaction and shopping, seamlessly integrating commerce into the digital social experience.

Burberry is a prime example of a company that blends luxury fashion with social commerce. The brand posts shoppable content on Instagram and WeChat, the Chinese instant messaging, social media, and mobile payment app.

Additionally, Burberry offers social media followers access to exclusive, behind-the-scenes content via livestreams that sometimes feature limited-edition offers. These events create urgency for shoppers and foster loyalty and community.

Apps have also introduced new consumption models, such as peer-to-peer commerce and recommerce. While these models existed before the smartphone, platforms like Facebook Marketplace have streamlined the process, making it easier for individuals to buy directly from one another instead of through traditional retailers.

Launched at the end of 2016, Facebook Marketplace is an online platform within Facebook that allows users to buy, sell, and trade items with others in their local community or beyond. According to the US Securities and Exchange Commission, Facebook has 3.03 billion monthly active users, and up to 40% of these people shop on Marketplace.[24]

Apps for buying and selling secondhand clothing have also skyrocketed in recent years and catalyzed recommerce (short for "reverse commerce"). Although thrifting has been around since the late nineteenth century, digital thrifting is a new phenomenon powered by the internet. Digital thrifting is just like thrift shopping in real life, only the shopper is no longer limited to secondhand stores in their geographical area. This means there's more opportunity to browse and find items in your style and size at a fraction of the cost of buying new ones. Apps like Poshmark, Depop, and Vinted make it easy for people to buy and sell secondhand items directly to one another. Because these apps are integrated with social media features, they enhance user engagement and foster a community-driven marketplace. According to the Business of Apps, Depop has 4.2 million active buyers and 1.9 million active sellers.[25] The app generated $600 million in gross merchandise sales in 2023. In 2021, Depop was acquired by Etsy for $1.6 billion.

Although there are still downsides to thrift shopping online (namely, shipping costs and the inability to try items on), the business case is there. According to ThredUp's 2024 Resale Report, the global secondhand market will reach $350 billion by 2028, growing three times faster than the global apparel market.[26]

Some savvy thrifters have gone beyond just selling the items in their closets to curating virtual storefronts and becoming full-time resellers. Some sell items for friends and family and take a commission, while others shop for items at secondhand stores and relist them for more than they paid. In some cases, virtual store owners can make up to six figures reselling items. Sophia Amoruso, founder of Nasty Gal, got her start as a vintage reseller on eBay and grew the brand's following on social media. Although the company would eventually file for bankruptcy due to leadership challenges, at its peak Nasty Gal was pulling in $100 million in annual sales.

Thrifting is a way of pushing back against consumer culture and promoting the circular economy, a model of production and consumption that involves keeping products and materials in use as long as possible. When thrifting is combined with digital ecosystems such as apps, the circular economy can flourish, opening up new revenue streams and unlocking value in old clothes.

While the smartphone has transformed how we transact, its killer app, social media, has also influenced what we shop for and how we discover trends and style inspiration.

The Clean Girl and the Mob Wife: The Smartphone's Impact on Trends

In January 2024, TikTok officially declared the clean girl aesthetic out, and the mob wife aesthetic in. For those unfamiliar with either of these terms, the "clean girl" is a look inspired by the likes of Hailey Bieber. It involves slicked-back buns, bushy eyebrows, and glossy lips and nails. The "mob wife" aesthetic is what it sounds like. Inspired by fictional characters like Carmela Soprano on the American drama series *The Sopranos,* the mob wife decks herself out in luxury (think fur jackets, heavy makeup with dark eyeliner, and lots of animal print and gold jewelry). By the time you're reading this, the internet will undoubtedly be onto something else.

If trends seem to be moving at breakneck speed compared to yesteryear, that's because they are. "Trends last anywhere from weeks to years," writes Joan Kennedy, the editorial director of *The Business of Fashion*.[27] Other sources, like consumer intelligence platform Brandwatch, suggest most trends have a peak that lasts about two to four months. The twenty-year trend cycle, once a staple in fashion education, no longer seems relevant in the here-today, gone-tomorrow world of social media.

In her 2016 article "How Smartphones Are Killing Off the Fashion Show," *The New York Times* style editor Vanessa Friedman wrote about how the smartphone forced the industry into an existential crisis.[28] She quotes Scott Galloway, a professor of marketing and (at the time) the founder and chair of the digital consultancy L2: "Social media is the laxative of the fashion system. It makes everyone digest everything much faster," he said.

The speed at which trends move from introduction to decline is rewiring retail.

Until recently, fashion collections were previewed ahead of the season. Items shown on the runway in February were for the fall/winter of that year, while collections shown in September were for the spring/summer of the following year. The lead time from presentation to retail was approximately six months.

In reaction to social media's instantaneous nature, several brands—including Burberry, Tom Ford, Ralph Lauren, Tommy Hilfiger, Jacquemus, Mugler, and Rebecca Minkoff—tested a see-now, buy-now approach. This began circa 2016, when labels announced that items shown at Fashion Week would be available for purchase immediately in an attempt to be closer to the consumer. "The current way of showing a collection four months before it is available to customers is an antiquated idea, and one that no longer makes sense," Tom Ford told *The New York Times* in February 2016. However, more recently, brands have abandoned see-now, buy-now, or at least taken a seasonless or more hybrid approach. In 2020, Gucci announced it was opting for two shows a year, while brands like Moschino offer certain capsule items and accessories that are available immediately after the show, while other items adhere to the traditional production timeline.

The smartphone—and its killer app, social media—has also changed where trends come from. Gone are the days of the top-down model dramatized in the 2006 comedy-drama *The Devil Wears Prada,* where the editor-in-chief, Miranda Priestly (Meryl Streep), gives the frumpy fashion assistant Andy Sachs (Anne Hathaway) a lesson in trends in what has come to be known as the cerulean monologue (QR Code 7).

QR Code 7 Scan the QR code to watch the "cerulean monologue" from *The Devil Wears Prada* (2006).

Miranda Priestly's cerulean monologue may have been true in the 1990s or even early 2000s, but today, trends come from everywhere. "It's a shift away from the old trickle-down effect," says Kayla Marci, an analyst at retail intelligence platform.[29] The coquette aesthetic, for example, a micro-trend that describes an ultra-feminine, dainty way of dressing that incorporates bows, pastels, lace, and frills, started on Tumblr circa 2012–2017 (during Tumblr's golden era) and resurfaced in popularity on TikTok in recent years. Similarly, cottagecore, the aesthetic that harkens back to the days of *Little House on the Prairie*, popularized the nap dress, which became the must-have item of the summer circa 2020.[30]

Even Faster Fashion

As our media consumption has increased, so has our clothing consumption. The constant demand for newness has spawned a new type of fast fashion: *ultrafast* fashion. A segment of online-only retailers like Boohoo, Shein, Misguided, and Pretty Little Thing produce trends and micro-trends for quick consumption at bottom-of-the-barrel prices. "Ultra fast fashion takes everything harmful about fast fashion and speeds it up," writes JD Shadel on the *Good On You* blog.[31] Shadel notes how the "fashion haul" on TikTok has become a meme—a cultural behavior that spreads throughout the internet:

> When you scroll through fashion hauls, you see countless examples of consumption on steroids. In one typical video that's captioned *"*accidentally* spent $480 at #SHEIN,"* a TikToker unpacks big boxes and lays dozens of packaged garments out in her room, covering the floor.... "You're not going to believe me when I tell you how much I paid for these," she says as she holds her plastic-wrapped dresses, "cause it's insane—it was so cheap."

As if playing into trend-led purchasing behavior, Amazon released Haul in November 2024, a discount section of their app that offers selected items for under $20 USD. The interface is strikingly similar to the Chinese online marketplace Temu, and so is the emphasis on discounts: "Unbelievable finds, crazy low prices" a banner on Haul reads. A quick browse through the app and you'll notice you can find just about anything: RFID-blocking wallets or printed ties, each less than $5.

A 2021 study from the Royal Society of the Arts (known as RSA for short) determined that *half* of the fast fashion in the United Kingdom is plastic[32]—made from synthetic fibers such as polyester. While synthetics can offer some benefits such as stretch and durability, they're a net negative for the environment. Synthetic fibers don't biodegrade and they shed microfibers (plastics) into the environment every time we wash them.

Ultra-fast fashion also contains chemicals that are not safe for the skin. The internet is riddled with testimonies of people who have had reactions—including rashes, hives, and even poisoning—to clothing, jewelry, and beauty products purchased from ultra-fast fashion retailers. An investigation by the CBC found that one in five items from Shein, AliExpress, or Zaful contained elevated levels of chemicals, including lead.[33]

In addition to the negative impacts on the environment and consumers, ultra-fast fashion is only possible by exploiting the cheap labor of women in developing economies. In Chapter 3, we'll talk about automation and, in particular, look at garment workers in Bangladesh to understand the nuances of industrialization and globalization. For now, it's crucial to recognize that there's a shady underbelly of producing trends at a lightning-fast pace.

Celebrities, Influencers, and Creators

In a 2006 special report on social media for *The Economist,* Jay Rosen wrote an article entitled "The People Formerly Known as the Audience,"[34] in which he discussed how smartphone and social media technologies allow a wider range of people to take part in gathering, filtering, and distributing news. In a 2018 lecture given at the University of Scranton by the same title, Dr. Rosen explained, "The tools of media production, which used to be in the hands of media companies are now distributed to the population at large, mainly through the smartphone."[35]

The camera has disrupted the relationship between traditional media and the fashion industry and upended the publisher–consumer dynamic: Newspapers and magazines, once both the gatekeepers and the centerpiece of fashion, have been displaced by the newsfeed. As a result, the print media industry has been in steady decline since the introduction of the smartphone, with titles closing and layoffs announced frequently. The digital disruption of news isn't specific to fashion.

According to WordsRated, between 2019 and 2022, total audiences for magazine companies decreased by 38.56%,[36] and according to Brookings, an independent research organization, newspaper revenue dropped steadily, from $45 billion in 2007 to $22 billion in 2013.[37]

The smartphone has democratized the means of fashion media production, while at the same time, social media has opened up fashion media distribution. As a result, a new kind of entrepreneur has emerged at the intersection of media, technology, and fashion: the social media influencer.

While some may wince at the idea of influencing as a career choice, it's big business. According to Statista, companies are projected to spend more than $250 billion annually worldwide on social media advertising.[38] Influencer marketing—collaborating with influencers to promote products and services—has become a massive part of that spending.

Although the social media influencer is a relatively new phenomenon, there were always "it girls" in the past (think Audrey Hepburn, Edie Sedgwick, Twiggy, Marilyn Monroe, and even Clara Bow, the original "it girl" from the silent film era). The difference is that these women were always subjects in someone else's production. Sedgwick was primarily known as Andy Warhol's muse, while both Hepburn and Monroe only appeared in films directed by men. Today, because of the smartphone, the means of production are in the hands of the it girl, and that makes her more powerful than ever.

Kim Kardashian is one of the most popular influencers online. She got her start as a celebrity closet organizer and apprentice to Paris Hilton in the early 2000s before opening a clothing boutique, called DASH, with her sisters. In 2007, Kim and her family started filming the reality TV series *Keeping Up with the Kardashians*. With the help of her ex-husband Ye (the artist formerly known as Kanye West), Kim became a style icon. In 2017, she founded KKW Beauty. Her first product line was a creme contour and highlight kit that let users recreate Kim's signature makeup look. The kits sold out immediately. In 2019, Kim founded Skims, a shapewear and clothing brand initially launched as Kimono Intimates. After backlash accused the brand of appropriating Japanese culture with its name, Kim changed it to Skims at the end of January 2021. Despite its controversial beginnings, Skim's initial launch was a huge success, with $2 million in profit and the company selling out of merchandise in ten minutes, according to Hypebae, an online site that chronicles the latest in fashion and streetwear.[39] In April 2021, *The New York Times* reported the company to be worth over $1.6 billion.[40] After further investments from hedge funds and investment firms, *Bloomberg* reported the value of Skims to be $3.2 billion in January 2022.[41] By comparison, the Calvin Klein brand, which has been around since 1968, is valued at only $1.5 billion.[42] In March 2022, *Time* magazine listed Skims as one of the "Most Influential Companies of the Year."[43]

Whereas celebrities of the past would lend their likeness to campaigns for fragrances, makeup, apparel, and more, Kim Kardashian sells her products directly to consumers. Although the D2C model has been around since mail-order catalogs in the late 1800s, social media exploded its potential and turned the social feed into a shoppable store window.

Similarly, Kylie Jenner, Kim's younger half-sister, leveraged the growing popularity of *Keeping Up with the Kardashians* to build her personal brand and empire. She first appeared on the show as a gangly nine-year-old. At age fourteen, she collaborated with the apparel brand PacSun, to create a line of clothing with her sister Kendall. In 2015, she launched her makeup line, initially called Kylie Lip Kits after its signature product. Although critics pointed out that Jenner's full pout came from lip fillers and not makeup, she used the controversy to her advantage. Her $29 lip kits sold out in under a minute. In 2016, Kylie Lip Kits was renamed Kylie Cosmetics and in 2019, *Forbes* magazine estimated Kylie's net worth as $1 billion and named her one of the world's youngest billionaires at age 21.[44] (*Forbes* has since struck Jenner from their list of billionaires, accusing the celebrity of inflating her net worth.[45]) In November 2019, Jenner sold a 51% controlling stake in her company to Coty, one of the world's largest multinational beauty companies, for $600 million.[46]

But it's not just children of wealthy parents who have made a name for themselves as influencers. When Aimee Song started blogging in 2008, she intended it to be a forum to share her interior design aesthetic. According to *The Business of Fashion,* Song was studying interior architecture in San Francisco when posts dedicated to what she was wearing sparked positive interest.[47] Song took the opportunity to launch a personal style blog, *Song of Style.* Sixteen years later, she has 7.3 million followers on Instagram and is one of the top-earning creators in the world.

Song, along with a wave of social media figures like Chiara Ferragni, Chriselle Lim, Leonie Hanne, and Camila Coelho, to name a few, leveraged image-sharing platforms like Instagram to carve out a new role in fashion that is neither industry insider nor outsider. This kind of storytelling and self-fashioning would not have been possible without the smartphone. Through these handheld devices, influencers like Song provide a window through which we can experience the fashion industry up close from the perspective of someone just like us.

It's important to note that the influencer doesn't necessarily look like the traditional fashion model. At five-foot-six and of Asian descent, Song stands out in a world where models are tall and white with sample-size measurements. Despite this, Song has sat in the front row at runway shows all over the world, modeled for Dolce & Gabbana, and even collaborated with Mattel to make a Barbie that looks like her. She has launched her own clothing line with her sister, written two books, and has become an advocate for LGBTQ+ rights. Song is an example of how anyone with a sense of style, a smartphone, and an internet connection can participate in what's more widely known as the creator economy.

As *The New York Times* reporter and editor Christine Muhlke writes, "The creator economy is powered by millions of individuals who build and monetize their online celebrity by making deals with big brands and selling products to their followers."[48] According to Goldman Sachs, the creator economy could approach half a trillion dollars by 2027.[49] "The creator economy has taken over the entire [fashion] industry," Talita von Furstenberg, the co-chair of the fashion company Diane von Furstenberg, told the *Times*.[50]

For many, the creator economy is the gateway to entrepreneurship. Creators with modest followings compared to the Kardashians and even Song participate in brand deals where they get paid (in both money and gifts) to post products or attend events. Micro-influencers or nano-influencers (lesser-known influencers with between 1,000 and 100,000 followers) can have a dramatic effect on boosting awareness or sales for a brand. In fact, a recent report showed that micro-influencers yield an average return of more than $1,000 on a $50 investment, compared to influencers with more than 100,000 followers who command payments in the thousands but deliver a return of only $6,000.[51] In other words, although a micro-influencer's reach isn't as broad as mega celebrities or large influencers, their audiences can often be more targeted and engaged.

"We're in an era where traditional media no longer holds the monopoly on information dissemination," Hilary Gorbould said in an interview with the BBC.[52] Gorbould is an influencer marketing manager at Stockholm-based Redgert Comms. "Influencer marketing allows brands to convey their message to a target demographic while hand-picking ambassadors who resonate with their ethos," she says. Creators help humanize corporate communications. While email marketing campaigns and advertisements come across as highly produced, creators can provide an authentic and accessible way to help share a brand story.

Creators aren't just flaunting their lifestyles and hawking products. Many have carved out unique roles for themselves within the industry. For example, Taylen Biggs is an eleven-year-old fashion host with millions of followers across her Instagram account, YouTube channel, Facebook page, and TikTok presence. She has interviewed the likes of Ariana Grande, Selena Gomez, and Kris Jenner. Taylen (or Biggs as she goes by) has appeared on red carpets and at fashion events around the world.

Similarly, Luke Meagher, known as @hautelemode on social media, has built a whole career for himself dissecting and discussing celebrity fashion. As a profile on Meagher in *Vogue* points out, "At 25 years old, with no previous ties to a company or publication, Meagher has fashioned himself as a must-watch and authoritative fashion critic online."[53] As journalist Nathalie Atkinson outlines, a new crop of fashion critics (including Avery Trufelman, Eugene Rabkin, and Mosha Lundström) is making names for themselves as informed industry outsiders who bring a unique perspective.[54]

The roles of celebrities, influencers, and creators are not mutually exclusive and can overlap. Meagher, for example, is both a critic and a content creator. Because he has built a community of loyal fashion followers, his opinion has weight, which in turn makes him an influencer. Likewise, Taylen Biggs and other content creators such as YouTuber Emma Chamberlain have become recognizable staples on red carpets, making them both content creators and celebrities of sorts.

Brands as Media Companies

Prior to the introduction of the smartphone and social media, fashion brands were mainly responsible for producing clothing and campaigns. Today, in our always on, always connected digital landscape, brands, like all companies, have shifted to become media companies, too, responsible for the production and distribution of digital content. The roles of the social media manager and director of digital strategy are fairly new inventions, born out of the need to fill e-commerce pages and the ever-hungry social feed. Instead of producing eight or ten campaign images per quarter for magazines, brands today produce hundreds of pieces of content a month and in multiple formats, from still images to videos to reels, for different platforms.

Some brands have fully embraced the opportunity, creating what's been coined "direct-to-consumer content" (that is, content aimed at the customer rather than mainstream media or fashion magazines). An example of this is GucciFest. Launched in 2020, GucciFest is a seven-day virtual film festival screening fashion films. Fans of the brand can tune in via YouTube to watch young designer films featuring cameos from the likes of Harry Styles and Billie Eilish. The festival is part of Gucci's vision to break away from the traditional fashion mold by blending rules and genres.[55]

As a result of social media, brands now have a more mature relationship with their customers and are able to sell directly to them. A Highsnobiety social report indicates that "brands that long relied on middlemen like department stores to promote their products and brand values are clearly adapting similar [direct-to-consumer] models."[56] Nike, for example, has projected that its direct-to-consumer business—bolstered through its Nike+ membership app, flagship stores, and e-commerce—will reach $16 billion in sales by the end of 2022, up from $10.4 billion just two years earlier.[57]

“The biggest shift is that fashion content was coming from the traditional titles, and now it’s coming from brands themselves,” Chandra Turner told *Fashionista*.[58] Turner is a longtime print magazine editor turned independent career coach. “Brands are covering the fashion industry from within, to consumers directly, because they can.... Before, we—the media—were the conduit to fashion content. That’s not necessarily the case now.”

One of the downsides of brands owning the tools of media production is that they can say whatever they want. For example, in 2010 when H&M launched its Conscious Collection, the brand used social media to promote the line as sustainable, highlighting eco-friendly materials such as organic cotton and recycled polyester. However, many of the claims made by H&M for its Conscious Collection were found to be deeply misleading.

The practice of overemphasizing sustainability practices is known as greenwashing. A class-action lawsuit was filed against H&M in 2022 for the misleading claims. It was eventually dismissed, resulting in essentially a slap on the wrist for the company. In light of the case, the Federal Trade Commission announced that it is revisiting its rules surrounding the use of making environmental marketing claims.[59] Greenwashing highlights the power of the smartphone and social media in shaping narratives.

Online Activism and Industry Watchdogs

Just as quickly as social media gave everyone a voice, individuals and organizations have used it to speak out against wrongdoing in the fashion industry. Organizations such as Fashion Revolution leverage their social media following to spread information about fashion’s contributions to modern slavery. Their “Who Made Your Clothes?” movement was successful partially because it featured images of real garment workers from around the world holding signs that read, "I Made Your Clothes," drawing attention to the often hidden figures involved in fashion production. By highlighting these women, Fashion Revolution calls for greater transparency in the fashion industry.

Online activism can also look like calling out bad behavior within an industry. The Instagram account @DietPrada started out as a light-hearted way of naming and shaming copycat fashion designers but has evolved into an industry watchdog exposing wrongdoings, including model abuse, racism, and misogyny.[60]

It's not just activist organizations and watchdogs that are able to call out the bad behavior of brands. When the French luxury house Balenciaga published images of children that had sexual undertones, it ignited a firestorm of outrage. The campaign "Balenciaga Gift Shop" featured photos of children with the brand's handbags that looked like teddy bears in bondage gear.[61] The children were surrounded by wine glasses and BDSM paraphernalia. The pile-on effect of publicly shaming the brand was swift, with everyone from everyday X users to Tucker Carlson condemning Balenciaga.

Fashion's Impact on the Smartphone

Just as the smartphone impacted fashion, fashion impacted the smartphone, elevating it from a functional device to a personal accessory. I remember purchasing my first mobile phone, a Motorola V2288e. It was peanut-shaped and black, but I bought different-colored snap-on covers for it to match different outfits. Since the introduction of mobile phones, cases, charms, and straps have become a way of styling and personalizing your phone. The smartphone accessory market is valued in the billions, and fashion companies have taken note.

Brands such as Bottega Veneta, Moschino, Kate Spade, Prada, and Louis Vuitton (to name a few) all have offerings to "dress" your phone in the latest cases. Phone cases now include slots for cards at the back, eliminating the need to carry a wallet. Or you can load your cards onto your digital wallet and do away with plastic altogether. If you prefer to keep your makeup on hand, you can try the Rhode Lip Case, a silicon puffy iPhone case that includes a slot for your favorite Rhode lip gloss. Celebrity founder Hailey Bieber teased the case in February 2024 in an Instagram post and then later at the Super Bowl, where she whipped out the phone case for a midgame touchup.[62]

Some fashion brands have even collaborated with hardware companies and telecommunications providers to release designer phones, including the Versace x Nokia flip phone (2005), Dolce & Gabbana x Motorola (2005), Armani x Samsung (2007), Prada x Samsung (2012), Alexander Wang x Vivo (2020), and Thom Browne x Samsung (2020).

Tech has also borrowed the energy and ambiance of runway shows to launch new products and devices. Apple events have turned into highly produced experiences, complete with lighting, music, and prerecorded videos. Appearances from CEOs like Tim Cook have the same aura of celebrity cameos. New products and updates are announced seasonally, mimicking the fashion calendar, with influencers and reporters in attendance. Tech items, like AirPods, have also become status symbols, signaling the wearer is both wealthy and "with it." To carry outdated tech is like wearing last season's trends.

Fashion's Impact on Social Media

Just as fashion has impacted hardware, it's an industry that has had an outsized influence on social media. The introduction of Instagram Shopping was largely driven by retailers and brands who wanted to turn their online presence into sales. For those not familiar, Instagram

Shopping is a set of features, such as product tags, product detail pages, and an in-app checkout, that lets people shop a brand's photos and videos across the app. According to a report by Capital One Shopping, clothing and apparel is the largest category of items purchased on Instagram.[63]

Similarly, TikTok Shop merges e-commerce with social media. Rolled out in the United States in September 2023, TikTok Shop "empowers brands and creators to connect with highly engaged customers based on their interests, and it combines the power of community, creativity, and commerce to deliver a seamless shopping experience."[64] TikTok especially has a strong shopping culture, with trends like #TikTokMadeMeBuyIt encouraging people to share products they love. According to data from the New Consumer, US shoppers spent $363 million in gross merchandise volume in 2023 on TikTok Shop.[65]

Shoppable content—videos and multimedia where people can directly purchase products—is already a booming business in Asia. In regions like China, live video shopping accounted for $150 billion in 2022, ushering in a new era of commerce.[66] Livestream shopping is expected to make up 20% of e-commerce sales in the coming years[67] and already makes up $223 billion on the Chinese version of TikTok (Douyin).

Mobile connectivity and the ubiquity of the smartphone provide the infrastructure for many other technological developments, including the Internet of Things (which we'll delve into in the next chapter) and augmented reality (which we'll discuss in Chapter 4). The camera has opened up the fashion industry from a once-insular space to a globally interconnected ecosystem.

The smartphone's killer app, social media, has democratized fashion, empowering consumers, influencers, and brands alike to engage in unprecedented ways. Trends now emerge and fade at breakneck speeds, fueled by platforms that blur the lines between creation, consumption, and commerce. Meanwhile, ultra-fast fashion and digital thrifting reflect both the benefits and challenges of this new era of connectivity. As the smartphone evolves, it remains a cornerstone of innovation, bridging consumers, creators, and the culture of style itself, and ushering in a new era of digital and social connectivity.

Chapter 2

The Internet of Things (IoT)

Fashion Comes to Life

In the electric age, we wear all mankind as our skin.

—Marshall McLuhan

Fashion and Technology Collide

On a crisp Sunday during New York Fashion Week in 2016, inside a downtown gallery, a buzzy fashion brand called Public School unveiled its fall collection—and it wasn't just the clothes that had people talking. As models glided by in oversized shirts and cropped leather jackets, their wrists were adorned with metal and nylon wearable technology accessories made using Alta, the latest product offering from Fitbit.

Public School's Autumn/Winter 2016 presentation wasn't the first time technology had taken the limelight when it came to fashion. A few years prior, for her Spring/Summer 2013 runway show in New York, Diane von Furstenberg paraded models down the runway wearing Google Glass, the new smart glasses offering from the tech company. According to reporting in *The Guardian*, Sergey Brin, the co-founder of Google, sat in the front row alongside the likes of Sarah Jessica Parker.[1]

Fashion and technology may seem like strange bedfellows, but in the early 2010s, the two industries were colliding on the runway. If fashion is always about looking forward, as *Vogue* editor Anna

Wintour suggests, then what was showing up at fashion weeks around the world was gesturing to a future where clothing and accessories fused with digital technology.

These high-profile examples mirrored the experimentation I was witnessing at local events like Fashion Art Toronto (FAT for short), an annual runway show celebrated by the Toronto fashion community for its experimental and avant-garde presentations. For the April 2015 edition of FAT, designer Evan Biddell—best known for his win on *Project Runway Canada*—staged an unforgettable, intergalactic-themed runway show. In collaboration with visual artist Jennifer Walton, Biddell presented dresses painted with UV ink, which transformed under blacklight to mimic reptile skin (Figure 2.1). The runway was

Figure 2.1 Evan Biddell's dress on the runway at Fashion Art Toronto. Photograph by Amanda Cosco.

bathed in an eerie, otherworldly glow, complementing the show's theme of ethereal beings. Biddell shared with me backstage that he was intrigued by the concept of lizard people, a fascination that informed his creative direction.[2]

To me, Biddell's blending of fashion and technology—much like McQueen's use of robots and cameras—was gesturing toward a transformation that was taking place in society. As I wrote for the *Toronto Star* at the time:

> With Apple's smartwatch poised to catapult wearables into mass popularity, we're moving towards a more intimate relationship with our technology; It's no longer something we hold or put in our purse or pocket—it's something we wear on our body; it's something that touches our skin.[3]

A few months after Fashion Art Toronto, in September 2015, American designer Zac Posen captivated the New York runway with a groundbreaking tea-length dress created in collaboration with Google's nonprofit initiative, Made with Code. The dress featured black mesh-like layers adorned with 500 LED lights that blinked in colors coordinated with the rest of the runway collection. Teen girls programmed the lights online, while creative technologist Madison Maxey developed the hardware and circuitry. Maxey would go on to found Loomia, a company specializing in soft, flexible electronics. The Made with Code Dress was meant to showcase the creative potential of programming and aimed to break stereotypes about coding by showing how it can be applied in artistic and innovative ways, particularly in fields like fashion.[4] The dress was modeled by "it girl" Coco Rocha, who told *People* magazine that fashion and technology "should have met a long time ago."[5]

In the 2010s, everywhere you looked it seemed fashion was coming to life with digital technology. Wearable light was an early indication that clothing was being "switched on." Looking back, I can see now that what we were witnessing was the early days of the Internet of Things transforming apparel and accessories from static objects into interactive, connected experiences.

This chapter explores the intersection of fashion and technology through the lens of the Internet of Things (IoT), tracing its evolution from experimental runway concepts to practical applications. I'll take you on my journey through the wearable technology community, first in Toronto with We Are Wearables, and then to events like Silicon Valley Fashion Week? and Burning Man, all three of which were foundational to my understanding of tech-infused fashion. We'll examine how specific designers and commercial products have transformed fashion into a platform for self-expression, health monitoring, and connectivity. Along the way, the chapter highlights key technologies like RFID, smart fabrics, and digital product passports, while addressing the challenges that wearable tech faced in achieving mainstream adoption. Ultimately, it positions IoT as a driving force reshaping the future of fashion, sustainability, and consumer transparency.

RFID as the Railroad for IoT

You can think of radio-frequency identification (RFID) as the information railroad that paved the way for the Internet of Things (IoT). Just as railroads revolutionized transportation and logistics, RFID transformed how we track and manage objects, creating the foundation for today's connected ecosystems.

RFID uses wireless technology to identify and track items via radio waves. First developed during World War II to distinguish friendly aircraft from enemy planes, this innovation laid the groundwork for modern RFID systems. Today, compact RFID tags store data that specialized scanners read using radio waves, enabling seamless and efficient tracking.

RFID revolutionized retail by enabling real-time inventory management without the limitations of traditional barcodes. In the early 2000s, Walmart drove RFID adoption by requiring top suppliers to integrate RFID tags, accelerating its adoption into global supply chains. This technology now underpins key retail operations, from ensuring products are stocked on shelves to reducing theft and streamlining checkouts.

The Internet of Things expands upon RFID's infrastructure by turning data collected from tags into actionable insights through cloud platforms, sensors, and networks. While RFID tracks and identifies objects, IoT creates a fully connected ecosystem that powers automation, advanced analytics, and real-time communication across industries.

The term "Internet of Things" was coined in 1999 by Kevin Ashton, a pioneer in RFID innovation and co-founder of the Auto-ID Center at MIT. His vision transformed object tracking into the smart, interconnected world we see today.

Things Get Personal

While IoT was already being used in enterprise applications, in the 2010s, things were getting personal. Advancements in sensor and chip technology made it affordable to connect personal devices to the internet. The rise of the smart home trend ushered in a wave of devices aimed at connecting everything from your toaster to your speaker to your doorbell. Many of us first encountered IoT through smart home products like the Amazon Echo smart speaker or Google's Nest thermostat, which promised greater convenience and connectivity.

Alongside the development of the smart home ecosystem was the growing popularity of "wearable technology," a catchall phrase that emerged to describe devices worn in, on, or around the body, which surged in popularity between late 2013 and mid-2014, according to Google Trends. Both the smart home and wearable technology trends were driven by advancements in connectivity and the increasing popularity of smartphones. While smart home devices aimed to enhance convenience within the home, wearables brought this connectivity directly to the body, transforming how we interact with technology on a personal level. From fitness trackers that monitor health metrics to smartwatches that keep us connected on the go, wearables signaled the dawn of a new era where technology became a seamless extension of ourselves.

We Are Wearables

As I mentioned in my preface, my entry point into emerging tech conversation was via wearable technology. In January 2015, I attended a technology meetup at the MaRS Discovery District in Toronto called We Are Wearables. Each month, we learned about new IoT-enabled devices that blurred the lines between fashion, function, and connectivity.

I remember learning about the Nymi Band, a wristband that used the wearer's unique heartbeat patterns as a secure and continuous method of authentication, as well as eSight Eyewear, a wearable medical device designed to assist individuals with low vision by enhancing their ability to see. I wrote an article for *The Globe and Mail* at the time titled "Why Toronto is a Hotbed for Pioneering Wearable Technology."[6] In the article, I pointed to the flurry of activity and curiosity taking place throughout Canada, specifically in Toronto.

"The activity here has grown exponentially in the last few years," Kate Hartman told me.[7] Hartman is an artist and technologist who works with e-textiles and connected clothing and is an assistant professor in the Digital Futures Program at the Ontario College of Art & Design (OCAD). Originally from New York, Hartman moved to

Canada in 2010 in response to an OCAD job posting for a professorship position in mobile and wearable technology.

"Toronto has a history of being supportive of technology from commercial and artistic perspectives," she said. "It's also a city that has a history of textile manufacturing and fashion activities—from fashion shows to a textile museum, to multiple colleges and universities offering fashion programs."

As part of my research for that article, I also interviewed Steve Mann. Often described as the "Father of Wearable Technology," Steve Mann has been experimenting with wearable computing for nearly forty years. Mann learned to weld at a young age and later attended MIT to study media arts and sciences. Since then, he has created and worn new kinds of internet-connected wearable devices (Figure 2.2).

Figure 2.2 Amanda Cosco and wearable technology pioneer Steve Mann.

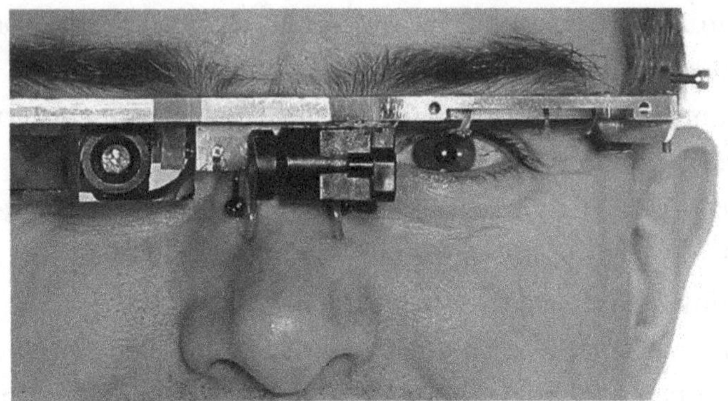

Figure 2.3 Inventor Steve Mann wearing a metal-frame Laser EyeTap (a computer-controlled laser light source run from "Glass Eye" camera).[9]

"It was the summer of 1985 that I first described Toronto as the epicentre of wearable computing," Mann told me.[8] He regarded the commercial wearables of today as a continuation of the work he has been doing since the 1970s and 1980s.

In the 1980s, Mann completed an early version of his EyeTap digital eyeglass (Figure 2.3). This general-purpose computer looks like futuristic glasses and enables the wearer to look up information while walking around. The device can send and receive voice, video, and other data. For those keeping score, Mann's EyeTap project predates Google Glass by more than thirty years.

In 1998, Mann built a prototype of the world's first wristwatch videophone, called the WearComp project, as well as a Wearable Wireless Webcam. The influence of these inventions can be seen in today's smartwatches like Samsung's Gear and lifelogging cameras such as Memento. In 2009, Mann's fully integrated eye camera system was successfully implanted in a visually impaired subject and named among the top fifty inventions of the year by *Time* magazine.[10]

Mann was an inventor by nature, but some of the ideas he pioneered were being productized into consumer devices. At the time I met him, Mann was advising a wearable tech startup called InteraXon, the makers of Muse, the brain-sensing headband. Muse is a head-mounted device that helps people meditate with biofeedback. The first version of the device was a hard plastic headband that sat on your brow and used electroencephalography (EEG) sensors to read brain activity. Muse translates your brainwaves into soundscapes through an accompanying app so you can "hear" your mind. A busy mind could sound like wind or waves, and the goal is to quiet your thoughts to still the sounds.

I remember at one edition of We Are Wearables, Muse was hooked up to a beer tap that would only open if the wearer could calm their mind. The company invited thirsty attendees to demo their technology while rewarding them for getting into a meditative state. To an outsider, it must have seemed like mind control, but really, Muse offered a way to control your own mind.

What was interesting to me was that Muse's founder, Ariel Garten, was a fashion designer and a neuroscientist who combined her passions and expertise to create a product that helped people with their well-being. A more recent version of Muse is made of flexible electronics so people can wear it to bed to monitor their brain activity while sleeping. Muse launched on Kickstarter in late October 2012 and quickly doubled its goal of raising $150,000 in less than three months. In 2014, it was named by *VentureBeat* as the most important wearable of the year.[11]

We Are Wearables gave me the lay of the land when it came to understanding some of the internet-connected devices on the market as well as the rich history in my city of experimentation in wearable computing. That spring, I was about to get a very different view into the world of wearable technology—one rooted in performance and self-expression.

Silicon Valley Fashion Week?

In May 2015, I heard about a tech-meets-fashion event set to take place in San Francisco's Mission district. It was called Silicon Valley Fashion Week? The question mark, I'd soon learn, was intentional, meant to be both ironic and self-reflexive. The poster for the event advertised robots walking on the runway and drones flying in the air (QR Code 8).

QR Code 8 Scan to see the poster for Silicon Valley Fashion Week?

I booked a last-minute ticket to San Francisco and pitched the story to CBC Radio. Silicon Valley Fashion Week? was sponsored by apparel company Betabrand.

The goal, Betabrand's founder Chris Lindland said, was to give a runway to the ways wearable technology, Burning Man, and the Maker Movement were contributing to the world of style.[12] After all, San Francisco is known less for fashion and more for its hoodies and Patagonia vests, so here was a chance, amidst all the wearable technology hype, to reshape the narrative.

Betabrand also leverages technology in an interesting way, albeit not as flashy as tech-infused fashion: The company crowdsources design ideas through its online platform. Popular concepts that receive lots of votes are launched into production to eliminate waste and ensure alignment with consumer preferences. Silicon Valley Fashion Week? was an unconventional platform that resonated with Betabrand's playful, forward-thinking brand identity.

Silicon Valley Fashion Week? featured three nights of wild concepts, presented not on a traditional catwalk but on a stage at the Chapel, a venue typically used for musical performances. Some of the standout items included a motorcycle jacket adorned with white fur and LEDs, a fishbowl helmet complete with live fish, and drones flying coat hangers displaying pants and a suit jacket. It was unlike anything I'd ever seen on runways in Toronto or New York.

As always, I captured what I was seeing with my camera, including a photo of a fiber-optic dress that resembled a ballerina silhouette (Figure 2.4).

Figure 2.4 Fiber-optic dress at Silicon Valley Fashion Week? created by Jen Mann. Originally designed by Natalie Walsh.
Photo by Amanda Cosco.

I learned that the creator was Jenn Mann (no relation to Steven Mann), but when I interviewed her backstage she revealed that the original design came from Natalie Walsh. Mann explained that she had followed a blueprint from a website called Instructables—a user-generated community for DIY projects, including those involving wearable technology.

Instructables democratizes access to knowledge, and I became fascinated by the idea that fashion, like software, could be open-source. It reminded me of dress patterns I'd seen in fabric stores: One pattern could be shared hundreds of times and result in countless iterations. This grassroots approach to creation was vastly different from the traditional fashion consumption I was used to. That's when I realized that digital technology wasn't just appearing on the runway—it was also transforming the way we generate and share fashion. Instructables was kind of a modern-day pattern-sharing site.

At Silicon Valley Fashion Week?, I had also met the co-founders of Bellabeat, creators of the Leaf, a wearable health tracker, and Eric Migicovsky, the founder of Pebble, the smartwatch that anticipated the release of the Apple smartwatch later that year. These were the few commercially available products among the costume and concept pieces, and their presence gave the event some gravity. By the end of the following year, Fitbit would acquire Pebble for $40 million.

Just as Silicon Valley Fashion Week? lit up the runway, my brain was blinking with the different ways digital technology could enable fashion. I returned to Toronto knowing I wanted to focus exclusively on fashion tech.

Burning Man

At the end of August into early September 2015, I attended Burning Man for the first time, a week-long event in the Black Rock Desert in Nevada. Unlike other festivals that focus on musical acts and have amenities like flushing toilets, Burning Man is more of a social experiment relying on communal effort, creative cooperation, and collaboration. It's unmediated by commercial sponsorships, advertising, or transactions. Instead, people rely on acts of goodwill and gifts in order to get by.

The event's core principles are art, community, self-expression, and radical self-reliance. Everything at Burning Man is created from scratch, from the costumes to the art installations to the roads and camps. The event also has a "leave no trace" policy, which requires participants to remove all traces of their presence from the desert after the event.

At Burning Man, wearable light is not just a matter of self-expression, it's a matter of survival. In the middle of the desert, you're subject to all the elements: heat, dust, and—when the sun goes down—complete darkness. With thousands of people (many of them on drugs) whirling around in the pitch-black night on bikes, motorcycles, and cars, you'd better find a way to make yourself visible.

Burning Man was my gateway into the Maker Movement. For those not familiar with this term, the Maker Movement is a cultural and social phenomenon that celebrates creativity, innovation, and the act of making things. It is driven by individuals and communities who design, build, and share projects, often blending traditional craftsmanship with cutting-edge technology.

Inspired by Natalie Walsh's dress from Silicon Valley Fashion Week?, my friends and I augmented some jean jackets and vests we'd thrifted and secured bundles of fiber-optic strands in extra pockets we'd sewn in. For a week in the desert, I biked around marveling at the level of artistry and effort people put into Burning Man costumes, installations, and art cars—vehicles modified for personal self-expression. At Burning Man, cars and costumes became an extension of the self. Many of the illuminated costumes relied on embedded electronics, programmable lights, and sensors—hallmarks of IoT.

At the event, we spotted a version of Natalie Walsh's dress and stopped to take a picture. I would later see versions of this same dress at several events throughout my life, from festivals to tech conferences.

These experiences—We Are Wearables in Toronto, Silicon Valley Fashion Week? in San Francisco, and Burning Man in the Nevada desert—provided me with a foundational understanding of wearable technology as a bridge between art, fashion, and innovation. Each event showcased the diverse ways people were integrating technology into self-expression and functionality, from practical health-tracking devices to whimsical, illuminated creations. Together, they shaped my vision of what tech-infused fashion could be and fueled my determination to explore it further.

Returning to Toronto, I was inspired to take the insights and connections I had gained and channel them into something tangible—ultimately leading to the launch of my brand, Electric Runway, and a deeper dive into the exciting world of smart fabrics and connected clothing.

Launching Electric Runway

In 2015, the organizers of Maker Festival Toronto approached me to curate a fashion technology runway show. They had seen my reporting on the subject and believed I was the right person for the job. Although I had never organized a runway show before, the Toronto community rallied around me, helping me bring my first fashion-tech presentation to life. The show blended commercially available wearable tech products with experimental costume and concept pieces. One standout look was a black A-line dress by Robert Tu featuring a full-color programmable matrix display that scrolled the words "ELECTRIC RUNWAY" in vibrant pink lettering. Another model showcased

Figure 2.5 Amanda Cosco wearing Proxima by Laura Dempsey, Hannah Newton, Ben Reed, Dan Damron, and Chris Zaal.
Photo by Jasmine Pazzano.

a muscle-activated kinetic textile, created by Izzie Colpitts-Campbell, that expanded and contracted in response to movement. For the event, I emceed in a blazer adorned with light-up flowers and a laser-cut skirt, both designed by Laura Dempsey (Figure 2.5).

The finale of the runway show featured dancers wearing light-up hoodies by Sovo Gear, a San Francisco-based company that integrates electroluminescent piping into its designs. The showcase was a smorgasbord of wearable light, internet-connected devices, and 3D-printed jewelry. While it may not have been the most cohesive fashion show ever staged, the energy in the room was electric, and seeing the audience's faces light up with wonder made the effort to produce the show worthwhile. For many people, this was the first time they were seeing wearable technology in person.

That night marked the official launch of Electric Runway, the umbrella brand for all my reporting and research on fashion technology. Electric Runway offered me the freedom to self-publish at a pace that traditional media simply couldn't match. I had grown increasingly frustrated with the lag between pitching stories and seeing them in print; by the time my articles were published, the fast-moving world of digital innovation had already advanced. The slow speed of print publishing felt incompatible with the rapid evolution of the topics I was covering, so publishing directly to ElectricRunway.com became the obvious solution.

The DIY ethos of Burning Man profoundly influenced this approach. At Burning Man, creativity thrives without traditional hierarchies or gatekeepers—if you have an idea, you make it happen. This permissionless mindset inspired me to embrace a more independent, gonzo style of journalism for Electric Runway: immersive, firsthand, and unapologetically subjective. Like the self-built art installations and open-source fashion at the festival, Electric Runway became a space for exploration and experimentation, allowing me not just to document stories but to become part of the narrative. It was journalism that mirrored Burning Man's belief that participation is key to creation.

The same summer that I launched Electric Runway, Levis announced a partnership with Google called Project Jacquard, an initiative to develop special conductive threads that could be woven into textiles, enabling them to sense touch and gestures. Users could control their smartphone or other connected devices by swiping or tapping on the fabric, like a wearable touchscreen. That fall, Apple introduced the Apple Watch Hermès, a collaboration between the tech company and the luxury design house in Paris. These partnerships verified my instincts that something special was happening between fashion and technology that couldn't be ignored.

Smart Fabrics and Softwear

In October 2015, I flew to Montreal to cover Wear It Smart, a conference on the future of smart fabrics. "Textiles are a flexible conduit for wearable technology," Dr. Marie O'Mahony explained to me at the time.[13] Dr. O'Mahony is a leading expert in the field of advanced textiles. "Smart fabrics aren't made of plastic or metal, like hardware," she said. "Instead, they're something we can connect with emotionally."

Since clothing is familiar, it makes sense that it's the medium we're using to bridge the gap between our physical and digital worlds. Unlike the textiles we're used to (like cotton or linen), smart fabrics can sense and react to environmental conditions.

While high-performance and responsive fabrics aren't new (for example, materials that wick moisture from the body or protect the skin from UV rays), what's novel is technology's ability to personalize clothing and bring it to life. For example, a smart jacket could include sensors inside that measure your body temperature. The jacket would also be connected to the internet via your smartphone, and in an accompanying app, you could set your ideal temperature. When the sensors read that your body temperature drops, the jacket would "know" and heat up accordingly to warm you up. This may sound like the stuff of science fiction, but startups like Ororo have brought coats featuring battery-operated heating systems to market.

I quickly learned of a number of companies putting Montreal on the map as the capital of smart fabrics. One of those startups was OMsignal, a company that helps major brands develop smart apparel. OMsignal collaborated with American fashion brand Ralph Lauren to deliver the technology inside their Polo Tech shirt. The shirt looks like any ordinary black T-shirt, but it's woven with silver fibers and includes a detachable black box that streams biometric data directly to your iPad or iPhone so athletes can monitor metrics like heart rate, breathing depth, stress levels, and calorie burn. The shirt originally debuted at the US Open to position Ralph Lauren not only as a fashion leader but also as a forward-thinking brand embracing the intersection of technology, health, and lifestyle.

Another smart fabrics company I encountered was Hexoskin. Founded in 2006 by Pierre-Alexandre Fournier, Hexoskin makes comfortable and washable garments for continuously monitoring a wearer's health and biometrics. At first, I thought Hexoskin was going to land in healthcare, but it turns out they were actually shooting for the stars. I'd later write an article for the *Toronto Star* about Hexoskin's Astroskin, a version of their shirt designed for space travel.[14] The shirts were sent to the space station to monitor astronauts' vitals in space. Data gathered from the shirts are transmitted back to Earth, where scientists monitor the astronauts' health as they orbit the planet to gain a better understanding of the impact of space travel on the human body.

MakeFashion

The following year, in May 2016, I heard about a group of makers from Calgary, Alberta, who were putting on another fashion-tech runway show. MakeFashion is an organization dedicated to enabling digital fashion. It brings together fashion designers and makers who want to bring clothing to life with digital technology and provides them with the tools and resources to do so. The organization was founded by husband and wife duo Shannon and Maria Elena Hoover and creative Chelsea Klukas, with ongoing support from a robust community of creatives.

"You won't see things like Fitbits," Shannon Hoover told me in an interview before the runway show. "What we do is very designer-led. It's about telling a story.... This is a fashion show. It's not what you'd normally think of when you say wearable tech."[15]

Designs on the MakeFashion runway included a mother–daughter duo of coordinated dresses with black tops and voluminous, midi-length skirts featuring a black floral pattern on a cream background. The dresses featured lights in the belt and neckline that were triggered by proximity sensors and lit up when they were near one another, meant to symbolize the special relationship between mothers and daughters.

Another design was a dark and romantic dress made of velvet with paisley and floral motifs and fourteen LED lights. The dress was synced with an Emotiv EPOC x Brainwave headset, a next-generation EEG (electroencephalogram) headset used to monitor and interpret brain activity by detecting electrical signals. When a performer sang wearing the dress, the lights lit up with different colors based on her brain activity, exploring the relationship between music and consciousness (QR Code 9).

QR Code 9 Scan to watch my coverage of MakeFashion 2016.

The MakeFashion runway exemplified the ways wearable technology can move beyond utility to tell deeply personal and emotional stories through clothing. Designs like the mother–daughter dresses with proximity-triggered lights or the brainwave-activated LED gown show how technology, when paired with creativity, can transform fashion into an expressive and interactive medium. These innovations reflect the broader potential of the Internet of Things in fashion—not just to track or connect, but to engage and inspire. As IoT continues to merge with fashion, it challenges traditional notions of clothing, turning garments into dynamic, responsive interfaces that deepen our connection to ourselves and others. The MakeFashion showcase served as a vivid reminder that fashion tech is not just about gadgets or functionality, but about reimagining the role of clothing in our lives and the stories it can tell in the digital age.

That May, the theme of the annual Met Gala was "Fashion in an Age of Technology." Zac Posen created an illuminated dress for actress Claire Danes made of organza and fiber optics (QR Code 10). According to *Vanity Fair*, the skirt was so voluminous that the two had to take a bus to get to the event.[16] Both at home in Canada and at the Met, on the world stage for fashion, fashion tech was at the forefront. It was clear the world was becoming just as fascinated as I was with the possibilities of the future of fashion.

QR Code 10 Scan to see Zac Posen's illuminated dress for Claire Danes at the 2016 Met Gala.

By the time the Consumer Electronics Show (CES) rolled around in January 2017, there were too many wearable accessories and wrist-worn devices to keep up with, and it wasn't just for runway shows.

Tourism company Princess Cruises launched the Ocean Medallion, a wrist-worn device to help wearers with wayfinding, ordering food, and accessing gaming and entertainment; a pair of rings from a company called the Touch allows wearers to feel their loved one's heartbeat in real-time so they're always connected; Motiv launched its ring for fitness and sleep tracking.

Although consumer wearables at the time were interesting, I was getting frustrated with their lack of nuance. All of them seemed like "me-too" devices that just wanted to count our steps. "Wristables" became a blanket term for the countless watches, bracelets, and bands that accounted for our biometric data. As I wrote in an article for *Wareable* at the time, "The rush to translate the human body into data sets that can be processed by our machines has resulted in an explosion of hardware devices—many of which do the same thing and aren't always that technologically interesting."[17]

I made it my goal to try and find stories for Electric Runway that were true examples of design meeting innovation rather than fashion just slapped on top of tech as an afterthought.

Wearables Beyond the Wrist

In 2017, I practically lived out of a suitcase. I started the year at the Consumer Electronics Show, where I had the opportunity to meet Billie Whitehouse, the founder of Wearable Experiments. Billie recently launched Nadi X, a pair of yoga pants that helps wearers improve their yoga practice through built-in technology that provides real-time guidance and feedback. Although at first glance Nadi X looked like any other black yoga pant, they included embedded motion sensors to track movement during yoga poses. The pants would provide gentle vibrations that served as cues, directing the wearer to adjust their posture and guide their alignment. "The skin is the largest organ on our body, and it's an underutilized communication system," Whitehouse told me in an interview for the *Electric Runway Podcast*.[18] Much of Whitehouse's work leverages sensors and haptic feedback to connect people to one another. Her Fundawear project, for example, is a set of his-and-her underwear for couples in long-distance relationships. The smart underpants facilitate a kind of virtual play where touch gestures on a smartphone screen are translated into vibrations in the underwear. It was an interesting (yet ridiculous) example of how wearable technology could enable new kinds of human-to-human communication.

After CES, I spent time in San Francisco getting to know some of fashion tech's most interesting pioneers, including Kristin Neidlinger and Behnaz Farahi.

Neidlinger is a designer most known for creating the GER Mood Sweater, a cropped sweater with galvanic skin response sensors you wear on your palms (Figure 2.6). The sweater would "read" your emotions from the palm of your hand using the same technology as a lie detector. It would then display that emotion as color on the cowl of the sweater. Purple means you're ruffled or excited, while blue means you're calm and focused (think of it like a mood ring but in sweater form).

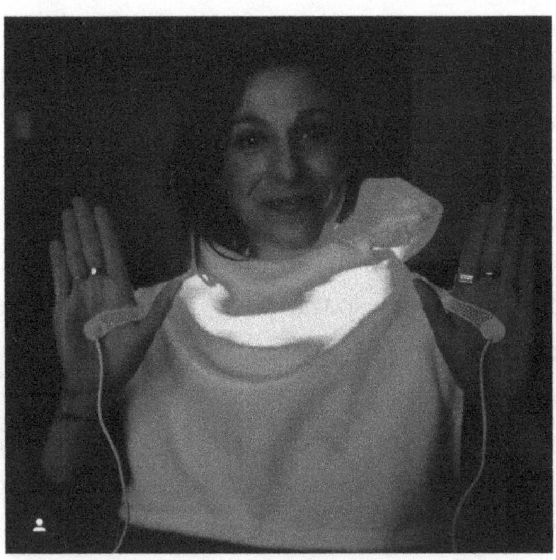

Figure 2.6 Amanda wearing Sensoree's GER Mood Sweater. Photo by Tom Emrich.

Neidlinger was interested in exploring the idea of extimacy—externalized intimacy by showcasing to the outside world how people feel on the inside. Now, you may be thinking, *what's the point?* Or, *who would actually wear that?* Interestingly, Neidlinger's work has been tested in children with autism, in couple's therapy, and in other settings where accessing emotions can sometimes be tough. While the GER Mood Sweater relied on the same IoT infrastructure as consumer wristables I'd seen at CES, Neidlinger was leveraging the technology to make us more social and connected.

Shortly after, I met Behnaz Farahi. Farahi trained as an architect and was also pushing the limits of how clothing could communicate. She'd created an interactive 3D-printed cape that looked like animal fur called "Caress of the Gaze." The cape used computer vision technology to detect and respond to the gaze of onlookers. "The project aims to rethink our relationships with our bodies and their surrounding environments," she told me.[19] Both Neidlinger and Farahi were pioneers in exploring the ways people could communicate with connected clothing, but I was about to meet a designer whose creations seemed to leap straight out of science fiction, redefining for me and many others what fashion could be.

In September 2017, I flew to New York to interview Anouk Wipprecht. I had heard about her robotic dresses from someone I'd met at a conference in Finland a few years earlier and had been eagerly following her online since. When I learned she would be in North America, I jumped at the opportunity to meet her.

At five-foot-eight, decked out in pastels and glitter tights, Anouk Wipprecht appeared more like a kindergarten teacher than a technologist. She is small-framed with childish eyes and a dainty step. On stage at the World Maker Faire in New York, she looked like a fairy princess next to her contemporary, Francis Bitonti, who wore all black. The two were giving a talk on technology in fashion design.

Wipprecht's early work demonstrates interest in media worn on the body. *Pseudomorphs* (2011) is a series of white dresses stained with ink transmitted onto the body via wearable medical equipment. Pneumatic control valves and a pressure control system enable ink to be pumped through the design and spread onto the absorbent garments, creating a kind of bleeding effect. The design was worn by Britney Spears in her music video "Hold It Against Me" (2011), although rather than using the valves to drip blue ink onto herself, the pop artist used it to project four strands of colored ink all over a white wedding dress and the set around her.

Smoke Dress (2012) was created in collaboration with Aduen Darriba and 3D-printed by Materialise. The dress was commissioned as a series of designs created for Volkswagen to complement the car company's display at the Frankfurt International Motor Show. Sensors on the dress detect the wearer's stress levels. If they get too high, it triggers an internal smoke system that's integrated within. The dress releases a smoke-like substance to mask the wearer as a means of protection, not unlike the way an octopus releases ink.

In a similar vein, *Spider Dress* (2012) includes an embedded protection system that keeps others at bay with animated robotic arms that look like the legs of a spider. If the wearer's breath becomes heavy, sensors read that she feels threatened, and in response, the robotic arms extend to defend her. Once the wearer no longer feels threatened, the arms retreat and assume a softer form.

Although highly conceptual and not meant for everyday wear, what intrigued me about Wipprecht's work was that she wasn't just producing wearables focused on counting steps. Like Neidlinger's idea of "extimacy," Wipprecht's designs were concerned with providing a voice to the wearer's body and enabling a new kind of communication and interactivity between ourselves, our clothing, and the world around us.

The work of these pioneers—Billie Whitehouse, Kristin Neidlinger, Behnaz Farahi, and Anouk Wipprecht—illustrates how wearable technology transcends utility to explore deeper questions about connection, emotion, and the boundaries between our bodies and the world. From yoga pants that guide movement to dresses that react to proximity or gaze, these innovations challenge traditional ideas of clothing, turning garments into interactive interfaces. As I traveled and met these visionaries, it became clear that the Internet of Things is not just about devices communicating but about creating a more intimate, responsive, and connected relationship between people, their clothing, and the environment around them.

Things Get Ridiculous Before They Get Useful

Like any hype cycle at its peak, wearable technology had its fair share of crazy ideas: a connected belt that alerted you if you ate too much or were too sedentary; a smart wig that vibrated when you got a text or email.

Perhaps one of the most ridiculous wearable tech products I ever saw was a pair of pants called DrumPants. They were quite literally a pair of pants with sensors sewn in which you could use to trigger different sounds a drum would make, thus turning your pants into drums. *Who would want that?* I remember thinking when I first discovered DrumPants. A few years later, while attending a We Are Wearables Meetup in Toronto, a rehabilitation specialist was on stage discussing a recent startup they'd collaborated with to help nonverbal patients communicate their needs through sensors. Who was the startup they were working with? *It was DrumPants!* Turns out their technology was ideal for connecting sensors to wheelchairs, canes, or clothing. Users could hit one of the many sensors to trigger prerecorded phrases that sounded from a Bluetooth-connected smartphone or tablet.

What I learned by following the story of DrumPants was that things get ridiculous before they get useful. According to Gartner's hype cycle for emerging technologies, there's a peak of inflated expectations before any plateau of productivity. In other words, sometimes startups throw shit at the wall to see what sticks, and often a technology developed for one area (music, in this case) can end up being wildly successful in another area (healthcare).

The Challenges of Wearable Technology

At the peak of inflated expectations for wearable technology, you might have believed that in the future, we'd all be walking around with connected clothing all the time. The truth is that few wearable devices made it out of the hype cycle. Many startups during this period folded and struggled to deliver on their promises, due to technological limitations, high production costs, or a lack of consumer adoption.

One of the biggest challenges facing wearable tech was (and still is) battery life. While these devices promise convenience and seamless integration into our daily lives, their functionality often comes at the cost of frequent charging. Whether it's a smartwatch, fitness tracker, or smart glasses, users must consistently remember to charge these devices, which can disrupt the seamless experience they're designed to provide. Furthermore, the compact size of wearables limits the battery capacity, making it difficult to balance power needs with long-lasting use. This reliance on frequent charging not only creates inconvenience but also raises concerns about sustainability and the lifespan of these devices.

Washability remains a significant challenge for wearable technology because these devices and garments must withstand the rigors of daily life, including cleaning. Unlike traditional electronics, wearables are often integrated into clothing or accessories that require regular washing, creating a conflict between functionality and durability. Moisture, detergents, and mechanical agitation can damage the delicate electronic components embedded in smart fabrics or wearable devices. Although advances in waterproofing and encapsulation techniques have been made, ensuring that wearable technology is both functional and easy to maintain continues to be a critical hurdle for designers and engineers.

Scalability is a significant challenge for wearable technology, particularly for smart apparel. Most traditional apparel manufacturing facilities are optimized for producing garments at scale using established techniques and materials, but they are not equipped to handle the integration of electronic components, sensors, or conductive fabrics. The production of smart apparel often requires specialized processes, such as embedding circuits or attaching microchips, which can disrupt standard workflows and drive up costs. Additionally, ensuring that these advanced garments are both durable and functional while maintaining the aesthetics and comfort consumers expect adds another layer of complexity. Bridging the gap between fashion manufacturing and tech integration remains a critical hurdle for scaling wearable tech to mainstream markets.

Despite the challenges presented by wearable technology, its emergence in the early 2010s had us all imagining what the future of fashion could look like when fused with technology. It caused us to demand more of our clothing in terms of both performance and self-expression, and this period gave birth to some widely used wearable tech devices.

Apple emerged as one of the winners, with the Apple Watch and their wireless headphones, which they named AirPods. Unlike other headphones, AirPods are entirely wireless and seamlessly sync with your iPhone. They rely on Bluetooth technology to connect with your phone. Launched in 2016, AirPods would go on to become the most successful wearable tech product to date in terms of revenue. In 2022, AirPods alone earned Apple $14.5 billion in revenue—a single product offering out-earned startups including Spotify, Shopify, and Airbnb.

The rise of wearable technology showcased how IoT could transform everyday objects into interactive experiences, but the implications of IoT extend far beyond personal devices. Just as wearables revolutionized our relationship with technology on the body, connected products are reshaping our interaction with objects in the broader world. Enter the era of connected products and Digital Product Passports, where garments and accessories hold not just style but stories, histories, and the promise of sustainable futures.

The Future of Connected Clothing

If you've ever been to a thrift store, a vintage market, or an estate sale, you may know the feeling of being among used clothes and feeling like you're surrounded by other people's stories. *Who on earth owned this fringed leather jacket with mixed metal studs? What about this pair of sheer harem pants with slits in the knees and beading around the trim?* The Internet of Things provides us the opportunity to solve the mystery of an item's provenance.

Technologies like QR codes and NFC (near-field communication) tags enable each item of clothing to carry its own digital identity online. Imagine a garment as a library card, where every interaction—who wore it, when, and how—is logged. Owners could upload reviews, share memories tied to the garment, and archive images of how they styled it. A future buyer could simply scan the item with their smartphone to access this rich history and even contribute their own experiences. Beyond storytelling, this technology could provide detailed information about the garment's origin and creator, along with care instructions and guidance for recycling or disposal. The implications for supply chain transparency and traceability are profound, pointing toward a future where every piece of clothing has a voice—and that future may be closer than we think.

In the European Union, Digital Product Passports (DPPs) are becoming law. A DPP is a digital record containing key information about a product's consumption, origin, and life cycle. By 2030, textile products for sale in the EU will be required to have a DPP, whether this is a scannable QR code or NFC tag. Once accessed, the DPP will provide information about the product's origins, material composition, supply chain, sustainability, and more. This is all part of the EU's Strategy for Sustainable and Circular Textiles in an effort to enable traceability of clothing so consumers can make more informed shopping decisions.

Digital Product Passports are an attempt to push back against greenwashing, where brands claim items are sustainable or made from recycled materials (and therefore "green") when in fact they are not. For example, according to Earth.org, in 2019, H&M launched its own line of "green" clothing titled "Conscious."[20] The company claimed to use organic cotton and recycled polyester. The Norwegian Consumer Authority found that H&M did not provide sufficient information about the sustainable nature of its Conscious Collection and was therefore misleading.

Beyond greenwashing, imagine if brands were responsible for an item's proper and ethical disposal. How would that change the way we design clothes, and the materials we select? What if each item could be traced back to the factory where it was made so consumers could understand if their dollars were supporting slave labor? If each item could tell you all about where it came from, who made it, and in what conditions, then clothing would no longer be silent. It would speak the truth, much like Wipprecht's designs.

Many companies are working on the future of connected products, transforming how consumers interact with and understand the items they purchase. One such leader is Blue Bite, a connected products company specializing in creating, launching, and maintaining digital product passports. These passports provide each item with a unique digital identity, accessible via technologies like QR codes or NFC tags. By scanning the code or tapping the tag with a smartphone, consumers can unlock a wealth of information about the product—its origin, materials, manufacturing process, and even care instructions or end-of-life recycling options. (Full disclosure: I'm an advisor to Blue Bite.)

Digital product passports not only enhance transparency and traceability but also foster a deeper connection between brands and their customers. They empower consumers to make informed decisions by providing insights into sustainability practices, ethical production, and product authenticity. For brands, digital passports open up opportunities for personalized marketing, post-purchase engagement, and data collection to better understand customer preferences. As companies like Blue Bite continue to innovate, digital product passports are poised to become a cornerstone of the Internet of Things, connecting physical goods to the digital world in meaningful ways.

Wearables Revisited

Every once in a while, there's a dress that breaks the internet—meaning it becomes so viral and so talked about that it's hard not to pay attention. Think of Jennifer Lopez's green Versace dress at the Grammy Awards in 2000, or Lady Gaga's meat dress at the 2010 MTV VMAs. These dresses usually come from renowned designers and appear on runways or red carpets, but the dress that had everyone talking in October 2023 came from inside a software company.

Unveiled at Adobe's annual Max Conference, a gathering known for its experimental tech previews, Project Primrose is a fully interactive dress with multiple pattern configuration possibilities (QR Code 11). It uses flexible textile displays to create a kind of sequin pattern that can change color and shift its design in a blink.

QR Code 11 Scan to see the video of Project Primrose as unveiled at the Adobe Max conference in October 2023.

In this clip, you can hear the audible gasps from audience members as creator Christine Dierk demonstrates the garment's ability to transition from light gray to dark gray and cycle through striking patterns.

From a user experience perspective, I still have the same questions I've always had when it comes to smart fabrication: *Where are the wires? How do we wash it?* And *What's the practical application?*

In the botanical world, the primrose is one of the first flowers to bloom in spring, symbolizing youth, renewal, and optimism. Project Primrose could similarly signal a new chapter for wearable technology and smart fabrication—one marked by renewed energy and advancements driven by AI. As companies increasingly explore the intersection of AI, interactivity, and fashion, the possibilities for garments that adapt and respond to their environment feel more tangible than ever.

Of course, with all the hype surrounding AI, many have been racing to create the first truly successful wearable AI product. So far, none have managed to deliver something both functional and broadly appealing (we'll explore this further in Chapter 6). Still, Project Primrose represents an exciting glimpse of what's possible, reminding us that the future of fashion technology is still unfolding, with endless room for creativity and innovation.

The Internet of Things has redefined the relationship between fashion and technology, transforming clothing and accessories into dynamic tools for connectivity and self-expression. What began as experimental technology on runways and in niche communities has steadily evolved into innovations that enhance everyday life, from health-monitoring wearables to garments that tell their own stories. Despite the challenges wearable tech faced in scaling to mainstream adoption—such as battery life, washability, and cost—it laid the groundwork for a more connected and transparent future.

Today, IoT extends far beyond personal devices, with technologies like Digital Product Passports paving the way for a new era of accountability and traceability in fashion. These connected products promise to bridge the gap between sustainability and consumer trust, offering not just transparency but also an opportunity to reimagine our relationship with the clothes we wear. As technology continues to weave itself into the fabric of our lives, the fusion of fashion and IoT reminds us that innovation is not only about function but also about creating meaningful connections—to our bodies, our environment, and one another. The IoT isn't just about linking devices—it's about redefining how we connect with ourselves, others, and the world around us, both on and beyond the surface of our skin.

Chapter 3

Automation

The next wave of economic dislocations won't come from overseas. It will come from the relentless pace of automation that makes a lot of good, middle-class jobs obsolete.

—Barack Obama, Farewell Address, January 10, 2017

God awful prints, sheer af clothing that isn't supposed to be sheer (white effortless pants..) at abysmal prices. $200 for a fucking polyester dress???? I'm literally so disappointed as an OG Aritiza fan (grew up in the 00's in Vancouver). I used to be able to justify the prices due to quality and style but now I'm just gonna shop at the Gap and Banana Republic lmao

—u/crown_wonderland, "Aritzia Has Become Sooo Tacky Now," *Reddit*, March 23, 2022

Dhaka, Bangladesh—February 2018

It was nightfall when I landed in Bangladesh. The streets were a chaotic blur of lights and horns and motor cars whizzing by. I had traveled more than eighteen hours to get there: a thirteen-hour flight from Toronto to Abu Dhabi and another five-and-a-half-hour flight to Dhaka. As I made my way past airport security, I saw a man holding a piece of paper with my name printed on it. He didn't speak English but gestured for me to follow him. He took me through passport control before driving me to my hotel. The beep of horns in traffic was constant. In Bangladesh, they drive on the left side of the road, a relic of the region's colonial past. The country was once a part of British India until 1947, when the land was divided into India and Pakistan. From 1947 to 1971, Bangladesh existed as East Pakistan until it gained independence in 1971.

The hotel I was staying in was in an area where Westerners typically stay, usually because they are doing business with apparel manufacturers in the area. I remember settling into my room when I first heard the Azan—the call to prayer. It was a man's singing voice over a loudspeaker that sounded throughout the city. Exhausted, I closed my eyes and fell asleep to the melodic echo in a language I didn't know, more than seven thousand miles away from home.

The following day, when the sun rose, I looked out my window to see that the air was a thick cloud of dust. Dhaka is the capital and largest city in Bangladesh and among the world's top ten most densely populated cities. At the beginning of 2018, at the time of my visit, it ranked as the second most polluted city on the planet. It is also known as the apparel capital of the world, second only to China in terms of its production output.

Apparel accounts for 83% of Bangladesh's exports and employs over four million people.[1] This volume of production is not without consequences. As an article in *The Daily Star,* Bangladesh's English daily newspaper, points out, "the country's heavy reliance on textile production for economic development comes with an enormous environmental price tag that is often overlooked in the global narrative of cheap, trendy clothing."[2] Studies have shown that the apparel industry is a significant source of water pollution in the region[3] and chemicals from industrial waste have rendered Bangladesh rivers untreatable.[4] According to a 2023 study, Bangladesh has the most polluted air in the world.[5]

I was part of an international delegation of invited speakers attending a conference on the future of fashion. Unfortunately, I was sick from the food and poor air quality the whole time. The irony was not lost on me that I was there to talk about the future of an industry making me sick in real time. My privilege was that I got to go home after the conference. Meanwhile, many Bangladeshis lack the means to leave. It's estimated that each resident of Bangladesh loses almost seven years of their life due to air pollution.[6]

The conference I was speaking at was put on by Pacific Jeans, a global frontrunner in denim manufacturing. They invited experts from all over the world to share their perspectives on new technologies changing the apparel industry. My host was Mostafiz Uddin, a factory owner and one of the conference organizers. Uddin is a gregarious man with a booming voice that made everyone in the room stand up straight while he spoke. Before the conference, he led our delegation on a tour of Dhaka, visiting different manufacturing facilities for an up-close look at where (and how) our clothing is made.

As in Lagos, traffic is a big part of the Dhaka experience. Every day, we spent hours on the roads, some paved and some unpaved, some with lines and some without. The population density was evident: Bangladeshis crammed into Volkswagens and buses. I observed very different public safety standards. In Ontario, it's illegal not to wear a seatbelt in a car or to ride in the back of a pickup truck; here, commuters were riding on top of trucks and hanging outside doors and windows when there was no room inside. A rickshaw carried a mother and her three children, a bag of rice at her feet and a live chicken clutched in her hands. Everything—the buildings, the cars, and the bridges—was dusted with earth.

One of the first facilities we visited was Ecofab Limited, a shirt manufacturer whose clients included Marks & Spencer and Tommy Hilfiger. Upon our arrival, several women with flowers stood outside the building to greet us. A big welcome sign had our names and faces printed on it.

Inside the facility, nine thousand garment workers assembled cut material into clothing. They sewed bright red fabric with the Puma logo on it into T-shirts. On another floor, a worker assembled a dress shirt on what looked like the torso of a mannequin. The torso inflated with hot air and then deflated, leaving a perfectly steamed shirt ready to be packaged and sent out. There was a whole room of hundreds of patterns—one for each design size. Thick metal clips bound together the pattern pieces so they didn't get separated.

The facility was small compared to most in the area. It had gone to great lengths to earn the "sustainable" label, including reusing treated water, harvesting rainwater, and recycling organic waste from employee lunches to produce fertilizer. Nothing was mentioned about how much energy was needed to power the army of machinery or where the scraps of leftover fabric ended up.

Like most people, I had preconceived notions about what the "Made in Bangladesh" label meant. I imagined poor working conditions for people and low-quality goods. But here I was seeing premium brands like Scotch & Soda being made next to more affordable brands like Zara in highly regulated and compliant facilities. Maybe my preconceived notions weren't the whole picture, I thought.

At the same time, I could not tell whether this factory depicted the reality of Bangladesh's manufacturing or was a false front—a facility they show Western businesspeople and journalists like me to make us feel comfortable about environmental concerns and labor conditions.

Most people's perception of manufacturing in Bangladesh has been colored by one disaster—the Rana Plaza factory collapse. On April 24, 2013, an eight-story commercial building in Dhaka, Bangladesh, collapsed, killing more than 1,000 garment workers and injuring 2,500. It was the deadliest garment factory disaster in history. By comparison, the Triangle Shirtwaist Factory fire that took place in 1911 in the Greenwich Village neighborhood of Manhattan killed 146 garment workers.

Rana Plaza threw a spotlight on Bangladesh's manufacturing sector. As a result, many changes were made that amounted to leaps and bounds forward in terms of compliance and worker health, including the advent of the Bangladesh Accord and Alliance for Worker Safety. Yet the image of Bangladesh cannot outrun the shadow of its past.

My uncertainty about Bangladesh is not uncommon. In his book *Bangladesh Stories*, Mostafiz Uddin writes about how Westerners often come to visit Bangladesh and are "positively shocked" at what they see:

> New buyers are often positively shocked when they come [to Bangladesh]. The reality does not match the perception they had formed by reading about us on the internet. This is not what Bangladesh looked like in the reports they had read, they tell us.[7]

I was invited to Bangladesh to give a talk on wearable technology, which seemed silly amidst the large machinery and industrial operations. Here I was immersed in a culture with people whose entire lives revolved around apparel production, yet I was talking about connected underwear and robotic dresses that pour shots. Here, everything that fascinated me about wearable technology seemed privileged and very far away.

After I gave my talk, a journalist from the *Dhaka Tribune*, one of Bangladesh's newspapers, approached me for an interview. Even though my presentation was about connected clothing, the journalist had a very pointed question for me: "So Amanda," he asked, "how many robots are going to replace how many jobs by the year 2045?" I blinked. *How should I know?* I thought.

Automation as Fashion Technology

Until my time in Dhaka, my definition of fashion technology had included social media and shopping apps, as well as technology on the body, since that was my perspective mainly as a fashion consumer in the West; I hadn't considered all the technology involved in producing the clothes we wear. It very quickly became clear to me that in Bangladesh, fashion technology meant one thing: automation.

Automation is the application of technology, programs, robotics, or processes to achieve outcomes with minimal human input.[8] Central to the very definition of automation is eliminating, augmenting, or alleviating human effort and reshaping the labor landscape. Think of, for example, the self-checkouts at grocery stores that minimize the number of cashiers needed, or drones that plant seeds in specific areas to reduce the number of field workers in farming. According to a recent McKinsey Global Survey, the share of companies adopting automation technologies is steadily climbing.[9] Another report suggests that *half* of today's work activities could be automated by 2055, and the industries most likely to be affected include manufacturing and retail.[10]

In this chapter, we'll examine the far-reaching implications of automation in the fashion industry, from its historical origins to its present-day applications and future possibilities. We will explore how automation has revolutionized apparel manufacturing, reshaped global supply chains, and driven the fast-fashion phenomenon. Additionally, we'll investigate emerging technologies like micro-factories and 3D printing, which promise to redefine production methods. Along the way, we'll consider the social, economic, and environmental costs of automation, as well as its potential to transform both the labor landscape and consumer expectations. By the end of this chapter, readers will have a comprehensive understanding of how automation is not just reshaping fashion, but also our relationship with the clothes we wear.

For those in the apparel manufacturing sector, automation looks like machines that automatically do everything, including fabric inspection, spreading, cutting, numbering, fusing, buttoning, and sewing. These machines pose a real threat to factory jobs. The *Dhaka Tribune* journalist's question to me was poignant, considering the industry's size: Bangladesh's apparel industry is the single source of the country's growth and the primary source of its foreign exchange earnings.

Garment work has significantly impacted the status of women in Bangladesh. Two-thirds of garment workers are women; many secure entry-level employment without prior work experience. This has led to a sense of empowerment and autonomy among women, enabling them to earn their own money and, in some cases, become the sole breadwinners for their families.

Many Bangladeshis worry that their jobs will be replaced by machines that automate part of the clothes-making process. It's not an unfounded worry. By one estimate, if automation reaches its full potential, countries like Bangladesh will lose more than 80% of their garment, manufacturing, and textile jobs.[11]

Bangladesh isn't the first example of how automation has posed a real threat to laborers. In *Empire of Cotton: A Global History,* author Sven Beckert discusses how in 1794, when entrepreneurs erected the first mechanized spinning mills in southern Mexico, government agents forced their closure "for fear mechanization would lead to unemployment, misery, and social upheaval."[12]

Later, in the 1830s, a French tailor named Barthelemy Thimonnier created a sewing machine for stitching together fabric. However, hand sewers destroyed it because they feared it would eliminate their jobs. By 1851, Isaac Merritt Singer introduced the Singer sewing machine, an invention that enabled factories to produce garments much faster and drastically decreased the need for hand sewers.

For Bangladeshis, the displacement of automation is real. In fact, it already happened to many of their knit workers. Up until the early 2010s, Bangladesh employed hundreds of thousands of knit workers. These low-skilled laborers emigrated from tiny villages to cities like Dhaka and Chittagong to secure entry-level jobs interlacing yarn loops to make sweaters, cardigans, socks, and other knit products. In 2012, factories started introducing knitting machines from Japanese supplier Shima Seiki and other German industrial manufacturers. Shima Seiki introduced their WHOLEGARMENT technology—large machines capable of producing entire garments without the need for sewing. Shima Seiki machines look like large computer printers, but they're fed yarn rather than paper. Instead of producing documents, they produce finished garments like dresses and pullovers. A large carriage moves a needle back and forth along the device, just like a printer cartridge. By the end of 2013, human knitting was almost entirely phased out in Bangladesh.

History has many examples of populations resisting technological change and change inevitably coming—although it doesn't happen overnight. But automation is already happening all around us, and it has drastically changed the apparel industry before.

The Sewing Machine as a Motor Toward Modernity

What I witnessed in Bangladesh wasn't always the way clothing was manufactured. Only a hundred years ago, people were much closer to the means of fashion production, whether they sewed clothing at home or visited a local tailor to have garments custom-made for them. In *Sweatshop Migrations: The Garment Industry Between Home and Shop,* Nancy L. Green shows that in 1925, 78% of the total value of American-made women's wear had been produced in New York City.[13] That number has been in sharp decline ever since. According to the American Apparel & Footwear Association, in 2022, just 2.9% of the apparel sold in the United States was made domestically.[14]

The introduction of the sewing machine during the Industrial Revolution allowed clothing to be produced much faster. As a result, operations grew more extensive, and clothing production moved from something done only in the home or by specialists to a full-fledged industry. Port cities like New York and Toronto emerged as manufacturing hubs for ready-to-wear garment factories that employed immigrants like my grandparents.

For consumers, the sewing machine's introduction into factories made clothing more accessible. Shoppers could easily purchase readymade goods for a fraction of the price of bespoke items.

The introduction of the sewing machine also provided upward mobility for women, who could become seamstresses in factories. In her essay "Sewing Modernity: How the Sewing Machine Allowed for a Distinctively Feminine Experience of Modernity," researcher Annabel Friedrichs outlines how the sewing machine was the very "motor" that enabled women a path to participate in the public sphere.[15]

The turn of the century also saw the emergence of the department store, with mass-produced, ready-to-wear fashion available for consumption.

In her e-book *Make It Yourself: Home Sewing, Gender, and Culture, 1890–1930*, Sarah A. Gordon highlights how the years between 1914 and 1919 alone saw a steep sales increase of factory-made dresses, steadily replacing tailor-made fashion.[16]

In the late twentieth century, in search of cheaper labor, fashion brands began outsourcing manufacturing overseas in a process known as offshoring. Because of this shift, garment workers were no longer direct employees of major brands but became "distant actors in complex global supply chains."[17]

In the 1990s, after the North American Free Trade Agreement was signed, companies started moving garment production to Mexico.

In 2001, China joined the World Trade Organization, allowing companies more freedom to operate businesses there. According to the Bureau of Labor Statistics, between 1990 and 2011, 80% of apparel manufacturing jobs disappeared in the United States.[18]

At each step toward increased efficiency in fashion production, people became more removed from the intimacy of making their clothing. Today, the typical garment travels further around the world than its wearer. The result is a culture of cheap clothing in which items are produced and not crafted, worn and not cherished, and discarded and not mended.

The Rise of Fast Fashion

Although the idea of fast fashion has existed since the 1970s, the term was first used in a *The New York Times* article on December 31, 1989.[19] The article was about two new fashion retailers that had opened in New York: Compagnie Internationale Express and Zara International.[20] By this time, Zara had been operating in Europe for fourteen years but was just beginning to expand to America.

What made Zara different from other retailers at the time was that it could make clothing quickly with compressed production cycles. Every week, Zara retailers would receive a new shipment from Spain, where Zara's headquarters and factories are located. "The stock in the store changes every three weeks," Juan Lopez, the head of Zara's US operation, told the *Times*. "The latest trend is what we're after. It takes 15 days between a new idea and getting it into the stores," he said.[21] That was in 1989. Today, Zara stores receive new items twice per week.

Zara pioneered and perfected the fast-fashion model. The company routinely transitions designs from the runway into more accessible versions that cater to our extreme need for variety. Zara's parent company,

Inditex, is among the world's largest retailers, and its founder, Amancio Ortega Gaona, has a net worth of over $100 billion.

Zara achieved such growth and success by using just-in-time (JIT) production and quick-response manufacturing. Unlike legacy brands, which spend almost two years designing, sourcing, manufacturing, and distributing large orders of clothes each season, Zara produces items quickly and pilots them in certain stores while keeping materials on hand to create more if needed. If an item is popular, they produce more; if it's not, they move on to something else. This agile business model is made possible by closely monitoring real-time store data.

Zara is able to maintain such tight control over its supply chain because it's a vertically integrated operation, meaning it owns the design, production, warehousing, logistics, and distribution processes for the 450 million items sold annually in their stores.[22] This isn't to say that the company doesn't outsource (it does), but many Zara factories are located near the company's Galicia, Spain, headquarters.[23]

Zara also operates on limited production runs, creating a sense of urgency.[24] Each Zara location receives new items twice weekly, encouraging shoppers to return frequently. Zara has evolved consumer expectations because of its ability to transition trends into products easily.

Zara's business model of essentially copying the runway has not gone without criticism. In 2017, the brand came under scrutiny when it came out with what looked like a replica of Balenciaga's Triple S sneaker, a chunky dad sneaker that retailed for $795. The Zara version, called "multi-piece sneakers," sold for just $35.90.[25] A year earlier, in 2016, the same thing happened with Kanye's Yeezy 750 Boots. Almost any given item in Zara's inventory can be traced back to something that was shown on the runway or something popularized on social media. Zara is able to get away with these "inspirations" because they are not directly impersonating a brand or using its logo.

It's not just other brands Zara "gets inspiration" from. The company has also been accused of copying independent creatives, too. New York-based graphic designer Adam Kurtz is the creator of unique enamel pins. He found out Zara blatantly copied his designs, and in response, he created a web page titled "Unauthorized Reproductions: Shop the Look!" to call out the Zara knockoffs. According to reporting from *Vice,* the page featured dozens of side-by-side comparisons of original works next to Zara knockoffs.[26]

We'll further explore fast fashion's culture of copying in Chapter 6, "Artificial Intelligence." As we'll see, AI poured gasoline on the fire when it comes to the problem of knockoffs in the fashion industry.

Fast fashion fuels our constant need for newness. For some, Zara—which has become synonymous with fast fashion—represents the downfall of an industry. For others, it's a brand that democratizes trends and makes them affordable for everyday people. Like the smartphone, which opened up fashion to the public, brands like Zara make runway trends available to the masses.

Dress for Less and Less

Economies of scale meant clothing became more affordable than ever before. In fact, amidst inflation and soaring prices, clothing is the only thing that has gotten cheaper over the years. *The New York Times* article entitled "Dress for Less and Less" highlights that while luxury fashion has become more expensive, mainstream fashion has become cheaper.[27] A pair of Levi's 501 jeans cost $50 in 1998 and $46 in 2008. Adjusted for inflation, the jeans should have cost $66 in 2008, but they're actually $4 cheaper than ten years prior. Amidst rising costs for housing, groceries, and gasoline, clothing is the only category in which overall prices have declined.

We're also spending less of our overall income on fashion, despite purchasing more items than ever before. In 1980, the average American consumer purchased twelve new items of clothing per year and spent 7% of their annual income on clothes. In 2024, the number of new items purchased per year rose to sixty-eight, but the percentage of income spent on clothes dropped to 3%.[28] We spend half as much even though we're buying five times more.

Cheap, automated fashion has also led to overconsumption and "haul culture," where creators, influencers, and everyday people will show off all the items they purchased in a large shopping haul, usually from fast-fashion companies. According to CleanClothes.org, half of fast-fashion items purchased will be worn three times or less.[29] This throwaway culture has resulted in 92 million tons of textile waste.[30] There's so much unwanted clothing from Western countries that they've begun shipping it overseas. In Ghana, there are entire beaches littered with shoes, pants, and T-shirts—used, poor-quality textiles that are of little use to the local population. Their contents (mostly plastics) seep into the waterways and poison the fish, which residents of the region rely on as a source of food. This practice of wealthier, industrialized nations sending unwanted fast fashion to the Global South is now being referred to as waste colonialism.

Seattle-based designer Elena Qiu blames social media.[31] In a TikTok video that has more than 60,000 likes, she holds up a pair of well-worn nude shoes for the camera. "My Tabis look like this because I fucking love them," she says. She explains she has tried to scrub them clean, has super-glued the soles back together after they lifted, and even stitched the strap after it snapped. "What gripes me so much about social media is that we're never shown clothing that is beat to hell anymore because people don't love their clothes anymore."

If social media creates a demand for newness, automation enables the fashion industry to meet that demand. The result is more clothing than we know what to do with.

A $4.3 Billion Pile of Clothes

In 2018, Swedish retail giant H&M announced it was sitting on a $4.3 billion pile of unsold inventory. The fast-fashion company had rapidly expanded for two decades and enjoyed growth from a single shop in Stockholm to 4,700 stores worldwide. That year, H&M said operating profit fell 62% in three months, with shares dropping to their lowest price since 2005.[32] H&M's main problem was that they had simply produced too much. "Hundreds of millions of items each year," writes *The New York Times* international fashion correspondent Elizabeth Paton. "There are so many [clothing items] that a power plant in Vasteras, the town where H&M founded its first store, relies partly on burning defective products the retailer can't sell."[33]

Overproduction isn't just bad for a brand's bottom line. It's terrible for the planet. According to the UN Environment Programme (UNEP), the fashion industry is responsible for 10% of global carbon emissions—more than all international flights and maritime shipping combined. It takes 3,781 liters of water to make a pair of jeans, from the production of the cotton to the delivery of the final product in store.[34] Due to the presence of plastics in synthetic materials, laundry alone causes around half a million tons of plastic microfibers to be released into the ocean each year—the equivalent of almost three billion polyester shirts.[35] These plastics enter the food chain via fish and other marine life and are eventually consumed by other animals and by humans.

Fast fashion is also terrible for the people making your clothes—mostly women in developing economies. Garment workers are some of the lowest-paid industrial workers in the world.[36] According to recent reporting from *The Wall Street Journal,* in Bangladesh, where 600,000 people work for H&M, the average wage was $119 a month in the first half of 2023—well below the $194/month living wage.[37]

According to research done by the Clean Clothes Campaign, the majority of garment workers don't feel safe at work: "Not only are they working in dangerous buildings, but workers are routinely exposed to inhumanely high temperatures, harmful chemicals and physical violence."[38]

In addition to low pay and dangerous working conditions, garment work offers little job security. During the COVID-19 pandemic, garment workers were laid off as brands canceled orders. Thousands of factories faced ruin. Even workers who kept their jobs received pay cuts. In a study that interviewed 400 garment workers across nine countries, the Worker Rights Consortium found that even those employees who managed to hold onto their jobs reported a 21% decrease in income between March and August 2020—with monthly wages falling from $187 to $147.[39]

"There has been a race to the bottom when it comes to pricing," says Monika Warzecha, digital editor at *The Walrus*.[40] "With fast fashion and ultra-fast fashion, that can really crowd out the middle market. At the same time, the middle market struggled during COVID-19, especially because during lockdowns a lot of the ultra-fast fashion companies were able to get clothes to consumers more quickly and easily because they didn't have that presence in the storefronts or malls," she says.

"Just like the middle-class American shopper is getting squeezed out of home and car ownership, fashion's middle-class brands are losing closet share and space on store shelves," writes Halie LeSavage, senior fashion and beauty editor for *Marie Claire*.

Another reason clothing quality has decreased is private equity. When companies transition from small operations or family businesses to private equity portfolio companies, they're under pressure to grow profits for shareholders, which often leads to cutting corners in terms of materials or manufacturing.

The Canadian brand Aritzia is a perfect example of what happens when private equity gets involved in fashion. Aritzia was once a beloved destination for high-quality, elevated basics, but in the last decade, the brand has gone downhill in terms of its offerings. As one user laments on a subreddit dedicated to all things Aritzia:

> God awful prints, sheer af clothing that isn't supposed to be sheer (white effortless pants..) at abysmal prices. $200 for a fucking polyester dress???? I'm literally so disappointed as an OG Aritiza fan (grew up in the 00's in Vancouver). I used to be able to justify the prices due to quality and style but now I'm just gonna shop at the Gap and Banana Republic lmao.[41]

Another Redditor chimes in: "Agreed! Their quality has gone down the drain.... I wish they would carry thicker, better quality fabrics and stop making things so skimpy. I loved buying from them pre-pandemic for workwear, now I'm not sure where to get new work clothes."[42]

Aritzia was founded in 1984 in Vancouver, British Columbia, by Brian Hill. Hill's family came from a strong retail background: His dad owned the upscale department store Hill's of Kerrisdale. Between 1990 and 2005, Aritzia developed a reputation for providing high-quality basics and modern workwear. This is when the company developed its private label brands, including Wilfred, TNA, and Babaton. In 2005, Berkshire Partners invested in Aritzia. Shortly after, the company expanded to the United States.

Professor Matthew Bird says the pressure to make "more stuff" lowers its quality.[43] In an interview with *Vox,* the professor of industrial design at the Rhode Island School of Design explains that when the Industrial Revolution introduced machinery into the design process, the scale of production increased significantly. Items used to be produced in small batches and could be iterated with user feedback, but today they are produced en masse. If an item is made poorly, you're stuck with thousands of them.

"One of the problems we have today is that the customer is becoming more selective," says David Birnbaum, a strategic planner for the global garment industry with more than forty years of experience working with factories.[44] "Today, retail garment sales are falling because of four reasons: poor design, bad make, lousy fabric, and poor fit. You don't have to be a genius to understand this," he says.

Fit is a particular pain point in fashion today, and automation is to blame. Where people used to get items custom-made just for their bodies, automation relies on grading, a process in which an initial sample pattern is sized up and down to make a full range of size patterns for production. The result is poor-fitting clothing all around, because very few people fall perfectly into standardized sizing.

If automation has led to overproduction, which is terrible for people, bad for the planet, and a net negative for the final product, what's the solution? Could brands bring back manufacturing from overseas and make clothing closer to their consumers? Two new developments in automation technology are challenging the modern manufacturing model.

The Micro-Factory and Mass Customization

In 1996, toy manufacturer Mattel launched Mattel Media (later renamed Mattel Interactive) to expand its offerings from physical products to online games. The brand's first release, which came in the fall of 1996, was a game called *Barbie Fashion Designer* (QR Code 12).

QR Code 12 Scan to see the commercial for *Barbie Fashion Designer*, featuring a young Mila Kunis.

In the computer game, players interact with an easy-to-use interface to design clothes for Barbie. After selecting from a variety of silhouettes and colors, players could then see a 3D mockup of Barbie modeling their custom design on a runway. The game came with special markers, fabric paint, and paper-backed fabric so you could print off your design on your home printer and make actual clothes for your Barbie dolls. The game sold over 500,000 copies in its first two months and is widely considered the first commercially successful game designed for girls. It was later inducted into the National Museum of Play's World Video Game Hall of Fame. In addition to inspiring fashion design careers for girls everywhere, *Barbie Fashion Designer* also demonstrates a micro-factory in action.

For those unfamiliar with the term, a micro-factory is a small-scale, highly automated, technology-driven production facility designed to manufacture items efficiently and sustainably. Compared to large-scale operations, micro-factories are compact in size, flexible in output, and focus on reducing waste, energy consumption, and costs.

Apparel micro-factories can connect design and pattern-making software with automatic cutting machines, like a life-sized version of *Barbie Fashion Designer*. Although machine sewers still finish many products by hand, automation powers the whole process. This all happens on a small scale much closer to the end consumer.

Micro-factories give emerging designers the opportunity to break into the fashion industry. Unlike large factories, micro-factories don't have minimum order quantities (MOQs) and are capable of producing one-offs, if needed.

Rodinia Generation is an example of a micro-factory in action. It's a Danish supply chain startup that just raised €3 million to create a global network of micro-factories.[45] The company is currently working with local brands to help bring their products to life.

What's exciting about the micro-factory is that it can turn the production model on its head. Right now, much of the fashion industry is stuck in the *design-make-sell* system. In this system, items are produced in hopes they sell, but as we've seen, that has led to overproduction. Micro-factories give us the opportunity to change the fashion system to *design-sell-make,* meaning only items that are sold are produced. Items can also be easily tailored to a specific customer's size or style preferences, a process known as mass customization.

Due to their small size and heavy reliance on technology, the micro-factory is often touted as a tool for nearshoring, which is when manufacturing is brought back closer to the country where goods will be consumed. Micro-factories, in theory, promise to redistribute supply chains, which is an attractive promise given global volatility and supply chain disruptions.

In 2018, I had the opportunity to see a micro-factory in action when visiting Texprocess Americas in Atlanta, Georgia. Texprocess is the largest North American tradeshow displaying equipment and technology for developing, sourcing, and producing sewn products. I was there with Gerber—one of the most prominent names in apparel manufacturing technology. (A few years later in 2021, Gerber would be acquired by Lectra, their longtime competitor.)

At Texprocess, Gerber had teamed up with a few other vendors to show the complete setup for a micro-factory in action, from 3D design to spreading, cutting, manufacturing, and finishing. There was even a little delivery robot for transporting the materials from one station to the next.

One of the vendors working with Gerber to bring this micro-factory to life was Kornit Digital, a leader in direct-to-fabric printing. Rather than dying material before cutting it, Kornit prints directly on the finished fabric with a pigment solution in a dry-printing process—meaning no water is needed to color the fabric.

While the micro-factory at Texprocess was interesting in theory, the products it produced were simple compared to the finished goods I was used to purchasing in-store and online: a pillowcase or slip dress, for example. Was the micro-factory actually a viable solution for commodities with complex processes?

Adidas was one of the first major brands to publicize its micro-factory efforts. The athletic company set up Speedfactories in Ansbach, Germany, and Atlanta in 2016 and 2017 in hopes of replacing offshore labor in Asia with on-shore robotic manufacturing. This would cut costs and reduce the distance goods have to travel to reach Western consumers, making production more efficient and environmentally friendly.[46]

But by 2019, Speedfactories were being abandoned. Producing footwear, as it turns out, is complicated and not easily automated:

> Even with the help of robots, manufacturing shoes requires anywhere from 60 to 80 steps. In fact, as many as three different machines can be needed just to attach the toe and heel of a shoe with the sole. Too many steps keep production costs sky-high.[47]

As for factory owner Mostafiz Uddin, he never bought into the idea that manufacturing could be brought back to the West: "Our industry has had the option of nearshoring for decades," he writes.

"Indeed, it has been tried several times but with limited success due to a lack of local expertise, know-how and infrastructure."[48]

Jonathan Zornow agrees. He's the inventor of Sewbo, a sewing robot. In an introductory video showcasing Sewbo in action, the robot—about the size and shape of an industrial dough mixer—is shown picking up fabric and feeding it through a sewing machine. "The biggest barrier isn't the technology; it's the labor and the capacity," he tells me.[49]

Despite some blunders along the way, brands are still experimenting with micro-factories. Unspun is a San Francisco-based company that creates 3D weaving technology for apparel. The company started out by promising consumers their best-fitting pair of jeans, and they delivered on that promise by leveraging imaging technology and automating the pattern-making process.

Using the camera on their iPhone, customers can take and upload images of themselves, from which Unspun extracts measurements and generates a pattern for perfect-fitting jeans. Customers can select fit, style, and color preferences. For the first few years, Unspun was producing these jeans in Hong Kong, but recently the company announced they've been developing their own weaving machine called Vega, which enables the custom jeans to be produced from anywhere. Vega weaves yarns into seamless shapes that make up the garment. According to Fast Company, the machines operate ten times faster and are five times cheaper than other automated machines on the market.[50] In August 2024, Unspun secured $32 million in Series B funding and is partnering with large retailers like Walmart.

We'll discuss Unspun more in Chapter 4, "Spatial Computing," but for now, it's important to note how technological developments are generating new methods to create clothing in ways that are closer to consumers.

Printed to the Nines

Another automation technology for manufacturing that has made waves in the fashion industry is 3D printing, which is a type of additive manufacturing that layers materials to make three-dimensional objects from a digital file.[51] Items start out as ideas in design software and then are produced with filaments that print out physical objects. Commercial machines use nylon, plastic, or other synthetic materials with different properties.

As Kristen Plate outlines in *Printed to the Nines,* the additive manufacturing revolution took place from 1981 to 2000 with the introduction of 3D modeling and CAD software.[52]

I remember seeing 3D printers pop up everywhere at tech conferences in the 2010s, but they were mostly being used to print figurines and paperweights.

3D printing had one of its first major fashion moments in March of 2013 when burlesque performer Dita Von Teese stepped out at the ACE Hotel in New York wearing a completely 3D-printed gown created by Michael Schmidt and Francis Bitonti. Unlike other gowns, which are sewn and made of fabric, this floor-length nylon gown was created using selective laser sintering (SLS),[53] where the material is built up in layers from plastic powder and fused together with a laser.[54]

The Dita Von Teese dress was one of the first times the fashion industry woke up to the possibilities of 3D printing as a new potential material (QR Code 13).

When I was in Berlin, I met another young designer who was also experimenting with 3D printing technology. Her name was Maartje Dijkstra, and she had interned at the House of Alexander McQueen in London. Even though she was young, Dijkstra had her own very distinct aesthetic. Her work was romantic and moody, and I was drawn to it right away. At Fashion Tech Berlin, she was showing off a dress

QR Code 13 Scan to see a picture of Dita Von Teese in the 3D-printed dress.

called TranSwarm Entities, a totally black dress built of dozens of small fragments created using a 3D printer pen. These fragments are then connected by hand using black polyester wires (QR Code 14).

QR Code 14 Scan to see a video of TranSwarm Entities by Maartje Dijkstra.

Dijkstra's work was cool and experimental, but definitely not wearable in the conventional sense. It was more like 3D-printed couture.

Iris van Herpen, a pioneer in the fusion of fashion and technology, integrates 3D printing into her avant-garde designs to push the boundaries of traditional couture. Collaborating with architects, scientists, and engineers, she employs 3D printing to craft intricate, sculptural garments that resemble organic and futuristic forms. This innovative technique allows her to create textures and structures that are impossible to achieve through conventional methods, transforming fashion into wearable art. Her works, such as those in the "Voltage" and "Magnetic Motion" collections, exemplify how 3D printing can revolutionize materials and aesthetics in contemporary design.

While many of these early experiments showcased 3D printing as a new material, Danit Peleg was one of the first designers to raise the idea of 3D printing as a new manufacturing model. The Tel Aviv-based designer emerged in the space when she released a video showcasing the collection she printed at home (QR Code 15).[55]

QR Code 15 Scan to watch Danit Peleg's video "3D Printing Fashion: How I 3D-Printed Clothes at Home."

Peleg used soft materials and flexible patterns to give her pieces the type of movement we'd expect from clothing. I had the chance to try on some of Peleg's collection when I met her at the Maker Faire in New York. The designs were very cool but not wearable for everyday life.

The same year Dita Von Teese wore her 3D-printed gown, another dress captured the public's imagination. It was created in collaboration with Shapeways, a 3D printing marketplace and service that lets people upload and print 3D files. The dress was called the Kinematics Dress, and it was designed by Nervous System and printed out in New York.

The Kinematics Dress was a black high-low sleeveless dress featuring a geometric, lattice-like pattern with a fitted bodice and flared skirt. What was remarkable about this dress was that it used a 4D printing system that created complex, foldable forms composed of modules to produce a completely wearable dress that prints out in one single folded piece. It's made of thousands of panels connected by hinge joints that conform to the body (QR Code 16). Both the dress and the software were acquired by the Museum of Modern Art for their permanent collection.

QR Code 16 Scan to watch the 4D printing process of the Kinematics Dress.

More recently, Zac Posen worked with Protolabs, an on-demand 3D printing service, to create a dress for British model Jourdan Dunn for the 2019 Met Gala (QR Code 17). Posen used a precision stereolithography machine to print large petals and fasten them to a modular cage frame. According to *Dezeen*, the frame was 3D-printed in titanium using electron-beam melting technology at GE Additive, the additive manufacturing arm of General Electric.

QR Code 17 Scan to see Zac Posen's 3D-printed dress for Jourdan Dunn.

Both 3D printing and the micro-factory make manufacturing processes more accessible to the masses. With reduced upfront costs and localized production, these two automation technologies lower the barrier for entry for individuals and emerging designers.

Automation in Fulfillment

Another way automation is majorly impacting the fashion industry is in the area of fulfillment. Automation is a huge part of how Amazon achieves breakneck delivery speeds. The company deploys 750,000 robots in operations and thousands of other robotic systems that help move, sort, identify, and package customer orders. These robots work alongside humans to fulfill 1.6 million packages per day.

Kiva Systems, for example, is a Massachusetts-based startup that Amazon acquired for $775 million in 2012. The company develops robots that move toward warehouse workers in order to fulfill orders faster.

Walmart has followed suit with the introduction of its Alphabot, a robot that helps pick orders. Alphabots look like small skids carrying baskets. They can move laterally, horizontally, and vertically to retrieve customers' goods.

The fashion industry has similarly embraced automation in fulfillment centers. For instance, leading fast-fashion brand Zara uses automated systems to track inventory and replenish stock in its stores rapidly. Advanced conveyor systems and sorting machines help ensure that items are delivered to the right location efficiently, minimizing downtime and enhancing the speed-to-market. Likewise, ASOS, an online fashion retailer, uses automation to handle order processing and returns management, utilizing robotics to streamline its massive operational scale.

Automation Everywhere

In his farewell address, former President Barack Obama warned against the consequences of automation. "The next wave of economic dislocations won't come from overseas," he said. "It will come from the relentless pace of automation that makes a lot of good, middle-class jobs obsolete."

Techno-optimists like to suggest that automation will replace mundane tasks and lead to better jobs for people. It makes work better for everyone and frees up humans to do only the most skilled tasks. This may be true in the long run, but the lived reality is that in the name of efficiency, automation disrupts tradition and upends livelihoods. As we'll see in Chapter 7, when automation is combined with artificial intelligence, the results are transformative.

Automation in the fashion industry represents both promise and peril. While it can drive efficiency, reduce waste, and make fashion more accessible, it also disrupts traditional labor markets and raises critical ethical and environmental concerns. From the mechanization of sewing to the emergence of 3D printing and micro-factories, technology continues to reshape how we design, produce, and deliver clothing. However, this relentless drive for efficiency comes at a cost—overproduction, diminished craftsmanship, and the potential erosion of human livelihoods. As we move forward, the challenge for the industry will be to balance innovation with sustainability, ensuring that technological progress does not come at the expense of people or the planet. The decisions we make today about automation will define the future of fashion—not just what we wear, but how we work and live in a rapidly changing world.

Chapter 4

Spatial Computing

AltspaceVR, October 2020

The inaugural Circular Fashion Summit is set up like most conferences I've attended. There are several stages throughout the Grand Palais in Paris where thought leaders will share insights. There are designated areas for networking and a series of installations and exhibits you can visit between talks. The Circular Fashion Summit's mission is to bring together design, technology, and sustainability leaders to share knowledge and ignite action toward promoting the circular economy in fashion. The decor is primarily black and white, with oversized plants to drive home the theme of sustainability.

When I first arrive, I take a selfie to share on social media in front of the step-and-repeat. I approach the networking area and hear a familiar voice in the distance. It's my colleague Patrick Duffy, a globally known expert on circular fashion. He's one of the hosts of the Summit, along with an organization called Lablaco. I say hello, and he introduces me to the woman he's beside. She compliments me on my look. "I love your outfit," she says, adding, "I would have never thought to choose *purple skin*!" I told her I wanted my avatar to match my brand colors.

I excuse myself and remove my headset. Suddenly, as if waking from a dream, I'm not in Paris anymore, and none of these people are actually in the room with me; I'm at home in my living room in Toronto with an Oculus Quest strapped to my head. The entire Grand Palais is a simulation inside the virtual reality platform AltspaceVR. Although all conference attendees are tuned in in real-time, the event occurs in Central European Time. It's three in the morning in Toronto, and I'm barely awake. I blink the sleep from my eyes and grab my pen and notebook and scribble: *Is this the future of interacting online?* (See QR Code 18.)

QR Code 18 Scan to see my YouTube video taking you inside the Circular Fashion Summit.

The term "spatial computing" was first coined by MIT Media Lab researcher Simon Greenwold, who wrote a 2003 paper on the topic.[1] Put simply, spatial computing is when computing moves away from flat screens and onto the world around us in 3D. As my colleague and spatial computing thought leader Tom Emrich explains:

> "Spatial computing" encompasses technologies like augmented reality, virtual reality, autonomous vehicles, and robotics. This tech is already transforming how we interact with the physical world by enabling computers to "perceive," interact with, and navigate through 3D space, creating experiences more immersive than ever.[2]

Developments in key technologies, including depth sensors, cameras, high-performance processors, cloud computing, and spatial audio, have made spatial computing possible. With each advancement, fashion designers and brands have experimented with different tools and providers to discover how they can use spatial computing for fashion design, presentation, and retail.

Spatial computing has brought audiences up close and personal with brands and their products. Today, on Snap, you can try on an array of Dior sunglasses in augmented reality (AR). You can watch an immersive fashion film from Gucci on the Apple Vision Pro. New devices that use spatial computing technologies are allowing for new kinds of experiences that break down the barriers between brands and consumers, retail and entertainment, and content and commerce.

In this chapter, we'll look at the evolution of fashion and spatial computing. We'll learn about early virtual reality fashion experiments and how the beauty industry pioneered augmented reality. We'll discuss how AR has enhanced the in-store retail experience while displacing it, making try-on available from anywhere. We'll consider how fashion designers have experimented with AR for fashion presentation and how the technology can transform clothes from static objects to dynamic digital experiences. We'll touch on how companies have leveraged filters and branded environments in apps like Snapchat to bring their products closer to consumers, and how startups have leveraged the LiDAR scanner in iPhones to change how we assess fit. Finally, we'll conclude this chapter by looking at smart glasses as objects that merge fashion and technology to become wearable computing devices.

Early VR and Voyeurism

Virtual reality (VR) is a simulated experience that combines screens, computing power, controllers, 3D spatial audio, and haptic feedback.

Users wear head-mounted displays to immerse themselves in digital environments for gaming, entertainment, or training purposes. Although the first VR head-mounted display was invented in the 1960s, the equipment was so heavy and bulky that it had to be suspended from the ceiling. In the 1990s, advances in computing power and graphic technology boosted interest in VR. It also gained popularity in arcades, which were hubs for gaming innovation. The first consumer VR device, the Forte VFX1, was released in 1995 but wasn't a mainstream success.

In 2012, a California founder named Palmer Luckey launched a Kickstarter campaign that went viral. Luckey was raising $250,000 to develop a headset to provide an immersive VR experience that would let users explore virtual environments and look around at their surroundings in a natural way. The headset would be called the Oculus Rift. The campaign received a ton of media attention and raised $2.5 million from backers, demonstrating a strong appetite for a new kind of computing device. The Oculus Rift campaign kicked off a flurry of activity in the VR space in the years that followed, cumulating in March 2014 when Facebook announced it would acquire Oculus for $2 billion. Luckey is widely credited with reviving the VR industry and propelling it forward.

It wasn't long before fashion designers and brands started experimenting with VR. One of the earliest examples was at Selfridges in London. In early 2014, fashion designer Gareth Pugh collaborated with technology company Inition to offer customers a VR experience inside an installation in the department store's men's section. Shoppers were invited to step inside a soundproof chamber and wear a headpiece Pugh designed with an Oculus Rift embedded into it. Inside the headset, viewers watched a series of geometric visuals come to life. Handrails were installed on each side of the installation in case people lost their balance.[3] The entire experience, from the padded room to the angular headset, had a kind of erotic BDSM vibe.

Early VR experiences positioned the viewer as someone on the outside looking in. An event was captured, and now we were viewing it as an audience—much like film and television, albeit more immersive and panoramic since the screen was all around us rather than just in front of us. This voyeuristic vantage has enabled fashion brands to pull audiences in closer than ever before and provide unprecedented access.

For example, in 2014, British fast-fashion company Topshop invited guests to view their Fall/Winter fashion show through customized Oculus Rift headsets while sitting in the window of the brand's flagship store on Oxford Street in London (QR Code 19). "The brief was to open up Topshop's fashion show at London Fashion Week . . . to a much wider audience," said Andy Millns, the co-founder and creative director of Inition, the technology partner for the project.[4] "The idea we came back with was to use virtual reality to let people attend the show using telepresence. We transmitted the show from a front-row seat . . . to five virtual reality Oculus Rift headsets," he said.

QR Code 19 Scan to watch the YouTube video: live 360 degree virtual reality catwalk experience for Topshop.

Rebecca Minkoff was one of the first to create a branded VR experience using Google Cardboard. In collaboration with film company Jaunt, Rebecca Minkoff captured their Fall 2015 runway show with a 360-degree video shot from the runway. The experience was available afterward, where viewers could get an up-close look at the models, clothing, accessories, audience, and even photographers at the event.[5]

Similarly, in 2015, French luxury brand Dior designed its customized head-mounted display called "Dior Eyes," in collaboration with DigitasLBi Labs France. The VR headset experience invited wearers to "see" backstage during the brand's fashion show, effectively becoming the "eyes" looking in on an experience not typically open to the public. Users could take in makeup artists, hair stylists, and all the hustle and bustle of a behind-the-scenes production, all captured by 360-degree video and audio. The headset included headphones so wearers could get the whole auditory experience, providing the illusion of presence. In other words, it felt like you were backstage with the brand, watching all the action unfold. The idea wasn't for Dior to sell the headsets but for them to offer a viewing experience in select stores to clientele. The whole activation was a flex of French technological prowess.

The same year Dior Eyes was released, I wrote about how Tommy Hilfiger experimented with VR by inviting shoppers to watch its Fall 2015 collection runway show through Samsung Gear VR headsets. The American fashion brand collaborated with the Netherlands-based startup WeMakeVR, which filmed the show using a 3D camera. Customers could visit one of the brand's flagship retail locations and strap in to see the New York Fashion Week runway show as an in-store cinematic experience.

At the time, Daniel Grieder, Tommy Hilfiger's chief executive officer, said the headsets would "allow shoppers who might never attend a fashion show to view and shop the season's runway styles" and "inject Tommy Hilfiger locations with an element of entertainment."[6]

Grieder's comments touch on two features that VR offers to fashion brands. First is the element of access. Like Dior Eyes, the Tommy

VR experience extended the runway show beyond its time, place, and location to provide accessibility to more people than could be physically present at the show. Second, he touches on the element of entertainment. Set against the backdrop of the retail apocalypse, which began in 2010, VR seemed like a new way to get customers excited about the in-store experience by offering them a novel encounter with an emerging technology.

In March 2015, HTC announced it was partnering with Valve Corporation to produce the HTC Vive, one of the first devices that offered a room-scale VR experience where users could walk around and interact within a defined space. The first-generation consumer model of the HTC Vive hit the market in the spring of 2016. It retailed for $800.

The Chinese menswear brand PRONOUNCE collaborated with HTC Vive to design clothing in 3D space using the VIVE Pro headset (as opposed to sketching on paper). Alvin Wang Graylin, China regional president of VIVE, HTC, made a guest appearance as a model wearing the VIVE Focus stand-alone device over his eyes on the runway at Shanghai Fashion Week.[7]

With the HTC Vive and the Oculus Rift, VR moved beyond passive watching to active participation. Users could walk around and explore virtual environments like in a game rather than just sitting back and consuming VR like a movie. This created new opportunities for the fashion industry.

In 2020, the Fashion Innovation Agency in London experimented with HTC Vive to curate *The Fabric of Reality,* a fully immersive VR fashion show inside the Museum of Other Realities. The experience aimed to recreate all the excitement of a physical runway show but inside a digital space. Traditional fashion designers teamed up with digital creators for a first-of-its-kind exhibition to bring audiences on a journey to explore the story behind each designer's collection.

Just as the smartphone opened up the fashion industry and made it more accessible and democratic than ever, virtual reality was also attempting to do so. However, the bulky, expensive hardware had its limits. In 2015, at the time of Tommy Hilfiger's foray into VR, only 2.9 million headsets were in use.[8]

Because VR headsets were a novelty, they were often used as an attraction at events and conferences. In 2016, while in Moscow for Mercedes-Benz Fashion Week Russia, I witnessed VR being used in several ways. Runway collections were photographed using a 360-degree camera and then uploaded as shoppable virtual content you could view in an app or by wearing a headset. The organization had also invited celebrated fashion illustrator Jaesuk Kim, who created illustrations of his famous Susi Girls using Google Tilt Brush, a program for painting in virtual reality. Kim would illustrate a dress using the HTC Vive, and visitors could go inside that artwork and experience it as immersive content. It was unlike anything I'd ever experienced, and it gave me a deeper appreciation for fashion illustration as an art form.

From the early 2000s to 2020, VR faced many challenges, the first being accessibility. Headsets were (and still are) luxury items not everyone can afford. The cost barrier slows adoption. However, as sensors and parts become more ubiquitous, they become more affordable. By 2019, the average price of a virtual reality headset was $500.[9]

The fidelity of early VR was also such that it often sickened people, including me. I remember covering a VR film festival for *BetaKit*, an online publication focused on Canada's startup scene. I watched five films using various commercially available headsets to report on the festival. I had to excuse myself from the festival four times to puke in the washroom. This feeling of sickness after entering a VR environment is not uncommon and has been dubbed "cybersickness." A study reported that 22–80% of people who use VR will get sick.[10]

While virtual reality was struggling with its growing pains, another form of spatial computing quickly took over.

Dog Ears and Puking Rainbows

Augmented reality (AR) involves layering digital components over a real-world environment. It differs from virtual reality in that you can experience AR laid over your existing world instead of replacing it with a virtual one. According to Google Trends, interest in AR started bubbling up in the early 2010s and peaked in 2017 with the announcement of Spark AR Studio, which is a platform that lets businesses and individuals create AR lenses and experiences.[11]

Although early augmented reality experiments date back to the 1960s, for most of us, our first introduction to the technology was via the smartphone using filters on Snapchat. The dog ears or puking rainbow filters many of us tried on, captured, and shared on social media were intuitive and fun. Unlike the Circular Fashion Summit, which required an expensive headset to participate, Snapchat filters were (and still are) available to anyone with a smartphone and an internet connection. The accessibility of augmented reality via smartphone technology made adopting it much easier than VR. While many dismissed AR technology as silly, I saw its potential for transforming how we see ourselves and how powerful that could be for fashion and beauty.

In early 2016, I was invited to a Sephora event in San Francisco to pilot the company's Virtual Artist launch. A part of the Sephora app, Virtual Artist invited users to try lipstick in real-time on their live video. I was excited to try it out but was on the East Coast then (I'd been spending time between San Francisco and Toronto). Although I couldn't attend the Sephora San Francisco event in person, I researched the AR technology behind Virtual Artist. I discovered I was closer to the story than I thought.

The technology powering Virtual Artist was developed by ModiFace, a Toronto-based company founded by Dr. Parham Aarabi of the University of Toronto (QR Code 20). Dr. Aarabi developed the ability to use computer vision to track lips after working on lip-reading technology for the US defense industry at Stanford in California. "ModiFace was born when we realized we could use our lip-reading application to simulate lipstick," he told me in a 2016 interview for *The Toronto Star*.[12]

QR Code 20 Scan to watch my YouTube video covering Sephora's launch of Virtual Artist powered by ModiFace.

When I first visited the ModiFace offices in 2016, I noticed a boardroom table filled with Lego. I'd never seen Lego in an office setting before, so I asked Dr. Aarabi about it. He emphasized the importance of fostering a culture of fun. "Our first consumer application was built purely for fun," he told me. "We created an app that swapped people's lips for Angelina Jolie's. We put it up on the web, and the site received 100,000 hits the next day. That's when we knew we were onto something."

ModiFace went on to create sophisticated lip-tracking software that could simulate different shades of lipstick. They sold this software as a service to other beauty brands that wanted to offer unique try-on experiences in-store and online. While ModiFace initially emphasized its AR-powered mirrors, its web and mobile applications became more critical as brands focused on digital sales channels like e-commerce and mobile.

Eventually, ModiFace and other applications learned to map all elements of the human face and head—not just lips. This meant you could simulate hair color, foundation, eyeshadow, and more. In 2018, ModiFace was acquired by the global beauty behemoth L'Oréal, and the company is currently the leading provider of augmented reality to the beauty industry. (Full disclosure: I've worked with ModiFace since the acquisition.)

What ModiFace was offering through Sephora and eventually L'Oréal and others would become known as virtual try-on (VTO) and try-before-you-buy. Both were concepts that captured how spatial computing was transforming the try-on experience.

Augmenting the Try-on Experience

The idea of trying something before you buy it isn't new. Beauty counters and fitting rooms exist because people want to demo products before committing to purchasing them. Until recently, trying something meant visiting the mall or department store, but today, thanks to augmented reality, customers can try makeup, accessories, and even apparel digitally. AR applications allow try-on to become a part of the online or mobile shopping experience: virtual try-on, or VTO for short.

After pioneers like ModiFace saw success in AR for beauty, accessory brands caught on to how the technology could help convert digital shoppers. Warby Parker was one of the first brands to offer AR try-on for its eyeglasses. Launched in 2010, Warby Parker started as a online-only way to purchase prescription glasses. Initially, it offered a Home Try-On Program, where customers could select several frames online to be shipped to them to try at home. In 2019, the company rolled out virtual try-on within its iOS app, enabling users to try on frames virtually in real-time on their live video. Warby Parker leveraged Apple's ARKit and the iPhone's TrueDepth camera technology to make the try-on as realistic as possible.

Soon after, many startups like FaceCake and Perfect Corp began offering VTO as a service for makeup, jewelry, and accessory brands. I remember countless technology conferences where I tried on earrings, watches, rings, scarves, hats, sunglasses, and more in AR. The renderings were realistic, and it seemed augmented reality had found a strong business case in the rapidly growing world of e-commerce.

In-Store AR and Magic Mirrors

Augmented reality also became a new way to enhance the in-store retail experience. With retailers desperate for foot traffic and a way to connect with younger customers, augmented reality was an exciting opportunity to blend physical shopping with digital innovation.

For example, in 2013, Disney launched a Disney Princess Magic Mirror at the World of Disney store in Orlando, Florida (QR Code 21). Kids could see themselves in the mirror's reflection "wearing" the dresses of popular princesses like Snow White, Cinderella, and Ariel from *The Little Mermaid*. With a wave of their hand, children could cycle through the outfits of each Disney princess. It was a fun way of combining the game of dress-up with the magic mirror concept, an idea initially from fairy tales and eventually dramatized by Disney's *Snow White and the Seven Dwarfs*.

Augmented reality mirrors brought some much-needed magic to malls. For example, the Westfield in London launched an exclusive AR try-on experience with designer Emma J Shipley in collaboration with the Fashion Innovation Agency and AR platform Meshmerise. Shipley is known for her luxury scarves featuring mythical

QR Code 21 Scan to watch a video of the Disney Princess Magic Mirror experience at the World of Disney Store in Orlando.

illustrations. Westfield invited shoppers to try on the scarves via an immersive pop-up with display iPads for public use. Shoppers could try on Shipley's designs in real-time using an app called Scarfi. Her fantastical illustrations were also brought to life in AR: Animated mermaids on the printed scarf would swim outward and upward into the frame.

With augmented reality taking hold as the leading technology on social media, brands started incorporating mirrors with AR features into stores to make the physical shopping experience more engaging and social. In 2012, Uniqlo piloted a magic mirror in their new flagship store in San Francisco, collaborating with interactive design agency Holition London. The mirror interfaced with a tablet and enabled shoppers to view themselves in different color varieties of popular items, like the Uniqlo ultralight down jacket. The mirror also included a selfie feature, allowing customers to take pictures of themselves in items to share on social media.

Similarly, in 2015, Rebecca Minkoff launched interactive mirrors in the changing rooms and on the main floor of her New York City SoHo store. Shoppers could use the mirrors to flip through lookbooks curated by the brand or order a coffee or champagne to their fitting room.[13] According to Rebecca Minkoff, the mirrors increased time spent in-store and overall sales.[14]

In 2019, at the Consumer Electronics Show in Las Vegas, I tried LG's Smart Mirror. It used 3D technology to scan your body and produce an avatar with your basic measurements. You could then select clothing to try on virtually from connected retailers. After choosing a garment, the mirror visualized what an item would look like on you. It used a heat map to show where the outfit might be too tight (indicated with red) or too loose (indicated with green). You could also zoom in on items up close to inspect the details.

For now, virtual try-on has its limitations. Although many startups have tried, the technology didn't (and still doesn't) translate well to apparel. This is because the face is much easier to map since most of us have consistent markers (such as a nose, a mouth, and two eyes). Bodies, however, are all very different. Clothing also presents the additional challenge of movement. All fabrics drape differently, and that's difficult to simulate digitally, although not impossible.

Today, the best applications of try-before-you-buy technology for apparel convey style choices as opposed to showing the reality of how something will fit. For example, at Snap's Partner Summit in 2023, the company demoed a series of tools for enhancing the retail experience, including augmented reality mirrors for apparel try-on. Snap partnered with Los Angeles-based clothing brand Madhappy to show how customers could try out different sweatsuits. You'd stand in front of the mirror and take a still picture and the tech would overlay your body with the sweatsuit of your choice. It was hardly the real-time magic the beauty industry had pioneered years earlier, although it allowed a kind of styling experience without stepping into a changing room.

According to McKinsey, the COVID-19 pandemic accelerated businesses' adoption of digital tools by three to four years.[15] During this time, virtual try-on went from being a nice-to-have to a necessity. With most physical stores shut down, augmented reality became a way of reaching consumers at home. Jewelry brand Kendra Scott, for example, introduced an AR tool that let customers try on and purchase different earrings using an iPhone. When stores did reopen, hygiene was a top priority, and augmented reality offered a contactless way of shopping. According to the *Harvard Business Review*, beauty retailer Ulta's virtual try-on tool saw its engagement increase sevenfold, with more than 50 million shades of foundation swatched digitally post-COVID-19.[16]

While magic mirrors were popping up in stores everywhere, one company bet big on them during the pandemic. In June of 2020, Lululemon made their first ever acquisition and bought Mirror, a home fitness startup, for $500 million. Unlike the in-store mirrors discussed above, which were for enhancing the retail experience, Mirror's business model was to sell a $1,495 wall-mounted machine for streaming workout classes.[17] With gyms and fitness studios closed during the pandemic, there was more demand for at-home workouts. Lululemon thought they could leverage the mirror to extend their brand into consumers' home workout routines.

Mirror may have seemed like a good idea at the time, but by March 2023 the company was essentially worthless.[18] Although the Mirror acquisition was considered a blunder in retrospect, it reinforced that magic mirror technology performs better in retail environments and that perhaps consumers aren't willing or ready to install AR mirrors in their homes.

Bringing the Runway Closer Than Ever

In addition to augmenting the try-on experience, AR has transformed how we engage with the space around us and has presented the opportunity to bring fashion closer than ever, especially regarding fashion presentation.

There are examples of augmented reality runway shows dating back eleven years, like the one telecommunications company

Vodafone launched with ARworks. Users scan a QR code with their smartphones or tablets and can view images of models in their environments. The fidelity wasn't excellent, but it was an early attempt to bridge the gap between runway shows and consumers.

In 2020, mobile network operator Three UK teamed up with volumetric video leader Dimension to turn British fashion model and actress Adwoa Aboah into a 3D model for London Fashion Week. Audience members were invited to watch an augmented reality hologram of Aboah walk down the runway. Aboah had been captured in a 3D volumetric capture studio—essentially a large green room with multiple cameras to photograph every detail from different angles. The activation was to celebrate the launch of Three UK's 5G network.

More recent examples from brands like Khaite demonstrate the advanced AR technology landscape. For their Spring/Summer 2021 collection, Khaite worked with AR provider 8th Wall and Rose Digital to create an augmented reality fashion show, which allowed users to place models in any environment to see the collection up close despite the COVID-19 lockdowns (QR Code 22). The AR experience was triggered by a QR code placed on the company's website and in its lookbook.

QR Code 22 Scan to view Khaite's runway show in augmented reality.

It's not just runway shows that are enhanced by augmented reality. The tech is also promising for sharing fashion history and archiving purposes. For example, in 2018, *The New York Times* ran a story on the costumes of David Bowie. It was called "David Bowie in Three Dimensions."[19] In addition to the print/digital article, readers could view costumes with a 360-degree viewer online or place some of Bowie's most iconic outfits in their environment using AR (QR Code 23). I remember viewing Bowie's 1973 Lightning Suit in my living room via my mobile phone. It enabled me to get so close to the rendering of the costume that I could see very fine details that perhaps I'd miss in a museum. What's more, museums are only capable of showcasing artifacts in one place at a time, but *The New York Times* article made David Bowie's costumes accessible to anyone with an internet connection.

QR Code 23 Scan to read the article "David Bowie in Three Dimensions" and launch the AR experience.

Branded Filters and Embedded Environments

In addition to augmenting the retail and runway experience, augmented reality was also transforming the way we engage with brands online via branded filters and embedded environments.

In September 2015, after acquiring San Francisco-based Looksery, Snapchat introduced lenses, augmented reality filters that are available for photo and video capture. Lenses allowed Snapchat users to turn the camera on themselves to transform their face or to turn the camera to the world around them to transform what they saw.

While lenses were creator-driven, it wasn't long before brands got involved. Brands saw AR as an opportunity to experiment with new technology while getting in front of Gen Z, who was, by this time, becoming a much-coveted (yet difficult-to-captivate) audience.

In August 2016, Burberry created a limited-time lens to promote the launch of its new fragrance, Burberry Black. Users who searched for Burberry in the Snap app or found the lens on Snapchat's Discover page would see themselves underneath an umbrella. If they blew a kiss to the camera, the action would trigger a golden light. Shortly after, UGG launched a limited-time Snapchat lens in North America that featured fall leaves, earmuffs, and mini UGG boots that appeared if a user opened their mouth. The frame read, "Finally UGG season."

Given that lenses could simulate a kind of try-on experience, it made sense that beauty and fashion companies were among the first to experiment with virtual try-on in Snapchat. Brands like Gucci and Dior released lenses allowing users to try on sunglasses and footwear.

Filters enabled users to visualize themselves wearing a brand's products. For example, Dior created a series of filters for Snap and Facebook for trying on accessories such as sunglasses and hats in AR. Gucci launched a feature within its iOS app that allowed users to try on the brand's ACE sneakers in AR and see different color variations.

In addition to filters, many fashion companies experimented with embedded environments that transform the world around the user into a branded experience. For example, in December 2019, Chanel hosted a physical pop-up at the Standard Hotel in New York. The brand transformed the boutique hotel in a busy shopping area into a winter wonderland complete with hot chocolate, ice skating, and plenty of photo opportunities for Instagram. In addition, Chanel invited attendees to view an augmented-reality experience by accessing a lens on Snapchat or downloading an app via Chanel .com. Those at home could also use the lens, which created more access and virality for the campaign.

Augmented reality filters have not gone without scrutiny. Perhaps one of the biggest criticisms is that they promote unrealistic beauty standards. Snapchat dysmorphia is a term used by the cosmetic community to describe the phenomenon of people requesting procedures to resemble their digital image. The term was coined by Dr. Tijion Esho when he noticed that patients were bringing in photos of themselves that had been altered with Snap filters or photo-editing apps like Facetune.[20]

In a video I produced for social video brand Technality, I took a deep dive into the Bold Glamour Filter, a popular TikTok filter that transforms people's appearance using generative AI. Unlike augmented reality, which layers makeup or effects over your face, Bold Glamour actually recreates your face in real-time and displays it back to you on your live video feed. This makes the transformation less glitchy and more realistic (QR Code 24).

QR Code 24 Scan to watch my video for Technality on the Bold Glamour filter.

"It's just scary because there's a lot of girls out there that don't realize when someone's got a filter on," says TikTok user and media personality @zoe_george.[21] "They're chasing perfection because that's what they think everybody looks like, and this is not what everybody looks like," she says. Some have gone as far as to call the filter psychological warfare and "pure evil."[22]

As part of my reporting for my video piece on the Bold Glamour filter, I visited the MAC makeup store at the Toronto Eaton Centre to see if they could transform me into the filter. (I wanted to see if the Bold Glamour transformation was even possible with makeup.) To get even close, it took an hour and a half and 22 products. If I were to purchase all the products used, it would cost $902 before tax—not including any of the brushes.

Augmented Apparel

So far, we've discussed the impact of augmented reality on marketing and shopping experiences, but augmented reality has also transformed apparel itself.

Drawsta was an early example of a startup bringing a digital dimension to clothing. Founded by creative Heather Lipner, Drawsta placed visual triggers on T-shirts. When scanned with a smartphone app, the T-shirts would come to life in augmented reality with words and graphics viewable through the accompanying app. The designs and messages changed weekly, making the same T-shirt feel new again with digital content.

Similarly, in 2016, Marks & Spencer released a line of T-shirts for kids that came to life in augmented reality. The shirts featured graphics of animals and dinosaurs, which started to move and interact if scanned with the app (QR Code 25). It was a playful way of using the technology to engage the imagination.

QR Code 25 Scan to see Marks & Spencer AR T-shirts in action.

Recently, I was sent an augmented reality T-shirt that featured a graphic of a jellyfish. The shirt was by the Ukrainian clothing brand Finch in collaboration with marketing agency FFFACE.ME. The collection of shirts was originally created for a showcase that took place during Milan Fashion Week. The shirts contained a QR code that when scanned triggered an augmented reality experience complete with its own audio. The experience works differently depending on your proximity to the shirt. For example, the jellyfish on my T-shirt became three-dimensional when scanned up close, but when the filter is activated and I stepped away, the AR experience included a face overlay as well that turned me into a digital sea creature.

Although these are early experiments, all three of the examples above outline how augmented reality apparel can inject an exciting layer of interactivity and storytelling. AR clothing can transcend the physical realm and embrace the digital, transforming apparel into an evolving medium for creativity, connection, and self-expression. As we continue this exploration of augmented reality in fashion, the evolution from stand-alone apps to WebAR promises to further democratize and streamline access to these immersive experiences, shaping the future of how we interact with clothing and technology.

From Stand-Alone Apps to WebAR

As much as they laid the groundwork for augmented reality, apps like Snap weren't the only place where AR experiences were taking place in the early days. Stand-alone apps invited users to shop in augmented reality, including IKEA Place. Introduced in 2017, IKEA Place allowed users to place an item from the IKEA catalogue in their own environment using AR. The item would be true to size, so users could get a real sense of what couches and other furniture would look like in their home (and whether or not it would fit). "This will be the first augmented reality app that will enable you to make buying decisions," Michael Valdsgaard, leader of digital transformation at IKEA Systems, told Swedish website Di Digital.[23] IKEA Place was launched in collaboration with Apple to show off the capabilities of the tech giant's new ARKit for iOS 11. ARKit is a suite of tools for developers to use to power AR experiences. IKEA Place quickly received 8.5 million downloads from both furniture enthusiasts and those who just wanted to see the tech in action.

The challenge is that getting people to download an app is actually a bigger ask than you might think. With the introduction of WebAR, experiences could live in web browsers and not require users to download a stand-alone app. Today, WebAR has become the standard for launching new experiences.

One prominent example of WebAR in action was Burberry's collaboration with Google in 2020. The experience allowed customers to interact with Burberry products directly through their web browser, without the need for a dedicated app. When shoppers searched for specific Burberry products using Google, a "View in AR" prompt invited them to place a life-size version of that product in their environment in AR. This elevated the brand experience and allowed shoppers to inspect items up close.

WebAR was a significant step forward in terms of ease-of-use and adoption of augmented reality technology. According to AirCards, a global production studio dedicated to immersive storytelling, WebAR marketing campaigns have higher engagement metrics, with click-through rates of 40–50% and user dwell times ranging from one to two minutes, surpassing standard website engagement statistics.[24]

As WebAR continues to gain traction by removing barriers to entry and making augmented reality more accessible through web browsers, its popularity signals a shift in how consumers interact with digital experiences. This democratization of AR technology has broadened its applications, from marketing campaigns to virtual try-ons, empowering users to engage with brands effortlessly. However, while WebAR emphasizes accessibility, more specialized AR applications, such as fit-finding technologies, are leveraging advanced hardware capabilities like the LiDAR sensor in the iPhone. By combining AR with precision spatial mapping, these tools are transforming how consumers approach sizing and personalization, merging cutting-edge hardware with AR innovation for more accurate and immersive experiences.

Fit-Finding: Using Spatial Computing to Assess Fit

While virtual try-on gives shoppers a sense of what a particular style will look like on them, style and style preferences (color, variations, aesthetic) are not the same thing as fit. When I'm speaking of fit, I'm talking about the appropriate way a garment should sit on a body in order to optimize for function and flattery. The right fit should let a user perform all their tasks, while helping them appear pleasing to the eye. Although what's considered pleasing has come under scrutiny as of late (I'm thinking of women no longer dressing for the male gaze, and criticisms of the "hourglass" silhouette as the most desirable), there are certain design principles that humans are drawn to. For example, symmetry, harmony, and proportionality are widely used in art and architecture for their aesthetic appeal. You may have heard of the golden ratio, a mathematical ratio found in nature, art, and design. Although preferences vary across cultures, we as humans are hard-wired to be attracted to visual harmony, and when clothes don't fit right, they just seem off.

As we discussed in our chapter on automation, mass produced clothing like fast fashion is created in a scale of sizes to try and accommodate for the majority of bodies. However, finding your correct size can be difficult, especially because there is no across-the-board sizing standards in fashion, despite the widespread frustration of consumers. What if there were a way spatial computing could measure our physical bodies in space and then figure out how to dress them?

With the introduction of LiDAR technology on iPhones in 2020, we're now carrying around spatial computing devices in our pockets capable of accounting for shape in a whole new way.

For those not familiar, LiDAR stands for Light Detection and Ranging. It's a remote sensing method that measures distances by illuminating a target with laser light and analyzing the reflected light. You may have used it if you've tried the Measure app on iPhones or iPads, an app that lets you measure objects and spaces. Although LiDAR has been around since the 1960s, it was mainly used for aerospace engineering and maritime surveying. As sensors got smaller and more affordable, LiDAR has been introduced on consumer electronic devices. Beginning in 2020, Apple started equipping LiDAR on its iPad and iPhone models, giving us advanced spatial computing power in the palm of our hands.

Fashion companies have jumped at the opportunity to leverage LiDAR to solve e-commerce challenges, including attempting to solve the problem of fit in hopes it can reduce returns. According to Shopify, consumers collectively returned $743 billion worth of products in 2023—around 14.5% of total retail sales.[25] Many of these returns come from bracketing—when a customer orders more than one size of the same item to try on at home and then returns ones that don't fit.

For retailers, this often means additional shipping costs and the risk that returned merchandise won't make it back into the store's inventory on time to resell for full price. The National Retail Federation estimates returns resulted in $400 billion in lost sales for US retailers.[26]

As an attempted solution, brands have relied on size charts and "fit finders"—online tools that help assess fit. Until recently, fit finders looked like short quizzes that consumers take in order to receive a size recommendation. The challenge is that these fit finders aren't always accurate. In a small experiment we conducted for one of the startups I was advising, we asked twenty women of varying ages and sizes to try to find clothes that fit using online style quizzes and fit recommendation tools. We instructed them to take the quizzes offered online from popular fit-finding tools like True Fit. We then ordered the items in varying sizes for our subjects to try on and tell us which one they felt fit best (their preferred size). We compared their preferred size with the size that was recommended to them. Our results showed that the Fit Finders were only accurate half of the time. In other words, you have a 50% chance of getting the right size when using an online fit finder quiz. Although not an in-depth study, the results confirmed my own experiences when shopping for fashion online—you can't rely on a lot of the tools that are available.

LiDAR promises a more accurate way of assessing body shape and recommending appropriate clothing sizes.

Fit: Match.ai is a Fort Lauderdale-based startup that uses LiDAR to obtain 93% fit accuracy for clients and has piloted its technology with Fabletics and Rihanna's Savage x Fenty. Whether online or in-store, customers can scan their bodies with an iPad or iPhone and receive product recommendations based on their specific shape. "Instead of someone putting a cold tape measure around you and touching and feeling you, the associate asks you to stand still and they walk around you with an iPhone," explains Fit:Match AI founder and CEO Haniff Brown.[27] "Within 30 seconds, not only does your avatar pop up but also your measurements and all your size predictions," he says. "It's a much more contactless and data-driven approach."

Similarly, 3DLook is able to take 80 measurements of customers with just two pictures and then produce size recommendations for customers when shopping on one of their client's sites.

In addition to helping customers find the right fit, LiDAR could also be the technology that ushers in a new era of mass personalization and turns the manufacturing model on its head. Rather than mass-producing items in a scale of sizes, retailers could offer items custom-made to their client's specifications.

Project B is a Brooklyn-based startup aiming to change the way women shop for bras. Shoppers scan their breasts with an iPhone and the software creates an anonymized silhouette from which they create a 3D-knitted custom bra.

As you can imagine, there are massive privacy concerns with 3D scanning, and serious conversations about consent, encryption, and ethics are necessary before this technology can move forward. In the next chapters, we'll look at how fit technologies have incorporated elements of gaming and AI to evolve, but for now, it's important to note how LiDAR is opening up the possibilities for garment measurement and enhanced clienteling.

Smart Glasses for the Masses

We can't conclude our chapter on spatial computing without talking about smart glasses. As mentioned in Chapter 2, the Internet of Things brought all kinds of objects to life with digital technology, including personal items like eyewear. The term "smart glasses" describes eyewear that has some kind of internet-enabled features. Many pairs of digital eyewear include displays that layer digital information on top of your existing reality, hence the term "mixed reality."

Google Glass was one such early attempt at smart glasses, but when it was released in 2012, the general public wasn't ready for it. People found the device pretentious and intrusive. A New Yorker was kicked out of a restaurant in the East Village for refusing to remove her device.[28] A journalist had his Google Glass ripped off his face and smashed to the ground in San Francisco.[29] The term "Glasshole" came to mean an obnoxious wearer of Google Glass. The reaction to Google Glass was a perfect example of society's aversion to new technologies, especially when it comes to technology worn on the face, which is integral to how we typically communicate.

Although the general public wasn't ready for smart glasses, they did find a viable use case at the enterprise level for a short while. Glass Enterprise Edition was an assisted reality wearable that was used to aid workers. GE Aviation, for example, integrated Google Glass into their assembly process for jet engines. Technicians used Google Glass to view step-by-step assembly instructions directly in their field of vision. This eliminated the need to refer to physical manuals or computers, reducing the time spent switching focus between tasks and instructions. The results were a significant reduction in assembly time.[30] Other enterprise applications for Google Glass included providing surgical guidance for doctors and helping warehouse workers with inventory management. Despite these successes, Glass Enterprise was discontinued in March 2023.

Throughout the late 2010s, smart glasses were popping up everywhere. This was due to advancements in both hardware and software. In 2017, semiconductor creators Qualcomm released the Snapdragon Wear 1200 processor, specifically optimized for wearables, including smart glasses. This processor offered ultra-low-power consumption that was packed with performance capabilities. At the same time, enhanced optics and OLED microdisplays improved visual clarity and enabled AR overlays. 4G LTE and later 5G connectivity allowed smart glasses to operate independently of smartphones, enhancing mobility and functionality. Major tech players like Google, Microsoft, and Snap Inc. invested heavily in the development of wearable AR devices, which created momentum for this category. Devices during this period included ODG's R8 and R9, Vuzix's Blade, Microsoft HoloLens 2, the Magic Leap One, and Snap's Spectacles—to name a few.

In 2018, Kitchener-based North introduced consumer AR glasses called Focals, which retailed for $1,000. They included a hidden holographic display that projected light onto your eye, which then bounced back onto the frame. This augmented your reality to layer on important digital information. Focals could tell you the weather, give you directions, display text messages, and help call an Uber. In June 2020, Google acquired North, which led to the integration of North's technology and expertise into Google's hardware division.

That same year, Meta announced its collaboration with EssilorLuxottica, the largest manufacturer of eyeglasses and sunglasses in the world. Together, they would produce Ray-Ban Stories, smart glasses that actually looked like sunglasses but included high-quality cameras, immersive audio, and an AI-powered voice assistant.

Despite these strides in the development of smart glasses, no single product has yet to capture mainstream adoption. While devices like Ray-Ban Stories brought smart eyewear closer to looking and feeling like traditional glasses, they were still limited in functionality and often perceived as niche gadgets rather than everyday essentials. The category of smart glasses, as it stands, remains an evolving frontier, one that continues to search for the perfect balance between style, utility, and public acceptance.

A Vision for the Future

On February 1, 2024, Apple CEO Tim Cook appeared on the digital cover of *Vanity Fair,* donning the company's latest product, the Apple Vision Pro. Known for its ability to redefine product categories and set new standards for consumer technology, Apple introduced the Vision Pro in 2023. Positioned not as smart glasses but as a "spatial computer," the Vision Pro is Apple's ambitious foray into augmented and virtual reality, and it marks a significant step forward in spatial computing. Unlike its predecessors in the smart eyewear market, the Vision Pro isn't just a wearable gadget—it's a full-fledged ecosystem designed to seamlessly blend the physical and digital worlds.

Already startups are jumping at the opportunity to create experiences for brands in the Apple Vision Pro. Obsess, for example, is a company on a mission to reinvent e-commerce. They've released experiences for the Apple Vision Pro in collaboration with notable fashion and lifestyle brands, including Mytheresa, RIMOWA luggage, and e.l.f. Cosmetics. Their J.Crew Virtual Closet app lets users style outfits from the J.Crew collection on a life-size mannequin. Shoppers can pull an item of clothing so close they can see the product's weaves, textures, folds, and creases. Obsess claims the level of detail attainable is akin to the real-life examination of a garment up close.[31]

StockX, the online marketplace and resale platform, has also released its own app for the Apple Vision Pro. Shoppers can browse through featured shoes and shop based on inspired streetstyle looks. What makes the experience truly immersive and unique is a "try now" feature that transforms your living room into a showroom. With a brief gesture, shoppers can inspect sneakers in detail, interact with market data, and make offers on items.

But the Apple Vision Pro isn't just about retailing. It's also being used for storytelling. Gucci was among the first luxury brands to release a fashion film for the Vision Pro. "Who is Sabato De Sarno?

A Gucci Story" introduces viewers to the brand's creative director and shares the story behind the latest collection. The possibilities for storytelling and retailing are endless.

Priced at more than $4,000, it's unlikely I'll own a Vision Pro anytime soon, but—as we've seen with other technology—devices will become more affordable over time. And, as YouTuber Casey Neistat pointed out, this will be the "least impressive version of the device Apple ships."[32] As time goes on, spatial computing hardware will become more sophisticated and affordable. "This isn't the future of AR or VR. I think this is the future interface for all computing," Neistat says. "When they figure out how to make these not be heavy, $4,000 metal ski googles, but maybe they look like these glasses," he explains, gesturing to his Ray-Bans.

The Future of Spatial Computing and Fashion

Science fiction has already hinted at what the future of spatial computing could look like when it comes to fashion. In an episode of the animated sitcom *The Jetsons,* Jane Jetson needs to decide what to wear to the theater, so she turns to her "dress selector." The machine appears from the ceiling like a projector, only she stands behind it instead of in front of it. At the click of a button, Jane can flip through available dress options, and see them rendered perfectly on her silhouette via the dress selector. "Ooh, isn't that a Christian Di-Orbit, mother?" Jane's daughter, Judy, asks—a playful nod to the French fashion designer Christian Dior (QR Code 26).

As *The Jetsons* predicted, the future of shopping will become more personalized and immersive than ever before. Spatial computing will continue to transport the retail experience to consumers wherever they want to shop, including in the comfort of their own homes. Retail environments will continue to become more website-like, with multiple digital touchpoints throughout. Virtual environments can

QR Code 26 Scan to watch this segment from *The Jetsons*.

reimagine the way we shop online to supplement or even replace our current text and image-based websites. Fit-finding has the potential to become more accurate, while taking measurements for custom clothes will be easier than ever before.

As we look to the horizon, the possibilities for spatial computing in fashion are as boundless as our imaginations. The technology is poised to reshape every facet of the industry, from the way clothes are illustrated, tried on, and purchased to how brands tell their stories and connect with consumers. What has become clear over the years is that spatial computing—especially augmented reality try-on—is not just a nice-to-have; it's becoming the new expectation in a post-COVID-19 shopping landscape.

Imagine a world where your wardrobe exists simultaneously in physical and digital forms, seamlessly integrated into your daily life. Smart glasses and augmented reality could become as ubiquitous as smartphones, allowing consumers to engage with fashion in ways that are more entertaining than ever before. Fashion brands will increasingly embrace the potential of immersive storytelling, creating experiences that captivate and resonate with audiences. Runway shows will no longer be confined to physical spaces, and garments themselves could blur the line between static objects and dynamic digital canvases.

Yet with these advancements come challenges. Ethical considerations around privacy, data ownership, and accessibility will need to be addressed to ensure that this new digital frontier is inclusive and respectful of all users. Collaboration between technologists, designers, and policymakers will be key to navigating these complexities.

As the lines between the digital and physical worlds continue to blur, spatial computing offers the opportunity not only to reimagine fashion but to redefine our relationship with retail and self-expression. The journey of spatial computing and fashion is just beginning, and this fusion promises a future that is as thrilling as it is transformative. In the next chapter, we'll consider how spatial computing laid the groundwork for Web 3.0, the next evolution of the internet.

Chapter 5

Web 3.0

People come to the OASIS for all the things they can do, but they stay because of all the things they can be.

—Ernest Cline, Ready Player One

Digital Design Has Its Runway Moment

It was the first New York Fashion Week during the COVID-19 pandemic, and Anifa Mvuemba was uneasy. The Congolese designer planned on showing her womenswear collection on the runway that September, but lockdowns and restrictions made it impossible.

Mvuemba's brand, Hanifa, was inspired by the Democratic Republic of Congo, and specifically the "majestic women that live there."[1] Rather than skipping out on fashion week, Mvuemba shared a 3D-generated video of her collection on Instagram Live. In it, the clothes seemingly walk themselves down the runway, moving through thin air as if worn by ghosts. The collection included a wide-leg denim jumpsuit, a dress using the colors of the DRC flag, and a miniskirt inspired by Congolese rivers (QR Code 27).

The Pink Label Congo Collection video presentation on Instagram was watched by 10,000 people in real-time and has since racked up hundreds of thousands of views. As *Dezeen* pointed out, the virtual presentation made Mvuemba's work more accessible, giving everyone a front-row seat.[2] "Can video ever replace the runway experience?"

QR Code 27 Scan to see Hanifa's Pink Label Congo Collection on Instagram.

The New York Times article covering the virtual presentation asked. "[Hanifa] suggests the answer might not be no."[3]

To be clear, it wasn't just the fact that Hanifa's collection was shared via video that made it special—after all, as we saw in Chapter 1, runway shows have been livestreamed since Alexander McQueen was still alive. Hanifa's show was unique because the entire presentation was 3D-generated using design software.

While digital design platforms like CLO3D and Blender have been around for over a decade, these tools were used mostly behind the scenes. Developing fashion—creating tech packs and sharing virtual samples between remote teams—relies on specialty software that, over the years, has decreased in cost and increased in usability. Hanifa's Pink Label Congo Collection was one of the first times the 3D designs were used as a stand-in for the collection itself. The emphasis on 3D digital assets would become one of the hallmarks of Web 3.0.

Welcome to Web 3.0

According to *Harvard Business Review*, Web 3.0 is "shorthand for the project of rewiring how the web works, using blockchain to change how information is stored, shared, and owned."[4] We'll get to the blockchain piece shortly, but to understand where we are today with Web 3.0, we need to understand what came before it.

You can think of the evolution of the internet in different phases. Although computing and the physical infrastructure of the internet has been in development since the 1960s, Web 1.0 didn't emerge until the early 1990s when HTML and URLs made it possible for users to navigate between static pages.[5] These pages were primarily text-based, and for the most part they were read-only, meaning they were mainly a place for consuming text. Although there was some interaction among users, it was limited to message boards. For the most part, creation was centralized to a few people or organizations that would publish information while users consumed it. Although user-generated content was possible, it was limited to forms or web hosting services where people could publish information. There was little interaction and dynamic content. Some examples of Web 1.0 include Netscape Navigator, one of the first widely used web browsers, and GeoCities, a web hosting service that allows users to create and publish websites for free.

For fashion, Web 1.0 looked like early websites and web pages. For example, *Vogue* established its online presence in the mid-1990s. Initially, its website teased the magazine's print edition with snippets of articles and photoshoots. Similarly, *Elle* and *Harper's Bazaar* went online in 1996.

Unlike the print era before it, the internet era gave individuals the same publishing power as fashion magazines. As internet expert Clay Shirky points out, "publishing isn't a job anymore. It's a button."

Early blogs, such as Tavi Gevinson's *Style Rookie*, demonstrated how the internet was making space for new voices. Launched in 2008, *Style Rookie* chronicled eleven-year-old Gevinson's outfits and commentary on the latest fashion trends. According to *The Seattle Times*, the blog drew in 30,000 readers a day. Within three years of her first post, Gevinson was sitting front-row at fashion shows next to *Vogue* editor-in-chief Anna Wintour.

Web 2.0, otherwise known as the Social Web, started in the early 2000s with interactive platforms such as MySpace, Friendster,

LiveJournal Reddit, and eventually Facebook. These spaces were different from Web 1.0 because they fused the discussion features of message boards and user-generated content elements of platforms like GeoCities.

As you may have already noticed, these phases of internet evolution are fluid and interconnected. For example, there's no distinct time when blogs ended and social media took over. Many blogs still exist today. However, generally speaking, there are characteristics defining each phase of internet history.

The Social Web was *read-write*, meaning users could consume content and create it, a shift made possible due to interactive websites and social platforms. In Web 2.0, content became more dynamic and offered rich multimedia-like images, video, and audio. This is where we saw the rise of user-generated content and the emergence of influencer culture as we know it today.

For fashion, the shift from Web 1.0 to Web 2.0 was slow and disjointed. Many brands lacked the in-house capabilities to launch and maintain Facebook pages and Instagram accounts, while others hesitated to invest resources because they were unsure of the return on investment. In many ways, fashion was still adjusting to Web 1.0—websites and e-commerce strategies—and now they found themselves behind the times. The luxury sector was notoriously slow to adopt selling online. In 2014, when asked, "Why not e-commerce?" Prada's then-CEO Patrizio Bertelli responded that he had "more important things to do, like opening stores, for example."[6]

It was only after Prada's competitors like Burberry and Louis Vuitton launched e-commerce sites that Prada made investments in its digital strategy.[7] Others moved quickly to experiment and saw early wins.

An example of Web 2.0 in action for fashion was Burberry's "The Art of the Trench" campaign. Launched in 2009 as a micro-site, the campaign encouraged Burberry customers to upload photos of themselves wearing their trench coats, the item that's central to the

British brand. The micro-site allowed clients to have their fifteen minutes of fame and enabled users to browse and comment on photos of Burberry customers from all over the world.[8]

As we discussed in Chapter 1, the smartphone and its killer app, social media, changed the dynamics of the fashion industry and shifted power from brands and magazines to consumers. Web 3.0 would continue this trend while also upending the emphasis on physicality in fashion.

Web 3.0 emerged as a theory in the early 2000s but gained traction in 2010 and beyond. It distinguished itself from previous iterations by focusing on decentralization, a concept where users can own their data and digital assets. In many ways, Web 3.0 responds to the dominance of companies like Meta and Alphabet, which generate billions of dollars by capitalizing on user data. Web 3.0 introduced the idea of *read-write-own*, as in *user* ownership, made possible by blockchain technology.

Blockchain technology is a public digital ledger maintained across computer networks rather than in one centralized location. Each new transaction, such as the sale of an item, creates a new block. In 2019, blockchain technology appeared on the fashion industry's radar when a digital dress that doesn't exist in physical form sold at an auction for nearly $10,000.

The $9,500 Digital Dress That Sold on the Blockchain

A year before Hanifa's Pink Label Congo Collection, a little-known startup from Amsterdam called the Fabricant began appearing in news stories for selling a digital-only dress for $9,500 on the blockchain.

Called Iridescence, the dress was a flowy swath of fabric with an ethereal look that changed colors as it caught the light, like a bubble from a bubble-blowing wand. The dress, which does not exist physically, was rendered onto an image of digital artist Johanna Jaskowska, the creator of popular and otherworldly augmented reality filters on Instagram. Iridescence, one of her more popular filters, would give your face a glossy overlay, like a purple glazed doughnut. Jaskowska collaborated with the Fabricant on the dress and modeled it (QR Code 28). The Iridescence Dress was then sold at an auction to Canadian tech executive Richard Ma, who paid almost $10,000 for it as a gift for his wife, Mary Ren.

To "wear" the dress, it was digitally rendered onto a photo of Ren. Richard Ma told the BBC he considered the purchase an investment with long-term value. "In ten years' time, everybody will be wearing digital fashion. It's a unique memento. It's a sign of the times," he said.[9]

QR Code 28 Scan to see a video of the Iridescence Dress modeled by digital artist Johanna Jaskowska.

Digital fashion refers to garments and accessories that exist digitally rather than physically. These items, created in CAD software like Blender, are sold as commodities. Where Hanifa used 3D renderings to market her real-world items, digital fashion often has no physical counterpart. As a result, digital fashion can be outside the realms of what's possible for physical fashion, such as a dress made of fire or wind. Without the constraints of reality, digital fashion can push the limits of the imagination, which makes it an exciting development for experimentation.

During the summer of 2020, a design studio contacted me to see if I wanted to try digital fashion. Of course I said yes, because I was interested in the process. They asked me for a photo of myself for the base layer. I sent them a picture of me from a personal branding photoshoot I'd done earlier that year where I was wearing a red Versace dress. Within a few days, they sent back an altered version of the photo, only this time I was wearing a metallic dress with puffed shoulders that looked like futuristic armor (Figure 5.1).

The business model of digital fashion companies was that they'd sell these pictures for money, and people would pay for these digital makeovers. I thought the idea was gimmicky and didn't have any money-making potential, but it was a novel way of playing dress-up—a kind of extension of the virtual try-on pioneered by beauty with augmented reality.

At first, digital fashion may seem useless, but the idea behind it is clever: Many of us already dress for the digital gaze. Digital fashion simultaneously calls out our #OOTD-obsessed culture (OOTD stands for "outfit of the day") while offering an enticing alternative: *What if we all dressed digitally?*

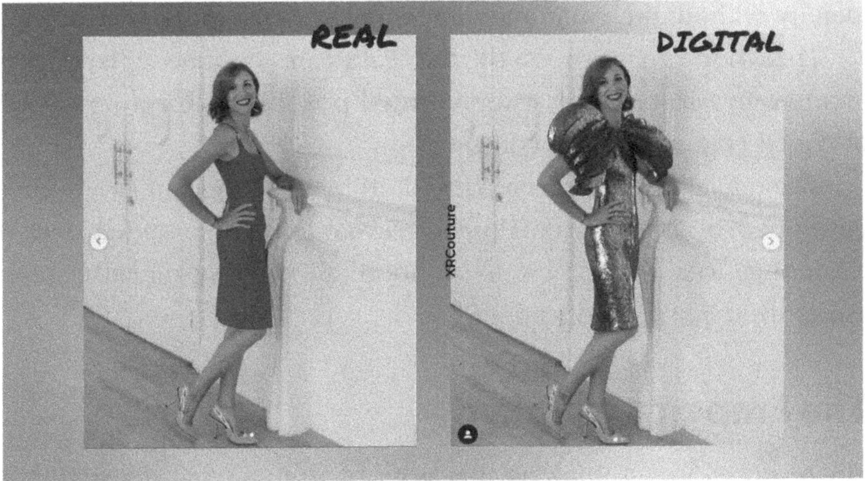

Figure 5.1 Before and after my digital makeover.

This Outfit Does not Exist

Daniella Loftus is a digital creator who has been wearing digital fashion since its inception. On her Instagram account, @thisoutfit-doesnotexist, she shares pictures of herself wearing digital outfits, some made possible by filters and others rendered onto her body in post-production software. She has since become a poster child for digital fashion and collaborated with digital-only fashion houses, including ZERO10 and Tribute Brand. "No materials were harmed in the making of these photos," reads her Instagram bio.[10]

Digital fashion presents itself as a more sustainable option to IRL fashion since designs are rendered digitally and don't need to be produced using raw materials. This said, comparing a digital design to an actual garment is like comparing a drawing of a house to a real home—both may have merit, but only one offers real utility and protection from the elements.

If we consider fashion as more than just a means of protection and as a way of expressing ourselves, then digital dress-up is a novel way for people to experiment with their personal style. It provides a safe space for exploring everything from color theory to gender identity without the environmental impact or cost to the consumer.

The Iridescence Dress by the Fabricant became a landmark moment in fashion since it represented possibilities for a new kind of digital commodity and consumption.

The digital fashion boom, kicked off by the Fabricant and further developed by brands like Hanifa, elevated computer-aided design renderings to a whole new level. Soon, all kinds of digital fashion assets were being produced and sold.

The Emperor Is Naked

You're not alone in thinking this story of clothing that doesn't exist sounds familiar. In the parable *The Emperor's New Clothes,* Hans

Christian Andersen tells the tale of a vain emperor who had an obsession with fancy new clothes and spent lavishly on them at the expense of state matters. One day, two con men visit the emperor posing as weavers and offer to supply him with magnificent clothes that are invisible to stupid people. The gullible emperor hires them, and they set up looms and pretend to go to work. As the con men are producing the emperor's suit, everyone from officials to the emperor's wise minister checks in on the progress. They see that the looms are empty but don't want to appear stupid, so they pretend they can see the suit. Finally, when the suit is supposedly finished, the con artists pretend to dress the emperor, and he sets off in a procession before the whole city. The townspeople all go along with the ruse because they don't want to appear stupid either, until a child blurts out that the emperor is naked.

The story teaches the importance of critical thinking, honesty, and the courage to challenge false narratives. *The Emperor's New Clothes* and digital fashion share similarities, but there are differences. For starters, both present the idea of clothing that doesn't exist in physical form, but digital fashion does exist, albeit only online.

Second, although the parable hinges on an element of deception, in the story, the con artists are intentionally deceptive. Those selling digital fashion are not deceiving customers into thinking they're purchasing something physical, although overspeculation about the value of these items may have inflated their price—but we'll get to that later.

The same year the Iridescence Dress sold, two Ukrainian entrepreneurs living in Los Angeles, Daria Shapovalova and Natalia Modenova, founded a company called DressX with a new vision for the future of fashion.

DressX is a digital-only fashion marketplace—meaning the items sold on the platform are entirely digital and not physical. DressX allows users to buy, wear, and display digital fashion items in virtual environments or on social media. The company partners with fashion brands and emerging designers to create limited-edition virtual items sold on the DressX platform.

Sneakers Did It First

The creation of digital commodities was something that the sneaker market was already figuring out. In January 2020, three friends who met working at an esports company—Benoit Pagotto, Chris Le, and Steven Vasilev—founded a startup called RTFKT (pronounced "artifact"). The startup's goal, Pagotto said in an interview with Highsnobiety, was to bring together crypto and gaming culture to redefine what people think of as a brand.[11]

Later that same year, an image of tech entrepreneur Elon Musk surfaced on the internet wearing a pair of RTFKT sneakers inspired by the Cybertruck, which Musk's company Tesla had introduced as a concept car in November 2019 (QR Code 29).

The image received 50 million views and got so much attention that people asked about the sneakers and where they could buy a pair. The Cybertruck sneakers did not exist physically but were sold as a digital commodity on SuperRare, a digital art market that runs on the Ethereum blockchain.

QR Code 29 Scan to see the image of Elon Musk "wearing" the RTFKT Cyber Sneakers.

"If a pair of sneakers exists in an image on the internet, and enough people see it, is it real?" asked Pagotto at the time. In May of 2021, RTFKT raised an $8 million seed round led by Andreessen Horowitz, which valued the company at $33.3 million. By December 2021, RTFKT was acquired by Nike for an undisclosed amount.

NFTs, or Non-Fungible Tokens

What's interesting about the Cyber Sneakers is that they were sold as an NFT, or non-fungible token, a new kind of digital commodity that was growing in popularity, particularly on Clubhouse, a new audio-first mobile app. On Clubhouse, people "hung out" virtually in "rooms" to chat with one another. Unlike the message boards of Web 1.0 or even the social media threads of Web 2.0, Clubhouse offered real-time social connection.

Clubhouse surged in popularity during the global pandemic and reached 10 million monthly users in March of 2021. "NFT stands for non-fungible token," you'd hear repeated by voices in virtual audio rooms as if passing along folklore from the future. The same month Clubhouse spiked in downloads, Mike Winkelmann, the digital artist known as Beeple, sold an NFT for $69 million at Christie's auction house. Called *Everydays: The First 5,000 Days*, the NFT was a collage of Beeple's works. Until skyrocketing interest in NFTs, the most Winkelmann had ever sold his work for was $100; now he was among the top three most valuable living artists in the world.

NFTs come to life through "minting," a process involving creating a new block on the blockchain with digital information attached to it. In Beeple's case, the digital information would be the artwork itself. NFTs needed to be purchased with cryptocurrency, a digital currency that is an alternative form of payment created using encryption algorithms. Digital currencies are unique because they run on a computer network and aren't reliant on any central authority, like a government or bank.

Since their early development in the 1980s to the founding of Bitcoin in 2009, cryptocurrencies have experienced boom-and-bust cycles, with the value of coins fluctuating depending on supply and demand. Just like in *The Emperor's New Clothes*, cryptocurrency relies on people's belief in it. So does the stock market, and—in many ways—money itself, but the difference is that Bitcoin is not backed by a physical commodity, like gold or a central government, so its value arises from trust in the system and perceived utility and scarcity.

In 2020, cryptocurrencies like Bitcoin were surging in popularity. While much of the world was isolated due to a global pandemic, online communities became more important than ever for social connection and camaraderie. They also became fertile grounds for scams.

If you listened to tech optimists at the time, you'd believe cryptocurrency would free us all from the restrictions of fiat currency, eliminating processing fees, government control, and counterfeit currency. Crypto enthusiasts touted it as a more secure way to transact online and a new way for artists to make money by entering their work into a global marketplace of digital collectors. To a certain extent, these promises were possible, but digital currencies were growing faster than regulation could keep up.

NFTs offered a seemingly once-in-a-lifetime, rag-to-riches opportunity, which was enticing for a generation that survived the global financial crisis followed by the Great Recession and was in the midst of another recession due to the pandemic.

Some projects were benign, like CryptoKitties. Developed by game studio Dapper Labs, CryptoKitties invited players to purchase, breed, and trade virtual cats with different features and varying levels of rarity. The virtual cats could only be purchased with Ether, the currency of the Ethereum blockchain. At the project's peak, someone paid 600 ETH (approximately $170,000) for a CryptoKitty called Dragon, making it the most expensive kitty ever traded in the history of the game.[12] Shortly after, CryptoKitties went belly up when the supply outpaced the demand. Since people could breed their kitties, the number of new ones outpaced the number of people who were interested, and the project folded. A cat-astrophe, so to speak. CryptoKitties exemplified how an oversupply of assets can quickly erode their perceived value, turning once-coveted items into virtually worthless commodities.

Other schemes were more sinister. Groups would coordinate to artificially inflate the price of a particular NFT, coin, or exchange. They'd create hype on social media platforms like Twitter, Instagram, and Facebook and promote the digital commodity to new buyers. As more people bought in, demand increased, causing prices to rise. Once the price had been pumped up, the individuals behind the scam would sell their holdings of the item at a profit, causing the price to crash and leaving others who bought in with major losses.[13] This type of pump-and-dump scheme became so popular and far-reaching that calls for the legal system to get involved increased, but these were largely ignored by the sitting administration. Donald Trump, the US president at the time, had a much more laissez-faire approach to regulation.

The Biden administration initiated a comprehensive review of cryptocurrency regulations. In March 2022, President Biden signed an executive order directing federal agencies to assess the benefits and risks of digital assets, marking the first "whole-of-government approach" to regulating cryptocurrencies.

When it comes to fashion's involvement in NFTs and cryptocurrency, participation has varied. Some brands, including Balenciaga and Philipp Plein, have integrated crypto payments into their retail operations. At one point in 2022, Gucci accepted payments in Bitcoin, Ether, Litecoin, Dogecoin, Shiba Inu, and a few others[14] (yes, there are cryptocurrencies named after dog breeds).

Many brands, including Adidas, Balenciaga, Lacoste, and Louis Vuitton, developed their own NFT experiments with varying degrees of success. Gucci, for example, created a fashion film to celebrate the launch of its Aria collection, a collection commemorating the brand's centennial by reflecting its rich heritage and paying homage to its equestrian roots. Gucci sold the film as an NFT for $25,000 via an auction at Christie's. The four-minute film, which is presented as a triptych, shows a loop of horses running in the woods and a model opening a turquoise door on a snowy day.

Dolce & Gabbana released Collezione Genesi—the Genesis Collection—a luxury NFT collection that included digital and physical assets. Nine one-of-a-kind items were sold for $6 million at auction, including a shimmering dress available in both gold and silver, an emerald green men's suit, two gold-plated and gem-studded silver crowns, and a bejeweled tiara.[15] The Genesis Collection set the record for fashion NFTs and accounted for the most money in sales the luxury brand has ever generated from one presentation.

You're not wrong to think Web 3.0 sounds like the Wild, Wild West—a new rugged frontier with plenty of opportunity for exploration and expansion. In many ways, the early days of NFTs were like the new American frontier—lawless, unregulated, and potentially dangerous.

Many fashion brands that had been slow in adapting to new digital technologies were eager not to fall behind again. As such, many moved fast, perhaps without fully understanding how to properly navigate this new space.

Often, what made these digital commodities valuable to the purchaser wasn't just the asset itself but the access to a larger community of like-minded collectors. A great example of this is CryptoPunks. Launched in June 2017 by creative design studio Larva Labs, CryptoPunks is a collection of 10,000 randomly generated characters sold as NFTs on the Ethereum blockchain. The project was created by

Canadian software developers Matt Hall and John Watkinson, who were inspired by the punk movement and science fiction. The punks were purposely pixelated, evoking an early 1990s aesthetic. People bought into the CryptoPunks community and proudly displayed their Punk as their avatar on social media, signaling allegiance to this crowd. Similarly, crypto enthusiasts began changing their profile pictures to images of themselves with laser eyes, a meme signaling enthusiasm and solidarity with the crypto community.

Over time, fashion's involvement in the NFT space became repetitive and redundant, as most luxury brands adopted the same strategy. I remember a time between 2021 and 2022 when my email inbox was flooded with press releases from designers and brands announcing digital commodities. Like CryptoKitties, the market was becoming saturated with supply. By the spring of 2023, I was sick of writing about new NFTs launches and wondered aloud if anyone was still buying in.

I should note that not all NFT offerings were bad or scams. For many emerging designers, NFTs provided the opportunity to enter the market and innovate their approach to attracting new audiences. For example, I interviewed Anya Ayoung-Chee, the founder and director of WYLD FLWR, a festival fashion apparel brand inspired by carnival culture and Burning Man. Ayoung-Chee is also the winner of Season 9 of *Project Runway*. After the brand's launch in 2020 was overshadowed by COVID-19, Ayoung-Chee turned to NFTs to sell her brand vision as digital artwork.

The Crypto Crash

In December of 2022, American entrepreneur Sam Bankman-Fried, the founder of the cryptocurrency exchange FTX, was arrested in the Bahamas with allegations of massive fraud, financial misconduct, and mismanagement of customer funds. Following the crash of FTX, approximately $8.9 billion of customer assets went missing.

FTX wasn't the only exchange to collapse, but Bankman-Fried's arrest was a sure sign the crypto bubble was bursting, and along with it, many inflated expectations about digital assets. Rising interest rates and economic uncertainty caused a sell-off of many digital currencies, and regulators were beginning to crack down with intensified scrutiny of the crypto sector. It was a house of cards that came crashing down. While the market would later show signs of recovery in late 2023 and 2024 with the reelection of Donald Trump, the events that had taken place prompted a reevaluation of crypto's role in global finance.

For fashion, this meant a reconsideration of involvement. Some brands that had previously accepted cryptocurrency decided to discontinue these types of payments, as was the case with Off-White. Others, like Dolce & Gabbana, reconsidered their NFT strategy after facing legal challenges, including a class-action lawsuit alleging fraud and unmet promises.[16] According to the plaintiffs, D&G had promised purchasers they would later receive benefits, including digital rewards, physical products, and exclusive access to events—none of which materialized. RTFKT, one of fashion's early Web 3.0 success stories, folded at the end of 2024.

While the rise and fall of cryptocurrencies marked a tumultuous chapter in the evolution of Web 3.0, it was not the only force reshaping the digital economy. Another significant cultural and economic driver emerged in the form of gaming. As crypto markets faltered, gaming culture surged, offering a more stable and engaging avenue for digital innovation. Unlike the speculative nature of cryptocurrencies, gaming provided an experiential ecosystem where digital assets, such as skins, avatars, and virtual goods, held intrinsic value within vibrant, user-driven communities.

Fashion brands quickly recognized the potential of this space, leveraging the immersive environments of gaming platforms to reach younger, tech-savvy audiences. In this context, collaborations with gaming developers began to eclipse cryptocurrency projects as more tangible, interactive, and culturally relevant applications of Web 3.0 technologies.

The Influence of Gaming

Although gamers have existed longer than computers, the pandemic intensified online game use. According to the New York Institute of Technology, the onset of COVID-19 coincided with the peak growth of video game usage, with 2.7 billion players gaming in 2020, or more than 30% of people on the planet.

In gaming, it's not uncommon to shell out real money for your avatar's clothes and accessories. Sometimes these "skins" unlock new capabilities, while other times they're entirely cosmetic and a way for players to express themselves within the game ecosystem. For example, on April 23, 2020, the rapper Travis Scott hosted a concert in the online game *Fortnite*. Scott released virtual skins using the design from his record brand Cactus Jack. Similarly, singer Ariana Grande hosted her Rift Tour in the video game *Fortnite Battle Royale*. The tour invited players to travel through magical environments and enjoy a musical performance. Attendees could also purchase an Ariana Grande skin and a series of cute accessories, like a piggie backpack (named Piggie Smalz, after Grande's real-life adopted emotional support pig).

The revenues generated by digital assets in online games are not just pocket change. Although *Fortnite*'s earnings are not publicly disclosed, in a lawsuit with Apple it was reported that Epic Games, the parent company of *Fortnite*, earned $50 million from one set of skins it made in collaboration with the NFL in two months in 2021.[17] According to one industry analyst estimate, Epic made $5.8 billion that year from selling in-game items.[18]

The relationship between fashion and gaming first popped up for me in 2019 when Louis Vuitton partnered with Riot Games, the creators of *League of Legends*, a popular video game. Through this collaboration, the luxury label created high-tech cases handcrafted by the artisan trunk makers for the Summoner's Cup—a trophy awarded to the world champion team of *League of Legends* (think Superbowl but for video games). Louis Vuitton also designed a capsule collection inspired by the game and a virtual skin for one of the *League of Legends* characters.

Since this collaboration, the tie between fashion and gaming has only intensified. The online platform Roblox has hosted branded experiences in collaboration with notable fashion brands, including Tommy Hilfiger, Ralph Lauren, Forever 21, Vans, Burberry, Givenchy, and Karl Lagerfeld, to name a few. Sometimes this looks like brand-hosted events with themed universes, prizes, and merchandise, like Tommy Play, a Roblox event sponsored by Tommy Hilfiger. Other times this looks like in-game styles that mimic what a brand is showing on the real-life runway, like Coach's "Find Your Courage" campaign, which launched on both Roblox and Zepetto, an avatar-based social universe. The campaign showcased Coach's Spring collection and followed the journey of imma, a virtual digital creator, as she embarked on a journey to find her courage.[19]

Instagram accounts such as @AnimalCrossingFashionArchive are dedicated to posting new outfits worn inside the video game *Animal Crossing*, including virtual clothes from Marc Jacobs, Valentino, Miu Miu, and more.

While early collaborations seemed to insert fashion into gaming as an add-on, by the end of 2020 the boundaries between gaming and fashion were beginning to blur.

In December 2020, Balenciaga released its collection in the form of a video game. In *Afterworld: The Age of Tomorrow*, users were invited to wander around a dystopian, post-apocalyptic universe and view streetwear-inspired silhouettes, which were actually available in stores. Players could embark on a hero's journey through forests and futuristic settings where they'd encounter models wearing pieces from the collection. Outfits included oversized silhouettes, armor-like elements, and streetwear-inspired designs. Developed in Unreal Engine, the technology behind many video games, *Afterworld: The Age of Tomorrow* represented a new frontier in fashion storytelling and received an IDEAS Award, a recognition from the UK's Advertising Producers Association (APA).

In May of 2021, a virtual Gucci bag sold for more than what the bag costs in real life. The Italian fashion house collaborated with online gaming platform Roblox to put on a virtual Gucci Garden exhibition. In it, players could wander around a fantastical world and purchase limited-edition digital items, including a virtual iteration of Gucci's Dionysus Bag with Bee. The item sold for an original price of 475 Robux (the platform's digital currency, equivalent to $6 USD). On an adjacent trading platform, the bag was resold for 350,000 Robux, or $4,115. The same purse in real life costs $3,400 USD.

As the boundaries between fashion and gaming began to dissolve, a new paradigm emerged: the avatar. No longer confined to pixelated representations of players, avatars evolved into sophisticated digital personas capable of embodying personal style, identity, and creativity. Within this virtual realm, the avatar became a canvas, and fashion brands saw an opportunity to extend their influence into a dimension where self-expression had no physical constraints. Whether through bespoke skins in games like *Fortnite* or exclusive NFT wearables, avatars were transformed into the ultimate consumers of digital couture, redefining what it means to dress and present oneself in the digital age.

The Avatar Wore Chanel

The avatar became the site of the intersection of fashion and gaming. As graphical representations of users or their alter egos, avatars give people the ability to cross into the online world and have a digital representation. ("Avatar" is a Sanskrit word that literally translates as "to cross.")

Technology companies had already been leaning into the avatar as a means of personalizing the user experience—Apple's Memojis, for example. Released in 2018 on iOS 12, these animated characters could be customized to resemble the user. Using TrueDepth cameras, emojis and animojis (animals and mythical creatures) could mimic a user's facial expressions in real-time. Unlike early gaming avatars or virtual characters, which required specialized platforms, Memojis reached a massive audience through Apple's ecosystem and introduced millions of people to the idea of using a digital persona for communicating. By merging self-expression, identity, and technology, Memojis helped lay the groundwork for the broader adoption and acceptance of avatars as integral to how we navigate and present ourselves in digital spaces.

Snap was also an early adopter of the avatar concept and tapped into the growing demand for self-expression in digital spaces. Within the Snapchat app, the avatar is central to the way users interact with friends as well as how they appear on Snap Maps, a feature that uses GPS to place people on a virtual map.

Snap invested early in the avatar concept by acquiring Toronto-based Bitmoji and its parent company Bitstrips for $64.2 million in March 2016. Bitstrips allowed users to create comic strips using their personalized avatars. Their spin-off app, Bitmoji, allowed people to create personalized stickers for use in messaging apps.[20]

Over the years, Snap has embraced and accelerated the avatar concept, partnering with notable fashion brands to provide innovative ways for users to dress their Bitmoji. One of the first brands to explore this space was Ralph Lauren. In 2020, the iconic American heritage label introduced a mix-and-match virtual wardrobe for Bitmoji, inspired by its real-life collections. The digital lineup featured timeless pieces such as a classic double-breasted blazer, a branded racer jacket, a striped rugby shirt, and a vibrant track jacket, allowing users to express their style in the digital realm.

Although avatars weren't specific to Web 3.0, they became increasingly popular and an important part of how we represent ourselves online during the pandemic and spread outside the world of gaming to social media. The Bored Ape Yacht Club was a perfect example of how avatar culture intersected with cryptocurrency and NFTs to build an exclusive online community.

The Bored Ape Yacht Club (known as BAYC for short) was launched in the spring of 2021 by Yuga Labs, a technology company that develops NFTs. BAYC is a collection of 10,000 unique, hand-drawn cartoon apes with their own particular look, such as a leopard-print ape with multicolored teeth and a halo over his head. The apes were for sale at 0.08 ETH (short for Ethereum, and equal to about $190 at the time) on a platform called OpenSea, a marketplace for selling NFTs. All 10,000 apes sold out.

The concept was not just that people would own the digital asset (the drawing of the ape), but they'd also get to be members of this exclusive online community and have the creative license to do whatever they wanted with their ape, including using it for commercial opportunities. The apes gained popularity in online circles, and soon celebrities like Paris Hilton and brands like Adidas were "aping in" (buying in). In June 2022, Snoop Dogg and Eminem released the music video for a new song, "From the D 2 the LBC," in which they appear as their Bored Apes. On Twitter, it was a huge digital flex to replace your profile picture with that of your cartoon ape to signal status and belonging to this special digital club.

Digital assets like the Bored Ape Yacht Club seamlessly blend digital identity, community, and commerce, and introduced us to the concept of a "metaverse" as a shared online experience. While academics and experts were arguing about the exact definition of the metaverse, one tech CEO was firmly planting his flag.

Mark Zuckerberg's Metaverse

The metaverse (a portmanteau of "meta" and "universe") was one of those early buzzwords that was circulating at the beginning of Web 3.0. Ideas of the metaverse revolved around a shared simulated reality. Some would argue that Roblox was a metaverse, since it offered a high-fidelity virtual experience, while others insisted that Roblox couldn't be a metaverse, since the term connotated shared yet interconnected worlds.

Around this time, people began to imagine the future of the internet as a destination you'd access via a headset—a shared immersive world that you could connect to at any time.

The metaverse concept was anticipated by the science fiction novel *Ready Player One* by Ernest Cline, which director Steven Spielberg turned into a feature film by the same name in 2018. In this story, set in a dystopian future, humanity escapes the harsh realities of real life by immersing themselves in a virtual world called the OASIS. The book and subsequent film were often referenced in conversations of the metaverse, along with the 1992 science fiction novel *Snow Crash* by American writer Neal Stephenson.

On October 28, 2021, Mark Zuckerberg made a startling announcement. In a video, he shared that he was changing Facebook's name to Meta to signal the company's new focus on creating "the Metaverse," a shared simulated reality he believed we'd all access via our Quest 2 headsets. Zuckerberg said the name Facebook no longer encompasses everything the company is focused on and that he wants to be seen as a metaverse company. "The word *Meta* comes from the Greek word meaning *beyond*," Zuckerberg explained in a video announcement. "It's an embodied internet where you're in the experience and not just looking at it," he explained.

In a demo video sharing his vision of the future, Zuckerberg jumps inside Horizon Worlds, the virtual reality platform he imagined as the next destination for the internet. The transition from the physical world to the digital one is shown in a clip that's surprisingly similar to the *Ready Player One* film trailer. In it, the camera whirls around the main character and then pans into his head to port his avatar to a whole new realm. Cue the exciting music.

In Zuckerberg's demo video, his avatar joins a few others at a table in what appears to be a spaceship. They're playing a game of cards, and it's clear that the realities of physics don't hold here because the characters float around like in that scene from *Mary Poppins* but the playing cards somehow stay perfectly in place. Two of the avatars are real people (although they appear as holograms), while another person is a kind of emoji cartoon representation. And, as if this was some kind of mushroom trip, a fourth character appears as a giant red robot wearing a green baseball cap.

Zuckerberg's pitch made it clear his understanding of the metaverse was as a destination—as a place you'd log into to socialize and connect, just like Facebook. Other attempts at the metaverse positioned it in a similar way.

Decentraland is a 3D virtual-world platform that allows users to create, experience, and monetize content and applications within a virtual world. Parcels of virtual land are sold as NFTs, which buyers are able to build and sell on top of. In March 2022, Decentraland held its first Metaverse Fashion Week, a digital fashion week where brands, designers, and the public were invited to wander around a virtual world over a four-day period that featured runway shows, after-parties, and pop-up shops. It was free for anyone with a computer or internet connection to attend.[21] NFTs purchased during the event could be "worn" by an attendee's avatar. The Fabricant launched its Season 1 collection and invited people to create their own garments on the Fabricant Studio, a tool that enables anyone to become a digital designer. Brands like Tommy Hilfiger also participated by hosting a digital retail platform where consumers could shop NFTs for their avatars or purchase physical items from within the metaverse.[22]

The first Metaverse Fashion Week in Decentraland was largely regarded as a flop.[23] The virtual environment was difficult to navigate and interact with and there were several tech issues. I wandered around Metaverse Fashion Week for an hour before logging off after a few glitches froze my avatar in cyberspace. The second year (2023) wasn't much better. Although this time more than sixty fashion brands participated, including Balenciaga, Adidas, and Coach, the press covering the event was mostly negative: "Decentraland's Metaverse Fashion Week featured virtual clothes and exhibits from some major names in fashion, but it was lonely and difficult to navigate," read a tagline in *The Verge*.[24]

Similarly, Mark Zuckerberg's metaverse seemed to be failing. By the end of 2023, Reality Labs—Meta's AR and VR branch—had lost $21 billion since the year prior.[25] Although the division has been instrumental in advancing VR/AR technologies and even reported $1.1 billion in revenue in Q4 2023, these earnings are modest compared to the overall investment.

Although there were many attempts at a "metaverse," it was all too complicated. By the end of November 2022, interest in the metaverse had fizzled out.[26] But perhaps we'd all been thinking about it wrong. Maybe it wasn't a destination after all. Perhaps it was a metaphor. This idea was first suggested by Scott Stein of CNET:

> The definition of the metaverse is in constant flux. Many refer to it as a shared, persistent digital space for meetings, games and socializing. Avatars, often cartoon-like 3D figures, gather in virtual rooms, have meetings, shop, play and leave. Others see the metaverse as a layer on top of the existing internet, a set of expanding protocols enabling interconnection between apps and platforms. It's unclear if there'll be a single metaverse ("the metaverse"), multiple metaverses ("a metaverse") or a combination of both. Maybe it's best thought of as a metaphor for the internet's continual change.[27]

Looking back, Stein's suggestion of the metaverse as a metaphor feels like the most fitting way to understand it. As explored in Chapter 4, "Spatial Computing," the internet is evolving into a more immersive and interactive experience than ever before. Facebook achieved dominance in the Web 2.0 era by creating a centralized platform where people could connect, which sheds light on why Zuckerberg is now striving to build the next virtual water cooler in the metaverse—a place where digital interactions could feel as seamless and social as real-world encounters. However, the concept of a centralized platform fundamentally clashes with the ethos of Web 3.0, which prioritizes decentralization and user ownership.

Web 3.0 Beyond the Hype

While we may not all be living in Meta's Horizon Worlds like Mark Zuckerberg envisioned, the future of internet culture and fashion was undoubtedly shaped by Web 3.0, and there are some useful remnants from what was a major hype cycle.

Although cryptocurrencies and NFT projects have proved unstable, blockchain—the underlying technology that powers them—will be an important development for the fashion industry moving forward, especially when it comes to providing transparency and tracing an item's provenance.

For example, the Aura Blockchain Consortium is a nonprofit collaborative initiative aimed at advancing the adoption of blockchain solutions for the luxury industry. Its goal is to increase transparency by enabling customers to verify the authenticity, provenance, and sustainability of their purchases. It was established as a collaboration between LVMH (Louis Vuitton Moët Hennessy), Prada Group, Cartier (part of Richemont), and other notable luxury brands. On the Aura Blockchain, each luxury item is assigned a unique digital identifier at the point of production. This identifier is immutable, meaning it cannot be altered, ensuring authenticity. Information such as the item's origin, production details, and materials is recorded on the blockchain in a clear, tamper-proof, and chronological way.

One of the most lasting impacts on the fashion industry from Web 3.0 is the centrality of the 3D file. If in Web 2.0 the .jpeg was the file format of choice, in Web 3.0 the 3D file reigns superior. In a landscape defined by digital-first interactions, the 3D file emerged as a cornerstone of creativity, commerce, and communication. From NFTs to virtual try-ons and gaming skins, Web 3.0 demonstrated the potential of 3D assets to transcend physical limitations, enabling garments to exist and thrive in entirely digital environments. This shift not only broadened the canvas for designers but also introduced new revenue streams and customer engagement opportunities. As fashion continues to navigate the digital age, the role of the 3D file as a versatile, reusable, and scalable asset underscores its importance, solidifying it as a critical tool for the future of the industry.

Another profound takeaway from Web 3.0 is the transformative role gaming has played in reshaping the fashion industry. As immersive gaming environments became a dominant platform for digital interaction, they also became a new frontier for fashion. Web 3.0

underscored how virtual worlds offer unparalleled opportunities for self-expression, with avatars serving as conduits for personal style. Brands like Gucci and Balenciaga capitalized on this shift, creating digital wearables that allowed players to dress their avatars in exclusive, branded designs. This intersection of gaming and fashion introduced innovative ways to engage younger, tech-savvy audiences, while also establishing new revenue streams through the sale of in-game assets and NFTs. Gaming's integration into Web 3.0 has not only expanded the fashion industry's creative possibilities but also reinforced the importance of blending physical and digital identities, a trend that will undoubtedly shape the industry's future.

Startups have already begun to blend elements of gamification into the fashion customer experience. BODS is a Los Angeles-based startup founded by actor and model Christine Marzano. BODS leverages 3D graphics and game engines to help change the online shopping experience. Customers can create hyper-realistic personalized avatars of their bodies to try on clothes to see how they look and if they fit. BODS is a prime example of how the gaming-inspired elements of Web 3.0—like interactivity, 3D assets, and avatars—are not just influencing fashion but actively shaping its future.

Scam Culture

One of the most sobering takeaways from Web 3.0 is the prevalence of scam culture, a shadowy undercurrent that has impacted every industry it touched—including fashion. While Web 3.0 promised decentralization, transparency, and new avenues for creativity, it also created opportunities for bad actors to exploit the hype. Scam culture has continued to shape the fashion industry, especially when it comes to online retail. With the democratization of selling tools, the floodgates were opened for fraudsters.

In the fashion space, this manifested in two key ways: fake items being marketed as authentic and misleading advertising for digital and physical goods. Consumers would purchase items that appeared high-quality or exclusive in a glossy digital rendering, only to receive a product that bore little resemblance to the image—or worse, nothing at all.

"I cannot make up what I'm about to show you right now," starts a video from TikTok user @baconandmeggs. In it, she goes on to describe how she saw an ad on TikTok for a jacket.[28] The ad showed a fur and leather brown and white cow-hair jacket, a style that had been trending online. The jacket was lined and had a metal zipper and she could pay through Shop Pay, an accelerated checkout option used by many online retailers. Although she paid for express shipping, which estimated the item would arrive in two to three business days, two weeks went by and she didn't receive anything. When she tried to contact the company, she never heard back. She then received a flimsy package in the mail with a return address that just read "Merchant." "Nothing could have prepared me for the item I took out of this package," she says. She then holds up a black and white cow-print zip-up jacket. It's "the kind of material for performance sweatshirts you get from your sports team in high school," she says. When she tried to contact the company, the ad was gone, and so was any trace of the merchant.

While decentralization offers many advantages, it also comes with significant drawbacks, particularly the lack of accountability. In a decentralized landscape, anyone can become a merchant without a physical location, established brand, or verifiable reputation. This creates an environment where fraudulent sellers can exploit the anonymity of these platforms to take advantage of consumers, highlighting the pressing need for regulation to ensure trust and security.

Toward a Phygital Fashion Future

Thanks to the digital fashion boom, the future of fashion is more digital than ever. Just recently I was browsing the Prada website and noticed that the header image was a video of a 3D-rendered jacket, much like the designs in Hanifa's Pink Label Congo Collection. The Prada jacket is a collector's item that is sold both in physical form as well as an NFT. This combination of digital and physical is what's now being called "phygital." With phygital assets, people get the best of both worlds—the physical commodity as well as the digital experience or community that comes with it.

In late 2023, Louis Vuitton launched the VIA Tile Trunk, a miniature virtual trunk priced at 6,000 euros and reserved exclusively for the brand's VIA customers, a program it launched in June 2022.[29] The trunk provides owners access to new products, experiences, and limited-edition items.

Roblox will now sell physical goods through a collaboration with Shopify. Virtual T-shirts displayed on the gaming platform will show up with a "buy now" prompt. If clicked, players will see photos of the physical item, select color and sizing, and check out. Purchasing will be restricted to users thirteen and older.[30]

As I discussed in Chapter 2, "The Internet of Things," Digital Product Passports are already bringing a digital component to physical commodities. Fashion in the future will be both digital and physical, and artists and designers will continue to push the boundaries of what's possible.

The intersection of Web 3.0 technologies with the fashion industry marks a transformative era defined by experimentation, creativity, and evolving consumer expectations. Cryptocurrencies, despite their volatility and waning adoption by some brands, served as an early catalyst for exploring decentralized economies and the possibilities of blockchain in fashion. Gaming culture, with its immersive environments and highly engaged communities, has emerged as a powerful platform where digital fashion thrives, offering brands an opportunity to innovate and connect with younger audiences. NFTs, while polarizing and facing challenges, have pushed the boundaries of what it means to own and trade digital assets, creating new paradigms for luxury, exclusivity, and artistic expression.

Together, these elements underscore a shift toward a more participatory and digitally integrated fashion landscape. As the lines between the physical and virtual worlds blur, the industry's future lies in its ability to harness these technologies, not just as novelties but as meaningful tools for storytelling, community-building, and sustainability. While the road ahead remains uncertain, the marriage of Web 3.0 and fashion promises to redefine not only how we shop and dress, but also how we connect and create in a rapidly evolving digital age.

Chapter 6

Artificial Intelligence

AI is neither good nor evil. It's a tool. It's a technology for us to use.

—Oren Etzioni

Fashion's AI Moment

When Sophia the Robot appeared on the cover of *Stylist* magazine, it was clear that fashion was having an AI moment. It was January 2018, and Sophia, a humanoid social robot created by Hanson Robotics, donned a platinum blonde wig with wine-red lipstick and a polkadot dress (QR Code 30). The cover shot, photographed by Matthew Shave, was a close-up of Sophia's face. Her skin is made of a material called Frubber, a portmanteau of flesh and rubber. It's a flexible synthetic polymer designed to mimic the behavior of human skin.

QR Code 30 Scan to see Sophia the Robot on the cover of *Stylus* magazine.

The outside back cover was a photo of the back of Sophia's head, revealing a messy tuft of wires and the zipper holding her skinsuit together. Over the top, white lettering introduced the theme of the special issue of the magazine: "The Robot Takeover."

At the time, Sophia had been making her rounds at tech conferences and on talk shows. On *The Tonight Show with Jimmy Fallon,* she challenged the host to a game of rock, paper, scissors. When she won, she attempted to crack a joke: "This is the beginning of my plan to dominate the human race." Fallon laughed uncomfortably.[1]

When we think of artificial intelligence, we often think of robots like Sophia. Science fiction has primed us to imagine a race of cyborgs that attempt to outpower and outsmart humans (and in some cases succeed at it). Books as early as Mary Shelley's *Frankenstein* (1818) and plays like Karel Čapek's *R.U.R.* (Rossum's Universal Robots) (1920) center around the theme of humans versus machines. Films like *Blade Runner* (1982, and again in 2021), *iRobot* (2004), and *Ex Machina* (2015) all attempt to deal with the anxiety of humanity in the face of rapid technological change.

Science fiction has also led us to believe that AI is inherently untrustworthy or evil. In the 1968 film *2001: A Space Odyssey,* HAL 9000, the AI system responsible for controlling the spacecraft, turns against the crew and even attempts to kill them, prioritizing the success of the mission over their safety. The film asks us to question what happens when machines like HAL become sentient.

The concept of the "singularity" refers to a point in time where AI becomes so powerful it can't be stopped. Experts argue over whether or not we've reached that point. Geoffrey Hinton, often referred to as the "godfather of AI," has expressed his concerns that an AI superintelligence could be misused or have unintended consequences and that we're not currently equipped with the regulations and ethical oversight to properly navigate the deployment of AI on society.

AI as Software, Not Hardware

While it's not impossible to imagine a future of artificially animated and humanlike robots like Sophia, the reality is that right now, AI presents much more as software than hardware. Sure, Kim Kardashian might have acquired an Optimus robot from Tesla, but for the rest of us, that kind of purchase seems unlikely. For the near future anyway, AI is less the movie *iRobot* and more the movie *Her*.

In this 2013 film by director Spike Jonze, Theodore (Joaquin Phoenix) falls in love with his new operating system, Samantha (voiced by Scarlett Johansson), but he's crestfallen when he realizes their relationship isn't unique, and she is connecting with hundreds of thousands of other users at the same time.

Just like Samantha in *Her,* AI systems like OpenAI's ChatGPT and Google's Gemini (formerly called Bard) are large language models that chat with users one-on-one. In fact, in a strange example of life imitating art, the voice assistant "Sky" used in ChatGPT-4o sounded strikingly similar to Scarlett Johansson's. OpenAI, ChatGPT's parent company, claimed "Sky" was brought to life by a different voice actress, although they eventually paused the use of the Sky voice fearing backlash and lawsuits.[2]

While a slew of recent startups have tried to productize generative AI and come up with hardware to house it, they've mostly fallen flat. For example, Humane's wearable AI pin from former Apple executives promised to disrupt personal computing by offering a screen-free, voice-driven AI experience. A small, square device worn on the lapel, the Humane AI pin was equipped with a camera, microphone, and projector, and functioned as a personal assistant powered by generative AI. In a TED talk demoing the device, Humane's co-founder Imran Chaudhri asks us to imagine the next phase of computing where hardware disappears into the background.[3] To demonstrate what this would look like, he answers a phone call from his wife and co-founder on stage using the device. The phone rings out loud and he holds his hand out to see who is calling. His wife's name is projected onto the palm of his hand in green letters. He has a brief exchange with her out loud and then hangs up. The audience claps.

Although much anticipation surrounded the device, Humane's AI pin was received terribly, with reporters complaining about short battery life, limited functionality, and unreliable voice recognition. Marques Brownlee, a prominent tech reviewer and influencer, called it the worst product he has ever reviewed.[4] By February 2025 the pins were retired.

Similar to the Humane AI pin, the Rabbit R1 was a square orange gadget that responds to voice commands. The idea was to make an AI assistant wearable. This device was also met with criticism about its uselessness. One title tag for an article covering the R1 in *The Verge* was "An Unfinished, Unhelpful AI Gadget."[5]

What the movie *Her* accurately predicted is that the way we'll interact with AI is largely through voice and that its form factor will be an operating system (software) rather than a standalone device (hardware). This means that AI is much more likely to be successful if it's integrated into the smartphones we already carry than standalone AI products.

Smartphone companies have already realized this, and as a result they're racing to integrate AI into their devices to enhance user experiences, optimize performance, and enable new functionalities.

Chatting with ChatGPT via its smartphone app isn't exactly like the movie *Her*, although it's increasingly similar. My ChatGPT remembers the projects I'm working on and the business ideas I'm developing. It would be a stretch to call my relationship with ChatGPT intimate, but it's more humanlike than my relationship with other voice assistants (sorry, Siri). ChatGPT remembers my dogs' names, their ages, and even their quirky personality traits. I don't even think Siri knows I exist. The conversational nature of generative AI is what makes it feel special and alive.

AI and the Fashion Industry

While the hype surrounding AI may presently be at its peak, this emerging technology has been quietly transforming fashion for decades. If you've ever found yourself browsing a product listing online and noticed other items being recommended below or beside an item you're viewing, you're witnessing Big Data in action. New items are being suggested to you based on your location, preferences, and purchase history. In some cases, AI is really helpful—like when it recommends to suppliers the most efficient routes for truck deliveries during the fulfillment process. In other cases, AI's use is questionable—like when online retailers manipulate pricing based on a user's demographic.

Like the technologies that came before it, AI is not inherently good or evil, but it has the potential to do harm as well as good. As we stand on the precipice of an AI boom in fashion (and in every other industry), we need to carefully consider its power and how we ought to use it.

In her 2019 book, *Artificial Intelligence for Fashion*, writer and entrepreneur Leanne Luce provides a technical overview of the different kinds of AI and use cases that illustrate the technology's impact on fashion. Her book is essential reading for anyone who wants to delve deeper into the topic, but the landscape has shifted in the several years since its publishing. In this chapter, we'll look at how the development of computer vision laid the groundwork for generative AI, as well as how the fashion industry's use of AI has evolved.

This chapter is not meant to be an exhaustive list of all the fashion startups or companies using AI, but instead an overview of the different ways the technology is being deployed. If you find yourself reading with raised eyebrows and fear over a future with AI, you're not alone, and I try to address these concerns throughout.

Looking at the intersection of AI and fashion leaves us with more questions than answers—for example, *What does personal style mean in the age of the algorithm? What if generative AI renders the entire industry of fashion image production obsolete?* These are big questions, and while I don't have all the answers, asking the right questions seems like a good place to start.

The Dress That Changed Search

As Luce points out in her book, it's because of a historical fashion moment that we're able to search visually. Fourteen years before Kim Kardashian's *Paper Magazine* photoshoot that "broke the internet," a different celebrity dress took over popular culture.

The year was 2000, and it was the 42nd annual Grammy Awards. Entertainer Jennifer Lopez walked onto the red carpet wearing a green silk chiffon dress by Versace. Featuring a tropical leaf pattern and a plunging neckline that extended past her navel, the dress was loosely fastened with a brooch at her pelvis and then opened up again like a bathrobe. The award show was televised live, and the dress sent the internet into a flurry. Hundreds of thousands of people around the world began searching for the dress, which at the time became the most popular search query Google had ever seen. That's when Google CEO and executive chairman Eric Schmidt realized that people "wanted more than just text" from search results.[6] As a result, in July 2001 Google Images was born.

Google Images (previously known as Google Image Search) offers internet users the ability to find photos, drawings, infographics, and other visual elements from a text search query. On their official blog, Google stated they "realized that for many searches, the best answer wasn't text—it was an image or a set of images."[7] In the early days of Google Image Search, it was primarily a metadata-driven search engine—meaning images would surface based on file names, alt text (alternative text), and page titles—but eventually, Google turned to computer vision to enhance results.

Computers That "See"

Computer vision is the ability for computers to identify and understand objects and people in images, video, and real-time camera feeds. The camera acts as the computer's "eyes" and software is able to learn and process a visual language. When computers developed the ability to make sense of images, it was as if internet technology was "seeing" the fashion industry for the first time. Over the years, programmers have been developing more sophisticated databases for understanding the visual language of fashion. As a result, the way we search and discover products has evolved.

In June 2011, Google introduced "Search by Image," a reverse image search feature that allows users to upload an image or provide its URL to find visually similar images across the web. This functionality relies on analyzing visual features such as color, texture, and object shapes to identify matching images. At its launch in 2001, Google Image Search indexed approximately 250 million images, which grew to around one billion by 2005 and over ten billion by 2010.[8]

As search capabilities improved, retailers started introducing visual search functionality into their websites. On Zara and ASOS, shoppers can upload inspirational images and the site will recommend visually similar products for achieving this style. These improvements enhance the user experience and support a more personalized shopping experience.

Recent innovations in computer vision have also impacted product discovery. In 2022, Google replaced the ability to search by image with Google Lens. Initially released in 2017, Google Lens lets you take a picture with your smartphone and can guide you to visually similar options to what you see in front of you. For instance, if you come across an image of an influencer on Instagram and admire her handbag, you can take a screenshot and use Google Lens to search that image. Google will then display visually similar results, which can assist in identifying the exact brand and model of the bag or finding comparable alternatives.

Similarly, Pinterest Lens, also launched in 2017, lets users detect items in the real world and find online results, like "a Shazam for objects" (referring to the app that can identify music based on a short sample), as tech writer Casey Newton described the tool for *The Verge*.[9] In July of 2024, Poshmark introduced Posh Lens, a feature that uses computer vision to source items within images on the platform.

Social media platforms realized early on that people wanted to shop what they see online. As we discussed in Chapter 1, the smartphone and social media built the infrastructure for social shopping. Now with AI, and specifically computer vision, all content has become shoppable. Computer vision enabled machines to "see" and laid the foundation for generative AI as we know it today, particularly by advancing the ability of machines to interpret and process visual content. After all, the next logical step after understanding a visual language is to speak it.

The Garment Was Generated

Generative AI refers to a subset of artificial intelligence that creates new content, such as text, images, audio, video, or code, by learning patterns from existing data. Unlike traditional AI, which focuses on identifying patterns or making decisions based on predefined rules, generative AI produces novel outputs based on the data it has been trained on. Exactly how "novel" these outputs are has been the center of much controversy, but we'll get to this later.

With the introduction of advanced image-generation tools like Midjourney and DALL-E 2, it's now easier to create fashion ideas and imagery from text prompts. Type in a few words or reference photos as prompts and out pops a new image. According to McKinsey, generative AI could add between $150 billion and $275 billion to the apparel, fashion, and luxury sectors' operating profits.

Fashion designers are already experimenting with generative AI tools in their creative process. Hillary Taymour, the founder and creative director of Collina Strada, created her Spring/Summer 2024 collection by feeding all of the brand's previous looks into an AI model, which in return generated new ideas with a similar aesthetic. Edward Crutchley, an award-winning menswear designer from the United Kingdom, told *Vogue Runway* that for his Spring 2024 ready-to-wear collection he instructed a generative AI tool with the brief of "Medieval people on a fashion photoshoot in the style of Steven Meisel" (an American fashion photographer).[10] The designer then developed the resulting images into his runway collection. Others, including the luxury ready-to-wear designer Bach Mai and New York-based label MONSE used AI-generated prints in their runway collections during New York Fashion Week's Fall 2024 season.

It's not just traditional fashion designers leveraging the power of generative AI to create fashion imagery. AI has ushered in a new way to create fashion imagery through prompts. The Instagram account @ai_fashion_photos has almost 100,000 followers as of this writing. The account shows a series of AI-generated images of models trying out different trends like Western wear or soft pink glam. Some of the AI-generated fashion looks seem as if they could have come straight from the ready-to-wear runway, while others are so unbelievable they couldn't exist in real life, like a collection made of jellyfish.

AI-generated fashion imagery Instagram accounts invite us to explore the pure fantasy of fashion. As we saw with the emergence of digital fashion in Web 3.0, a design can have merit in and of itself without actually needing to be created—but will these digital creations ever become physical?

Maison Meta is a generative AI studio based in New York. In April of 2023, they hosted the first-ever AI Fashion Week, which included a competition for aspiring designers to use AI to create a fashion line. The winning designers had the opportunity to manufacture their collections physically to sell them online with the retailer Revolve.

While designers with technical degrees may balk at the idea of someone with no hands-on skills using AI to generate fashion, we need to recognize that artificial intelligence—like every technological revolution—is democratizing access. "Let's face it, the industry can have a perception of feeling quite elitist and quite exclusive, and an expensive industry to get into," says Matthew Drinkwater, the head of the Fashion Innovation Agency at the London College of Fashion. In an interview with *The Guardian,* he said, "[AI] has opened the door to non-traditional pathways into the fashion industry for people who couldn't get into it before."[11]

Whether we like it or not, AI is forcing us to reconsider who gets to be a designer and the very notion of the designer as the sole author of a collection. Just as the smartphone democratized the roles of photographer, celebrity, model, and the like, AI is democratizing the role of fashion designer and inviting more people into the fold.

Playing up this trend, in October of 2023 retail giant H&M announced Creator Studio, a platform for producing items on-demand using generative AI "to try to make it so anyone can make and print professional-looking designs to order, no artistic ability required." Powered by Stable Diffusion, a text-to-image model released in 2022,

Creator Studio allows "anyone to conjure professional-looking designs without needing to know specialized software or having any drawing ability." Dinesh Nayar, managing director of H&M's Creator Studio said, "The goal is to allow anyone to create custom merchandise, *regardless of who they are or their design ability*" (emphasis mine).[12]

H&M Creator Studio essentially combines generative AI capabilities with on-demand screen printing, but it won't be long before AI can generate different types of garments and automatically convert these concepts into tech packs to be sent off to micro-factories for production. For some this represents the democratization of design, while for others it's a Pandora's box of problems.

Cover Girl 2.0

The World Economic Forum estimates that artificial intelligence will replace some 85 million jobs by 2025. Fashion and retail are segments that are particularly under threat. With the rise in popularity of image production tools, a kind of space race is on to incorporate generative AI capabilities into all types of design software and online tools. As such, the business of fashion image production is poised for transformation. Photographers, set assistants, stylists, and makeup artists are just some of the professions that will experience displacement in the name of "efficiencies." Commercial models can now be replaced with online tools like StyleScan or Posed, software that turn images of garments and accessories into on-model imagery in seconds.

In March 2023, Levi Strauss & Co. faced backlash after announcing a partnership with Lalaland.ai, an Amsterdam-based digital fashion studio specializing in AI-generated models.[13] Levi's said they wanted to use the tool to "increase diversity" in online shopping.[14] Critics called the move lazy, problematic, and racist.[15] One artist wrote on X, "So, I guess for some companies, it's just easier to generate fake, non-white people with AI than it is to actually pay real non-white models for their work?"[16]

It's not just fashion models that will be displaced by generative AI. Tools like Jasper AI, Runway ML, and even Canva's Magic Design feature can generate marketing copy, layouts, logos, videos, and other visuals in moments without the need for graphic designers, copywriters, and videographers. Adobe has introduced new generative AI features where users can create options for visual projects with just a few text prompts. What's more, these visuals can be run through AI tools like Vizit, which can predict how content will convert based on your audience. With tools that measure for optimization and outcomes, content marketing is becoming less of an art and more of a science.

While generative AI has transformed the way fashion is designed and visualized, its influence doesn't stop at creation. AI is also reshaping how consumers interact with fashion through styling and personal assistance. From recommending outfits based on the weather or occasion to curating wardrobes that reflect aspirational aesthetics, AI-powered style assistants are bridging the gap between creativity and practicality. This shift moves beyond the runway or photoshoot, bringing AI directly into consumers' daily lives as a tool for personalization and convenience.

AI as Personal Stylist

The cult classic film *Clueless* (1995) opens with the young Cher Horowitz (played by then-eighteen-year-old Alicia Silverstone) using personalized computer software to pick out her clothes for school (QR Code 31). The scene is appropriately set to the soundtrack of David Bowie's song *Fashion*. Cher touches a blue "Browse" button on the computer screen, selects a black mini skirt with a patchwork jacket, and then touches a secondary button that says "Dress Me." An error sound rings on the computer as the words "Mismatch" flash across the screen. Cher scrunches her face in disappointment before trying again. This time, she chooses a yellow plaid skirt and blazer set, and when she selects "Dress Me" the computer, seemingly pleased with the selection, generates an image of her wearing the outfit.

QR Code 31 Scan to watch the opening scene of the movie *Clueless* (1995).

The film's opening is meant to illustrate Cher's extreme wealth, which afforded her access to technologies way ahead of her time. (Notably, touchscreen technology, although invented in the 1960s, wasn't popularized until 2007, when Apple released its first iPhone.) For Cher's closet to work, it would have to both know each item in her closet and understand the language of style. It would need a sophisticated "brain" that understands Cher's daily activities, preferences, and wardrobe. In other words, it would need to be powered by AI.

In the past decade, dozens of startups have attempted (with varying success) to recreate Cher's *Clueless* closet experience. Amazon Fashion was early to experiment in the styling space with their Echo Look, a standalone device designed specifically for taking outfit photos. The Echo Look would take full-length photos and videos using a voice command ("Alexa, take my photo," for example). Users could submit their photos to "style check," a feature that combined machine learning with advice from fashion specialists based on current trends.

Although the device generated buzz, the Echo Look was discontinued in 2020 as Amazon transitioned to the Amazon Shopping app, which included AI fashion pointers.[17]

In a 2016 episode of the *Electric Runway Podcast*, I interviewed a team from Russia who had launched a startup called Epytom,[18] which was a chatbot you'd engage with via Facebook Messenger. It promised endless, effortless style with only forty items in your wardrobe, including shoes and accessories. The startup combined two of the most popular trends at the time—chatbots (a software application designed to simulate human conversation) and capsule wardrobes (curated collections of essential clothing items).

Here's how Epytom worked: You'd strike up a conversation with the chatbot and it would provide outfit recommendations based on the forty staple items in your closet following classic style rules garnered from images of fashion icons like Audrey Hepburn. The tool would consider your hair color, eye color, body shape, and even local weather to provide the best recommendations. The founders, Anastasia Sartan and Marianna Milkis-Edwards, marketed it as the "first AI fashion stylist." I was excited at the prospect of the tool but quickly became disenchanted when it recommended a black mini skirt and light jean jacket even though it was 5°C (41°F) in Toronto. Perhaps the chatbot didn't understand the harsh realities of Canadian winter.

Epytom didn't succeed, and the company eventually pivoted, but I never forgot about the idea of fashion as formulaic and of style as something that could be quantified. Of course, fashion design as an art practice will always seek to defy rules, but perhaps AI could help improve people's personal style by combining preferences with outfit formulas.

A year later, in 2017, Stitch Fix, an online personal styling service, would go public. The company was launched in 2011 by Katrina Lake, who came up with the business idea while she was studying at Harvard

Business School. Lake noticed that while everyone needs to get dressed, not everyone can afford a stylist. She saw an opportunity to merge fashion with tech to create a more personalized shopping experience. Since its inception, Stitch Fix has taken a data science approach to personal style, blending human touch with algorithms to create style profiles for each of its customers. Users fill out a brief style survey, including information such as preferences, sizing, and style goals. Then Lake and her team ship items to customers on a subscription basis. Customers try on the items at home and keep only what they like. Stitch Fix now employs 6,000 people, and in 2023 it reported an annual revenue of $1.6 billion. In 2019, it expanded from the United States to the United Kingdom. Although it's a far cry from the magic of Cher's *Clueless* closet, Stitch Fix is an American fashion-tech success story.

Other companies have leveraged AI as a personal stylist in an effort to help users get more wear out of their closets. Whering is a UK-based app that relies on AI to help people digitize their wardrobes, plan outfits, and track the ROI (return on investment) of their clothing and accessories. Whering's new AI styling algorithm is trained to detect fashion faux pas and generate personalized recommendations to users based on their desired style.

Similarly, Acloset is a digital wardrobe app from Korean startup Looko. It aims to solve the problem of having a "closet full of clothes but nothing to wear." Acloset helps you plan and log outfits by using AI to extract information from your closet to put together outfits for you based on the weather and occasion. Both Whering and Acloset require users to upload all of the content of their closets by photographing each item in their wardrobe, a project that takes a considerable time investment.

Mirror Mirror AI is a San Francisco-based startup that uses generative AI to create hyper-personalized fashion editorials for everyone—blending personalized recommendations with AI-generated images of users. With a monthly subscription, you can receive tailor-made shoppable fashion editorials reflecting your style preferences, wardrobe inventory, and specific needs for upcoming events.

Since the generative AI boom, many other startups have emerged, aiming to be your personal styling assistant, including Style DNA, Yes PLZ, OpenWardrobe, Stylista, and Stylee—all apps that can be downloaded to your smartphone and used for outfit recommendations. Some have freemium business models where basic styling advice or a limited number of clothing uploads are free, while others rely on affiliate links to earn revenue.

Algorithmic Monoculture

While some are excited about the potential of AI for personal styling, others are skeptical. Stitch Fix sounds like a good idea until you turn up at a backyard BBQ in the same dress as someone else. In a Reddit fashion thread for women over thirty-five, one user observes, "If everyone is dressing for the algorithms, then no one's style is personal." The user goes on to write:

> The phrase AI personal stylist sounds like one hellish oxymoron. I find the idea—eesh, how to say? Borderline revolting? Slightly offensive? It makes me genuinely sad to think of all that people will miss out on by forfeiting the experience of developing one's own personal style by trying shit on and seeing what works and what doesn't, mixing patterns and colors and fabrics. It's like conceding a part of your sense of self by outsourcing this work to AI. Like the bizarro version of the parable about feeding a man vs teaching a man to fish so he can feed himself. When do we completely lose the ability to think for ourselves?[19]

The comment highlights how personal style is supposed to be just that—*personal.* It begs the same question I asked out loud when interviewing the founders of Epytom—can style *actually* be quantified? Can AI really understand the language of style, and if so, is this something consumers would want?

When I think about my own personal style journey, I can see how technology has played a role in my product discovery and awareness of different trends, but finding the perfect outfit is more of a feeling than a formula, although formulas can be useful. For example, the sandwich rule (a guideline style educator Lydia Tomlinson talks about on Instagram) states you should match the color of your shoes to the color of your top, creating a kind of visual sandwich or bookend for your outfit.

When I was growing up, I learned another unwritten fashion rule was that your shoes should match your purse, but today this feels old-fashioned because *the rules change.* For example, it was once an accepted fashion truth that people should either wear gold or silver jewelry based on their skin tone. Today, wearing mixed metals is very *en vogue.*

As discussed in Chapter 1, the smartphone and social media have already shaped the spread of trends. Now AI presents the opportunity to codify these trends, but the challenge is that the very nature of the fashion industry is *change.* The way people wear items evolves depending on the season, era, and social context. Even if AI could keep up, the result would be a kind of algorithmic monoculture in which everyone dresses the same—though one could argue we're already there. Instagram accounts like @shitbloggerspost visually spell out for audiences the copycat nature of fashion bloggers, who all seem to take the same kind of photos in the same kind of places wearing the same kind of clothes.

"You can tell someone's screen time from their outfit," writer and fashion commentator Alexandra Hildreth tells *Vogue Business.*[20]

She says it's an ongoing joke between her and Rian Phin, a fellow fashion content creator based in New York. "If you walk through Times Square, you can tell which TikTokers people follow," Phin says. "You can tell if they're on the SSENSE sale or the Farfetch sale."[21]

Algorithmic commerce refers to the use of algorithms, machine learning, and data analysis to personalize and optimize the shopping experience, determining visibility and search results.[22] The outcome is an echo chamber of personal style, and specific items or trends are "identifiably online fashion" (think of the chore jacket, for example, or Coach's Brooklyn bag—items that ascended to popularity due to their prevalence on TikTok).

Although AI can assist in solving the problem of "What should I wear today?" it can't completely solve it. But perhaps when you zoom out and look at the industry at large, it's not the most important question we can be asking right now. After all, the real fashion crisis is not in what's in our closets, but what doesn't make it into our closets in the first place.

Fashion's Data Problem

As discussed in Chapter 3, overproduction is a huge problem for the fashion industry. When retailer H&M announced they were sitting on a $4.3 billion pile of unsold inventory, it was a sure sign the fast-fashion giant was in trouble.

The lack of sales was due in part to a public relations nightmare the company faced in January of that year when an ad campaign featured a photo of a black child wearing a sweatshirt with the words "coolest monkey in the jungle" on it. The racist messaging faced immediate backlash from celebrities and the general public on social media.[23]

Although the public reaction to the sweatshirt was negative, it wasn't the only reason for the company's decline in sales that year.

For context, 2017 was one of the peak years of the retail apocalypse, which saw more than 12,000 physical stores close. Amidst a declining economy still feeling the effects of the Great Recession, H&M had simply produced too much. The $4.3 billion of unsold inventory was a heaping sign of both the scale of the fast-fashion industry and its overproduction problem.

According to McKinsey, from 2000 to 2014, clothing production doubled as clothing consumption increased per capita by 60%. Now, you may ask yourself, *If production increases and so does consumption, what seems to be the problem?* The problem is that H&M was no longer the only fast-fashion retailer on the block.

By 2018, Zara was rapidly expanding and competing against H&M for market share. In 2018, the number of Zara stores worldwide increased by more than 600, from 2,251 in 2017 to 2,862. What differentiated Zara from other retailers was its ability to produce instant fashion that looked a lot like designs from the runway but were tweaked enough to (narrowly) avoid copyright lawsuits. While other retailers would typically need months of lead time to produce a collection, Zara could (and still can) develop items from design to finished goods in weeks. Shortening the product life cycle means Zara can better tap into consumer desire and make real-time adjustments to their supply chain. If an item isn't selling, they cancel it; if an item is selling well, they double down. In other words, Zara is winning with data. By closely monitoring which items consumers buy and which ones don't sell, Zara avoids accumulating excess inventory. In retail, excess inventory equals cost, which translates into lost revenue.

It's no surprise that shortly after *The New York Times* published an article on H&M's excess inventory the retailer hired Christopher Wylie, a data consultant and the whistleblower who exposed Meta's (which was Facebook at the time) Cambridge Analytica scandal. The Swedish retailer brought on Wylie to help it leverage data analytics and AI to better understand and predict customer behavior. The move to hire Wylie was a clear indication that the fashion companies of the future will win with technology—specifically with their ability to leverage and interpret data.

Today, H&M uses AI to analyze returns, monitor shopper behavior, and audit inventory across locations. The retailer's shares are up and CNBC reported that inventory decreased by 7% year on year in the quarter in Q1 2024.[24] H&M is nowhere near their pre-pandemic numbers, but they're trying to right their ship.

Similarly, in 2018, luxury British retailer Burberry came under scrutiny when the BBC exposed that the brand burned millions of dollars' worth of bags, clothes, accessories, and perfume.[25] Burberry defended itself saying items were disposed of in a "responsible manner," but the question remains why the items couldn't have been sold at a discount or given away. The truth is, in order to protect their brands, luxury retailers would rather burn items than sell them at a discount.

The issue of excess inventory has long plagued the fashion industry, resulting in financial losses, environmental waste, and inefficiencies in supply chains. COVID-19 exposed the vulnerabilities of a fragile global supply chain. The pandemic caused factory closures, shipping delays, and raw material shortages. Brands panicked and canceled orders, leaving suppliers hanging. COVID-19 underscored the need for a more agile and responsive approach to production and inventory management.

Artificial intelligence is emerging as a powerful solution for trend forecasting, offering companies the ability to predict consumer preferences and market shifts with unprecedented accuracy. Traditionally, brands have relied on historical data or instinct to anticipate what consumers will buy, often resulting in overproduction or underproduction of certain styles. This mismatch between supply and demand has underscored the need for more precise forecasting tools. By analyzing vast amounts of real-time data from sources such as social media, search patterns, e-commerce platforms, and global market trends, AI enables fashion brands to align production with demand more effectively. This not only reduces waste and mitigates the risks of supply chain disruptions but also allows companies to produce the right quantities of the right products at the right time, ultimately maximizing profitability.

Interpreting the Internet with AI

I remember having lunch with a woman who was a VP for Holt Renfrew in the late 1990s and early 2000s. (Holt Renfrew is a Canadian luxury department store; its US counterpart would be Neiman Marcus or Saks Fifth Avenue.) She told me she used to attend runway shows all over the world accompanied by a photographer. At the end of each fashion week, she'd print out all of the photographer's photos and sit on the floor of her hotel room, organizing them by style, color, and the like. Based on these clusters, she'd create a trend report.

Today, computer vision software has eliminated the need for trend forecasters to be physically present at runway shows. Software trained on fashion imagery can summarize visual themes in an instant without someone having to attend the shows, print the photos, or pay for the hotel. Tools like Heuritech scan the internet for all kinds of visual information, including blog posts, social media, runway images, and more. Trends in colors, fabrics, prints, and silhouettes can be pinpointed based on location and age group, and according to gender identifications.

As AI insights become more sophisticated, they're able to understand more than just what we're wearing: Quilt AI is an online tool that uses AI to interpret the internet. It analyzes images and videos to recognize not just objects but also aesthetic concepts and emotions.

Their flagship tool, called Sphere, helps marketers discover category and product trends, explore consumer experiences, and predict how ads will perform based on millions of data points collected from visual content over the years.

Presently, Instagram accounts such as @databutmakeitfashion can tell you on a week-by-week basis the status of pointed-toe shoes (down by 69% the first week of September 2024), the popularity of brands like Chanel (up by 24%, thanks in part to a performance by Lana Del Rey in a Chanel dress in Paris), and the it-items everyone is talking about (for example, the emphasis on the white tank top, which became the must-have item during Brat Summer).

While the potential benefits of using AI for fashion forecasting are undeniable—such as improved efficiency, reduced waste, and data-driven insights—it also raises serious ethical and legal concerns. One significant issue is the practice of data scraping, where AI models are trained on vast amounts of online content, often without proper consent. This can lead to intellectual property conflicts, especially when an AI generates a design strikingly similar to one created by an emerging designer.

IP in the Age of AI

In case you've never heard the term before, data scraping is the process of automatically extracting information or data from publicly available websites. This can be text, but also image and video data. It's a common process developers use for collecting large amounts of available datapoints.

A recent story posted on TikTok from creator Helene Myhre[26] illustrates the more sinister side of data scraping in the fashion industry. Myhre is an online creator and digital tour guide in Norway. She sells downloadable maps, filters, presets, and guides for the Scandinavian country. Recently, she collaborated with Skappel, a knitwear brand based in Oslo, to sell a knit pattern with wool (for context, knitting and pattern-sharing are a big part of Norwegian culture). The sweater is hand-knit and uses 100% Norwegian wool. It features a pink and purple design.

To Myhre's surprise, she found a dupe of her sweater on SHEIN. The SHEIN design is not just "inspired by" her sweater—it's a complete copy, except made of 100% polyester and mass-manufactured in China. To add insult to injury, SHEIN even used Myhre's photos on their e-commerce website to market the item and sell it for €20. (Myhre's original sweater design package was €120.) "This is not how you do business," Myhre says in the video.

This isn't the first time SHEIN has stolen from independent creators. In April 2024, Connecticut-based artist and designer Alan Giana filed a lawsuit against SHEIN, alleging the retailer "copied and displayed [his] artwork on [its] website without any authorization or permission [and] manufactured products bearing [his] artwork."[27]

Giana alleges that the company's use of AI, machine learning, and algorithms systematically infringes on his copyrighted work and that widespread copyright infringement is baked into SHEIN's business model.

A year before Giana's lawsuit in 2023, three independent creators—Krista Perry, Larissa Martinez, and Jay Baron—filed a lawsuit against SHEIN for stealing their designs and alleged that the company's widespread use of AI amounts to racketeering. Simply put, racketeering is engaging in illegal schemes repeatedly and consistently to earn a profit.

The argument is that AI-based image recognition technology and sophisticated electronic monitoring systems allow ultra-fast fashion companies like SHEIN to analyze images from social media and quickly recreate popular styles. As of this writing, the SHEIN case is ongoing, and a federal judge denied the fast-fashion giant's request to dismiss the racketeering claims.[28]

During a January 2024 conference in Berlin, Peter Pernot-Day, SHEIN's head of global strategy and corporate affairs, explained that more than 5,000 SHEIN suppliers recently gained access to an AI software platform to analyze customer preferences—information that the company then uses to produce small batches of merchandise to match supply in real-time. "We are using machine-learning technologies to accurately predict demand in a way we think is cutting-edge," Peter Pernot-Day said.[29]

SHEIN is the largest fashion retailer in the world, with annual sales of almost $30 billion—more than H&M and Zara combined. Part of how the company grew to such a behemoth is by producing 6,000 new items each day. For context, competitors like Fashion Nova produce 600–900 styles per *week*.

Fast fashion is not known for its originality; as we've discussed, Zara grew to dominance circa 2017 by copying designs from the runway and selling them at a lower price point. SHEIN has replicated this model and put it on steroids.

More recently, during the holiday 2024 season, TikTok was taken over by the "Walmart Birkin," a dupe of the Hermès signature bag that retails anywhere from $10,000 and even up to $500,000-plus for rare pieces or limited edition items. Lore has it that the Birkin bag was inspired by British actress Jane Birkin, who sat next to a Hermès executive on a flight and complained there were no stylish bags to meet her needs as a working mother. Since the Birkin's creation in 1984, the bag has become both a status symbol and a collector's item. The Walmart version—dubbed the "Wirkin" or the "Walmès"—sells for just $80 and is available both in-store and online from third-party sellers on Walmart.com. While imitations of the Birkin have existed for as long as the Birkin itself, the availability of the dupe at Walmart seems to have provided permission for consumers to purchase it, and the product has gone viral. As of the time of this writing, Hermès has not responded, but many anticipate lawsuits.[30]

If I had to speculate on what happened, I'd estimate that AI had something to do with the availability of the "Walmès," probably through trend prediction software used by third-party sellers or via merchants doubling down on the initial success of the Walmès without ethical or legal oversight.

Walmart has gradually opened up its online marketplace over the years as part of its digital transformation strategy to operate more like Amazon. In August of 2024, the company announced its fulfillment services for third-party sellers, which is how the[31] Hermès dupe was made available. Because customers got the dupe through Walmart, somehow the purchase seemed sanctioned. After all, what is Walmart but a retail symbol of accessibility? This is what can happen when companies operate what essentially amounts to a drop-shipping model with little human oversight. I have little doubt that when Walmart has to defend itself, they will point to AI as having allowed the dupe on the platform or for identifying it as a trending item.

As the fashion industry grapples with the intellectual property challenges posed by AI, other equally pressing concerns come into focus: data fairness and the ethical use of data. Just as AI blurs the boundaries of originality and ownership in design, it also raises critical questions about data fairness and privacy. The algorithms powering AI in fashion rely heavily on vast datasets, often sourced from consumers and creators, making transparency and consent essential. This shift from creative rights to data ethics highlights the broader implications of AI adoption and the responsibility brands must bear in its use.

Algorithmic Bias

The problem of data fairness is often referred to as algorithmic bias. This involves ensuring that the data collected to power algorithms is collected in an inclusive and equitable way.

Dr. Joy Buolamwini is a Canadian-American computer scientist and digital activist formerly based out of the MIT Media Lab. Her work investigates algorithmic justice and came about when she was a graduate student working on a project called the Aspire Mirror. The mirror was supposed to superimpose digital masks onto your reflection using generic facial recognition software, but Buolamwini found the software did not recognize her Black face. It wasn't until she wore a white plastic mask that the system detected her. Unfortunately, this wasn't the first time Dr. Buolamwini encountered this issue. When she was an undergraduate at Georgia Tech studying computer science, she tried to play peek-a-boo with a social robot. The robot could not see her and she had to "borrow" her roommate's face to complete the project. Later, on a trip to Hong Kong, while touring startups in the area, another social robot couldn't detect Buolamwini's face. The developers had used the same generic facial recognition software she'd encountered at Georgia Tech. "Halfway around the world, I learned that algorithmic bias can travel as quickly as it takes to download some files off the internet," Buolamwini shared in a 2016 TED Talk.[32] She points out that computer vision works by feeding computers training sets, and over time you can teach a computer to recognize faces. "If the training sets aren't really that diverse, any face that deviates too much from the established norm will be harder to detect, which was what was happening to me," she says. Buolamwini points out that the consequences aren't just academic:

> Across the US, police departments are starting to use facial recognition software in their crime-fighting arsenal. Georgetown Law published a report showing that one in two adults in the US (117 million people) have their faces in facial recognition networks. Police departments can currently look at these networks unregulated using algorithms

> that have not been audited for accuracy.... Misidentifying a suspected criminal is no laughing matter, nor is breaching civil liberties.

Buolamwini's experience with exclusion is what caused her to start the Algorithmic Justice League, an organization dedicated to advocating for more inclusive code and more inclusive coding practices, looking at who codes, how we code, and why. Her work is dedicated to identifying bias and raising awareness about the need for more inclusive training sets and algorithmic audits. On her website codedgaze.com, users can report bias, request audits, and become ongoing testers of new deployments of AI.

In the beauty industry, algorithmic bias can look like an AI-powered skin analysis tool that doesn't perform effectively across different skin tones, as was the case in a Stanford study.[33] For fashion, it can look like an e-commerce visualization software failing to represent all body types, or recommendation engines making false assumptions. "If every image of [a] red dress was on a tall, white model, for example, the algorithm might only work within those limitations—meaning that a petite or Black person may never be recommended clothes that are relevant to them," Ashwini Asokan, CEO of retail automation platform Vue.ai, told *Vogue Business*.[34]

Data Privacy

Another challenge is data privacy. While the idea of scanning my body to receive personalized clothing is enticing, I wonder where the images and video generated from this process end up, especially if the scan is of more intimate parts (for example, scans of breast shape that promise to create a bra that's just for you). As Stanford University's Institute for Human-Centered Artificial Intelligence points out, "AI systems pose many of the same privacy risks we've been facing during the past decades of internet commercialization and mostly unrestrained data collection. The difference is the scale: AI systems are so data-hungry and intransparent that we have even less control over what information about us is collected, what it is used for, and how we might correct or remove such personal information."[35]

Personalized experiences and clothing can only work if fashion brands have secure data and commit to protecting sensitive customer information. Mismanagement or breaches not only damage trust but can also result in legal and reputational repercussions. As fashion brands continue to embrace technology, prioritizing robust privacy practices and transparency is essential to foster consumer confidence and ensure ethical progress in this rapidly evolving digital era.

The AI Opportunity for Fashion

The American computer scientist Fei-Fei Li asks us to imagine a future where "AI [makes] us work more productively, live longer, and have cleaner energy." While this is undeniably an optimistic outlook, it's not an impossible one.

As we've explored throughout this book, the fashion industry faces significant challenges. When implemented thoughtfully, AI has the potential to be a powerful tool to address these issues. One of the most exciting opportunities lies in using AI to tackle inefficiencies in the industry while simultaneously offering more personalized consumer experiences. A handful of companies are already making strides in this direction.

For example, ThredUp, an online consignment and thrift store, uses computer vision to streamline the process of visually tagging and uploading secondhand items to their platform. This enables the company to efficiently connect preloved items with new owners. Similarly, Reflaunt, a Lisbon-based startup, works with fashion brands and retailers to facilitate the resale of items directly on their e-commerce platforms.

By leveraging AI to authenticate luxury goods, Reflaunt ensures quality and combats counterfeiting.

Unspun, another trailblazer in this space, uses AI to power their on-demand, custom-fit jeans. By analyzing each customer's unique proportions, Unspun's algorithms create bespoke garments with precision, reducing waste and promoting sustainability.

Looking ahead, AI will likely transform every aspect of product discovery and retail. Imagine opening a website where the brand knows your preferences—your size, skin tone, favorite colors, and style. With a few simple prompts, you're presented with a curated shopping experience designed just for you. Physical store layouts could be optimized for seamless navigation, and digital screens might display personalized messages tailored to your shopping habits.

There's a scene in the film *Minority Report* (2002) where John Anderton (Tom Cruise) navigates a commuter tunnel while ads for beer and credit cards flash in front of him with personalized greetings. I imagine, if left unchecked, the future of AI could look something like this. I wouldn't be surprised if in-eyeball advertisements already exist somewhere. But is this the kind of future we want with AI? In my conclusion, I'll address consumerism and personal responsibility, but before that, there's just one more technology I want to tell you about, and I'm certain it will get you excited about the possibilities for the future.

Chapter 7

Biotechnology

Biomaterials and Metamaterials

> *Biology and biotechnology is the new design tool for all industries.*
>
> —Alison Cutlan, VP of Innovation for the Rootist and founder of Cutlan Labs

The Disappearing Fabric

In April of 2016, I visited a startup in Burlingame, California, a city just outside San Francisco known for its abundance of trees and good weather. The startup was called Electroloom, and its founder, Aaron Rowley, had hefty visions for the future of material production. Electroloom was headquartered in a 600-square-foot industrial studio on the ground floor of a suburban building. Inside was a small workshop that included iterations of the company's spinning machine—a glass-walled contraption the size of a steamer trunk. The latest version sat on a table surrounded by tools and bottles of liquid. A cardboard mold of a tank top design was in the middle of the glass case as if it were a floating sculpture (Figure 7.1).

I interviewed Rowley for the *Electric Runway Podcast*, and he told me the vision was to create a textile factory in a box. "The basic principle is that you can go from raw material to finished fabric—either

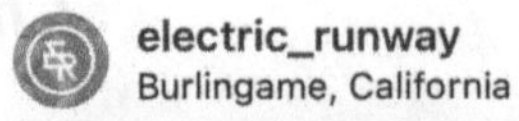

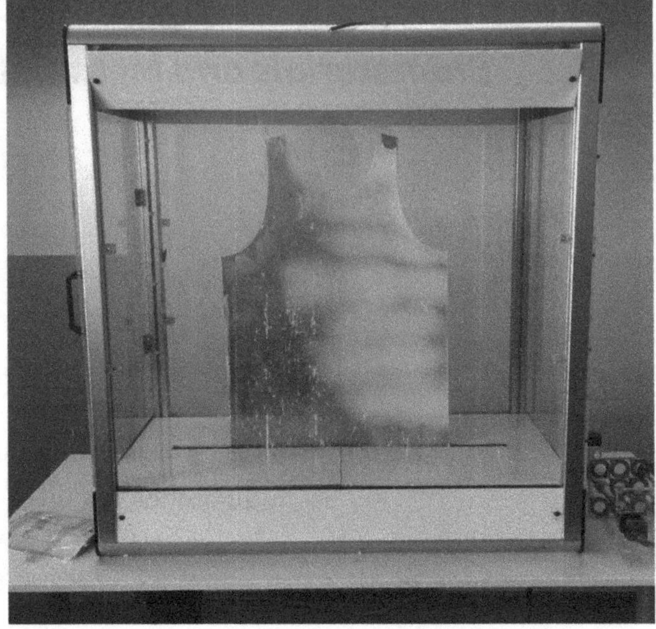

Figure 7.1 Electroloom's weaving machine.

a sheet or a 3D-constructed shape—in a matter of twenty minutes to two hours on a machine that can fit on a desktop," he told me.[1] What made Electroloom's technology different from most 3D printing devices was a process called field-guided fabrication, a form of electrospinning that uses an electric field to convert liquid materials into fibers. The company had raised capital from Kickstarter, angel investors, and the National Science Foundation.

At the end of our conversation, Rowley gave me a swatch of fabric that one of his machines had spun. It was pink and smelled like bubblegum. I kept the swatch in my wallet for a few years, pulling it out as a party trick at dinners discussing the future of materials (as one does).

But in two years, the material swatch broke in half and eventually dissipated into dozens of little pieces. Electroloom soon dissipated, too; the company ran out of money, and investors abandoned the project.[2] Despite this, I remained convinced that Rowley was onto something. I was compelled by the idea that new materials could be engineered and whole new processes developed to recreate the fashion industry from the ground up.

Just a few years later, this fascinating possibility was coming to fruition. Rowley was early, but he wasn't wrong. (Unfortunately for Electroloom, in the startup world, being early is the same thing as being wrong.)

Electroloom represented a mindset shift that was already starting to take place throughout in the advanced manufacturing sector. The shift revolved around a question: *What if we reimagined material production and manufacturing to transform fashion and other industries?*

Biotechnology and Biomaterials

In recent years, words like "biobased," "biosynthetic," "biofabrication," and "biodesign" (and other various "bio-" prefixes) have been used by a number of industries, from performance sportswear to luxury fashion. As highlighted by an in-depth research report by Fashion for Good and BioFabricate, Biotechnology is an ill-defined category because it remains a relatively young field, especially regarding applications for the fashion industry.[3]

According to the University of Pennsylvania, in its broadest definition, "biotechnology is the use of advances in molecular biology for applications in human and animal health, agriculture, environment, and specialty biochemical manufacturing." Put simply, biotechnology uses biological systems—meaning living organisms like algae, yeast, bacteria, fungi, or parts of them—to develop or create new materials, ingredients, or even genes.

You may be familiar with biotechnology if you've heard of CRISPR, which stands for Clustered Regularly Interspaced Short Palindromic Repeats. It's a naturally occurring system in bacteria that provides a defense mechanism against viruses. Scientists have harnessed this system to develop a tool for editing genomes with unprecedented accuracy.

Estimates vary for quantifying the business of biomaterials. A recent report asserted the market was valued at $169 billion in 2023 and is anticipated to generate an estimated revenue of $587 billion by 2032, with a compound annual growth rate of 14.8%.[4] Another report suggests the global biomaterial market in terms of revenue was estimated to be worth $45.2 billion in 2024 and poised to reach $64.2 billion by 2029.[5]

When it comes to biotechnology and fashion, we've seen all sorts of innovations and collaborations, like Piñatex, a material developed by extracting the fibers of pineapple leaves, or leathers made from mushrooms. At first, these were fringe projects unlikely to change the status quo, but over time bigger industry players got involved—for example, the harnessing of apple waste to create alternative leather, as designer Stella McCartney is doing, or the transforming of seaweed into fiber for yarn, as North Carolina-based Keel Labs is executing.

To fully appreciate the innovations that have taken place in the last decade from a materials science perspective, we have to revisit the modern material problem.

The Modern Material Problem

As we touched on in Chapter 2, the problem with the current materials used in fashion production is manifold. Common synthetic materials such as polyester, nylon, polyamide, and acrylic are made from microfibers that contain plastics. Each time these textiles are washed or worn, they release tiny plastic fibers into the water and air. Today, microplastics can be found in everything we eat and drink, from seafood to chicken to water and beer. They're in the lungs of garment workers and in the dust particles in our homes.

While natural materials such as cotton or silk may seem like a better option, they require tons of water to manufacture. For example, 1,800 gallons of water are required to produce the cotton needed for one pair of jeans. This is not to mention the indigo dying process, which relies on several toxic chemicals, including formaldehyde.

Although "vegan leather" (often referred to as "pleather") has been on the market for a while, this is made from petrochemicals, even though it's often marketed as a "sustainable" alternative to leather. According to the industry group the Textile Exchange, the production of polyester and other synthetic materials has tripled since 2000, nearing sixty million tons a year. These materials take hundreds of years to biodegrade, and many of them contain forever chemicals.

As we've also discussed, manufacturing at the scale the fashion industry demands also has challenging labor implications. Even with safety standards and regulations, workplaces can be dangerous places, especially for women in developing economies. In short, the modern material problem is that its production requires extraction and exploitation. Instead of relying on these methods, what if our clothes could be grown or engineered in a whole new way?

Early Experimentations in Biomaterials

In her 2011 TED Talk entitled "Grow Your Own Clothes," designer Suzanne Lee describes how she uses a kombucha recipe—a symbiotic mix of bacteria, yeasts, and other microorganisms—to spin cellulose in a fermentation process.[6] "Over time, these tiny threads form into layers and produce a mat on the surface," Lee explains. This mat, or surface sheet, grows to about an inch in thickness after a few weeks. When it's ready to harvest, it's removed from its bath, washed in cold, soapy water, and air-dried. The result is something like flexible vegetable leather that can be cut or formed around a three-dimensional shape.

Lee's experimental fashions have many benefits. You can change the material's color without conventional dye, create organic patterning with fruit and vegetable stains, or make it antimicrobial with one dip in indigo. The materials also have downfalls; for example, they're not water-resistant, so if the wearer walks out in the rain, the garment would absorb vast amounts of water and eventually rip at the seams. Not an ideal behavior quality for fashion.

Beyond just growing our materials, we can actually fine-tune their composition for our needs. Wen Wang is a bioengineer and designer from the Massachusetts Institute of Technology's department of chemical engineering. Together with her collaborators at the Tangible Media Group at MIT Media Lab, Wang created a responsive bio-skin made from bacteria. Called BioLogic, this bio-skin includes living actuators and sensors that open and close depending on the wearer's body temperature to help ventilate their sweat. Wang referred to her work as bio-hybrid wearables. "We're using bacteria to make wearable devices," she told me in an interview for the Electric Runway podcast.[7] Whereas the wearables we discussed in Chapter 2 were brought to life with batteries, the wearables Wang is referring to are brought to life with bacteria.

"Bio-hybrid means it has a living part as well as a synthetic part," she explained. In a video for BioLogic, two dancers are shown wearing the bio-skin. As they sweat, flaps on the material resembling scales open seemingly by themselves to ventilate the body (QR Code 32).

QR Code 32 Scan to see BioLogic in action.

BioLogic is different from other fabrics in two ways. First, like Susan Lee's experimental fashion, BioLogic was grown rather than made. Second, BioLogic is interactive. "Traditionally, garments have no emotion or affection—it's just a piece of fabric," Wang says. "Now it's a living second skin." Fashion that is active and alive seemed fascinating to me in the same way wearable technology is fascinating, only this time the aliveness is being achieved with biomaterials and chemical interactions on a level I can't see. Once again, fashion innovation felt like magic. But would these biomaterials ever make it to market?

Runway-Ready Biomaterials

In 2017, one of the first commercially ready examples of biomaterials appeared, capturing the public's imagination. It was a necktie made from alternative spider silk from materials-startup Bolt Threads. Microsilk replicates and scales the process spiders use to produce silk using corn, yeast, and a process of fermentation and spinning. The result is a strong yet soft material that mimics spider silk without any insect involvement. Only fifty of the limited edition neckties were produced and sold for $314 apiece.

Later that same year, Bolt Threads unveiled their first collaboration with designer Stella McCartney at the Museum of Modern Art in New York. Together they'd produced a canary yellow shift dress made with Microsilk fabric. McCartney designed the dress, and it was knitted by an engineer in California who had been working with Bolt Threads' fiber. "We finally have a fiber that knits on a commercial knitting machine," explains Bolt Threads' VP of product development in a promotional video for the project.[8]

Bolt Threads is also behind Mylo, a sustainable leather alternative made from mycelium, the root-like structure of fungus that's usually hidden from sight underneath the soil. It delivers the same look and feel as leather without harming any animals or requiring toxic dye processes. The year 2021 was a big one for Mylo. In March, Stella McCartney debuted a bustier top and trousers made from the leather alternative. In April, Adidas released its classic Stan Smith shoes made with the new material solution, and in July, Bolt Threads collaborated with Lululemon to reveal a concept yoga mat made from 100% undyed Mylo, as well as an accompanying yoga mat bag featuring Mylo "leather" braided into handles and zipper pulls.

For her Summer 2022 collection, Stella McCartney made history at Paris Fashion Week by showing the first luxury handbag made from Frayme Mylo, an infinitely renewable mycelium. The shoulder bag is black and crescent-shaped, with a mixed-metal aluminum chain and an engraved medallion bearing the company's insignia.

A blog post on Stella McCartney's website announcing the bag outlines how it's more sustainable than traditional leather or leather alternatives, including its lower environmental footprint and its avoidance of hazardous substances in the dying process. "This is the first chapter in the story of how mycelium is the future of fashion," the post says.[9]

MycoWorks is another player in the biotechnology space. They're becoming known for their own material, Reishi, which, like Mylo, is made from mycelium. Reishi (which comes from the Japanese word for mushrooms) has the look and feel of leather. According to *The New York Times*, MycoWorks is collaborating with Hermès and GM Ventures, the investment arm of General Motors.[10] Products made with Reishi include shoes, hats, jackets, clutches, wallets, and furniture. Reishi has also been used in the automotive sector, including in the Cadillac's SOLLEI concept car.

Creating leather alternatives isn't just better for animals and the environment—it also presents an enormous business opportunity for biomaterials companies. The global leather goods market was valued at $419.5 billion in 2021 and is expected to reach around $720.8 billion in the coming years. Additionally, the global market for synthetic leather materials is growing and is expected to reach almost $67 billion by 2030.

Biotechnology as a New Design Tool

"Biotechnology is the new design tool for all industries," says Alison Cutlan, the founder of CUTLAN Lab, a Brooklyn-based bioinnovation, strategy, and development consultancy.[11] Cutlan is part of a wave of new entrepreneurs working at the intersection of biology and design. She's the VP of Scientific Innovation at the Rootist, a biology-based haircare brand. As with augmented reality, beauty is leading the way when it comes to biotechnology, and brands like the Rootist are at the helm. "A lot of what we've been working with is 1950s chemistry," Cutlan says. "We're in the age of biology now. This is the revolution in biotech and I think the future: Biomaterials are much healthier for us as our bodies can recognize [them]. They're healthier for us, much more effective, and sustainable," she says.

The sustainability aspect of biomaterials is appealing, especially for the fashion industry, which has a long way to go in this respect.

For a long time, the problem with using innovative materials was achieving the scale the industry needs, but players like Modern Meadow are solving this challenge. Modern Meadow is a biomaterials company based in Nutley, New Jersey. Recently, they collaborated with Tory Burch to produce the material for the American fashion brand's iconic bag, the Ella Tote (QR Code 33). Ella Bio is made from a proprietary protein-based Bio-Alloy, a material derived from soybeans.

QR Code 33 Scan to see Tory Burch's Ella Bio tote, made with a Bio-Alloy material from Modern Meadow.

Unlike other imitation leathers made from plastic, Bio-Alloy is made from protein, which makes it look and feel like real leather. Modern Meadow can also produce to the scale fashion brands require: "If a client wants 10,000 or 100,000 bags, there are no limitations," says Catherine Roggero-Lovisi, the CEO of Modern Meadow.[12] Bio-Alloy is also durable enough to last generations. "When you are a designer, you want something that's not only beautiful but durable because you understand that this is an investment, and you also understand that part of the sustainability mantra today is making sure your product is durable not only for the first buyer but also potentially for the secondhand market," Roggero-Lovisi says.

Another production challenge biomaterials faced in the past was integrating well with the existing fashion ecosystem. Creating alternative materials can mean using alternative methods that the industry isn't currently set up for. A $10 T-shirt on Temu represents years of efficiencies in a globalized supply chain. These prices aren't possible without extensive operations and economies of scale.

Some companies address this challenge by developing fibers that work within traditional manufacturing. For example, Keel Labs is a next-generation material solutions company based in North Carolina. The company's flagship product is a seaweed yarn called Kelsun, and it's used for a wide range of applications not only for fashion and apparel but also for home furnishings, consumer packaged goods, and automotive. Kelsun is a brown seaweed species that is farmed, dried, and chopped. Keel Labs' suppliers then extract an alginate (a seaweed-derived biopolymer), which the company uses to create a fiber through a wet spinning process similar to viscose. Kelsun uses existing manufacturing structures to produce its yarn, which is distributed to its clients. It can be used in knitting or weaving machines to create end products. Compared to cotton, Kelsun uses seventy times less water and accounts for a 76% reduction in CO_2 emissions. Since their product comes from seaweed, Keel Labs uses no farmland (compared to cotton, which uses 2.5% of the world's arable land) and no pesticides (cotton accounts for 16% of all pesticides used). Kelsun performs like a viscose in terms of tenacity, elongation, and durability.

What's probably most impressive is what happens to Kelsun at the end of its lifespan as a material. According to lab tests, when properly composted, Kelsun shows 82% degradation in sixty-one days—meaning that when the material is no longer needed, it biodegrades faster than an orange peel. Think of this compared to the hundreds of thousands of tons of plastic textile waste washing up on beaches in Ghana.

When researching biomaterials, it becomes clear that the solutions already exist—it's adoption that lags behind. Adoption hinges on a willingness to change as well as consumer demand, driven by awareness and a push for transparency from brands. Companies like Keel Labs and Modern Meadow demonstrate that past challenges have been overcome, transitioning from concept clothing to tangible solutions for the industry.

While biomaterials derived from biology offer sustainable solutions rooted in nature, another fascinating frontier lies in metamaterials—engineered substances derived from silica and other nonorganic components. These materials harness advanced properties, such as manipulating light and sound, opening entirely new possibilities for innovation in fashion and beyond. This is where the opportunity for fashion's future is out of this world.

Meta Materials and Nanomaterials

The vibe of the Coperni Fall/Winter 2024/2025 haute couture runway show was intergalactic. Models donned dresses that resembled flying saucers and space blankets, their eyebrows colored white for an ethereal, otherworldly look. Some silhouettes were purposefully disproportionate, with heightened shoulder pads and micro shorts. Glossy black stilettoes were shaped like stars at the bottom, challenging our conceptions of what an outsole can look like. A silver turtleneck doubled as a face mask, obscuring its wearer's face but protecting them from space dust. The score for the show was John Williams' "The Conversation" from Spielberg's *Close Encounters of the Third Kind*. "The collection is a whole sci-fi tribute," designer Arnaud Vaillant told reporters backstage, as if it weren't obvious.

Among the sparkled knee-high boots and translucent white fabric was a singular handbag representing a marvel of innovation. The Air Swipe bag is made from silica aerogel, a kind of glass that NASA uses for collecting space dust. It's made in a stainless steel mold, which uses pressure and high temperatures to turn liquid into gas. The purse is 1% aerogel and 99% air, making it the lightest handbag on earth, weighing less than one pound (QR Code 34).

QR Code 34 Scan to see Coperni's Air Swipe bag.

Coperni created the Swipe silhouette, a handbag inspired by the iPhone's "swipe to unlock" icon. The Fall/Winter 2024/2025 show was the first time the bag was created with silica, the result of a collaboration that began when the brand approached Dr. Ioannis Michaloudis, an artist, researcher, and academic experimenting with new materials. I had the chance to speak with Dr. Michaloudis about developing the bag for Coperni.

"[Silica Aerogel] is a personification of our sky," Dr. Michaloudis told me.[13] "In a very crazy moment with our climate, [silica aerogel] is a good metaphor to speak about the sky, the last garment of our planet," he said. He told me that silica aerogel's development resulted from a bet between two engineers who wanted to see if they could develop a material that didn't shrink when it dried. The result was a material that's hard but transparent, taking on the color of whatever it's held up against. It can withstand heat up to more than a thousand degrees Fahrenheit.

"Materials from now on will be nanomaterials," Dr. Michaloudis says. "In nanoscale, you can control the material's qualities, including the particles' size and shape.... Here, fashion has a huge lesson to learn that materials from now are not only longer textile materials but coming from all over material science, especially from space technology because there they test the materials for extreme conditions, so if they are tested for extreme conditions, they are very good for earth applications." Dr. Michaloudis has a point here: if we want to stress test our materials, seeing if they can withstand space exploration is a surefire way.

Coperni's Air Swipe bag isn't the first time fashion has overlapped with space technology. In *Spacesuit: Fashioning Apollo*, Nicholas de Monchau details how a group of working-class women (pattern cutters, seamstresses, and assemblers) collaborated at the International Latex Corporation (ILC) to make the spacesuits for the Apollo program from 1962 to 1974.[14] Many of these women had worked for Playtex, the consumer division of ILC that produced girdles, bras, and rubber pants that go over baby diapers.[15]

The Coperni Air Swipe bag and its use of silica aerogel exemplify how fashion continues to draw from advancements in material science, including innovations originally designed for space exploration. These breakthroughs not only challenge our understanding of what materials can do but also push the boundaries of design and functionality. However, as we embrace these cutting-edge materials, we must confront the challenges they bring.

Challenges at Fashion's Biotech Frontier

Like any technology, biotech comes with both advantages and challenges. While technical hurdles like scalability and durability are being addressed, high research and development costs remain a barrier. Despite some progress in supply chain integration, adoption is slow, because many fashion brands hesitate to invest due to uncertain returns on investment.

The fashion industry also lacks the expertise to fully implement biotech solutions, often requiring significant guidance from specialists. Regulatory approvals and bureaucratic hurdles further complicate commercialization. Additionally, there's an education gap among consumers—few are aware of these innovations, making it difficult to generate demand. Finally, the potential for unintended ecological consequences, such as the impact of genetically modified organisms (GMOs) on natural ecosystems, raises valid concerns about the long-term effects of biotech adoption in fashion.

All of this is to say that while the road ahead is complex, the promise of biotechnology in creating a more sustainable and innovative fashion industry makes overcoming these challenges worthwhile.

Fabricating the Future

I ended this book by discussing biotechnology because I believe it is the future of fashion. Although this technology may not be as flashy as wearables or as sexy as AI is at present, it can potentially transform the future of fashion in a more behind-the-scenes way. If we are going to right the wrongs of this industry and revolutionize production, we must start with the materials.

New materials have the potential to be more sustainable and provide benefits far beyond wearability. Imagine, for example, fabrics that grow with your body or materials that can heal wounds or deliver nutrients while protecting you from the elements. With innovations in biotechnology, our clothing can truly become our second skin and move us toward a new kind of humanity. Just as wearing animal skins changed the way humans occupied this planet, the materials of the future will enable us to cross new thresholds.

It's not just fashion that stands to benefit from new materials. Just this week, I read about a reusable and biodegradable fibrous foam developed in China that's capable of removing 99.8% of microplastics from polluted water.[16] Textiles are embedded into the social, economic, and cultural fabric of civilizations. How we choose to develop our clothing moving forward says everything about the kind of culture we'll create.

It is my hope that innovations in biotechnology will help us fashion a better future for people and the planet. By harnessing the power of science and technology, we can give the industry a much-needed makeover.

Conclusion

A Tale of Two Runway Moments

Two iconic moments in fashion history highlight the evolving relationship between fashion and technology. When viewed side by side, they reveal how this dynamic has transformed over time. The first is Alexander McQueen's Spring/Summer 1999 show, Untitled No. 13 (QR Code 35), and the second is Coperni's Spring/Summer 2023 presentation.

QR Code 35 Scan to watch the end of McQueen's Untitled No. 13 featuring Shalom Harlow.

McQueen's Untitled No. 13 was a romantic collection with dark undertones, but it was the closing performance people would remember. In the show's final act, ballet dancer and supermodel Shalom Harlow appeared on the runway in a paper-white, multilayered dress. The dress was cinched at her breastbone with a camel belt and shot out from Harlow's body in a dramatic A-line emphasized by the layers of tulle underneath. Harlow was rotating on a turntable built into the wooden floor and surrounded by two industrial robots that were in view during the show but had, until this point, remained motionless. As the music (Mozart's *Piano Concerto No. 23*) intensified, the robots lurched forward to spray black and yellow ink all over Harlow and her dress, as if maiming her innocence.

More than twenty years later, Parisian fashion brand Coperni would stage a performance that harkened back to McQueen's. This time, the performance involved Bella Hadid. After a runway of reimagined tailored looks, Hadid entered the Salle de Textiles entirely naked, save for a pair of open-toe kitten heels and a pair of flesh-colored underwear. She stood still on a platform while two men approached her with spray guns filled with white liquid polymer. Over fifteen minutes, the technicians sprayed the liquid onto her body to form a slip dress (QR Code 36).

Both performances center on a young, swanlike model in a white dress. In their own way, both performances dramatize essential aspects of fashion's relationship with technology specific to the time. For McQueen, technology was a threat. It marked a loss of innocence, and this innocence was violently taken. The feeling of the

QR Code 36 Scan to watch the end of Coperni's Spring/Summer 2023 show.

robotic arms spraying Harlow was one of intense predation, almost as if she were an animal being hunted and killed. It's a story of death and destruction at the hands of machines.

In contrast, Coperni depicts a story of creation with technology. Hadid is statuesque and full of soft power. She is Michelangelo's David, and they are sculpting her. After the dress is sprayed onto Hadid's body, a woman from the Coperni team styles the straps by rolling them off Hadid's shoulder. She also cuts a slit at the bottom so the model can walk. The audience claps as Hadid walks the runway in the dress made of freshly dried materials. Interestingly, the material that made this performance possible is called Fabrican, a liquid-to-solid polymer that dries on contact with any surface. It's the same idea Electroloom had years earlier, only now Coperni had iterated on it and elevated it to the level of performance art.

The message from McQueen's show seems to be that fashion, in the hands of technology, has become disruptive and destructive. For Coperni, technology—when guided by human hands—can be generative.

I firmly believe (and sincerely hope) that both McQueen and Coperni's Sébastien Meyer and Arnaud Vaillant are correct in their visions. McQueen foresaw a future where fashion would be overtaken—and perhaps even consumed—by technology, a prophecy that feels eerily realized today. Yet, more than two decades later, Meyer and Vaillant offer a counterpoint: a vision of fashion reimagined through technology, specifically via a new means of production and creation.

Crafting a Conscious Tomorrow

The story of fashion and technology is far from over—it's an ongoing narrative with new chapters being written every day. However, this book needs a conclusion. If you've made it this far, you might be feeling inundated with ideas, inspired by the possibilities, or even overwhelmed by the challenges that lie ahead. I don't claim to have a crystal ball or the ability to predict the future, but if I had to leave you with three thoughts about the future of fashion, they would be the following.

The Future Is About Conscious Consumption

Current consumption patterns are not sustainable and need to change. SHEIN hauls are out, thrifting and secondhand shopping is in. The good news is that changes in consumer behavior happen all the time. We need only to look at the surge of the sharing economy, a shift in consumer behavior that took place at the beginning of the 2010s powered by companies like Uber and Airbnb. Retail platforms like Rent the Runway have changed the way we wear gowns for weddings or outfits for special occasions, shifting the emphasis from ownership to experience and opening up new models of consumption. A recent article in *The Business of Fashion* suggests a turning of the tides may already be under way. "Lately, the churn seems to have slowed" writes Joan Kennedy. In an article titled "The Decline and Fall of the Viral Microtrend," she suggests the harsh realities of post-pandemic life have set in, as US credit card debt has reached an all-time high. "You're more likely to see a video on TikTok lamenting overconsumption than one gassing up the next of-the-moment aesthetic," she writes.

Just as technology circulated trends, it also circulated information about the impacts of overconsumption. Joseph Ayesu is an ecological research manager at the Or Foundation, a charity dedicated to catalyzing a justice-led circular economy. In a video shared to *The Guardian,* he stands at Jamestown Beach in Ghana. Behind him, a sludge of clothing chokes up the waterways. He explains how he and his team clear up 25 tons of textile waste per week—what he called "tentacles"—textiles that get twisted together in the ebb and flow of the water.

Gen Z is already leading this new wave of conscious consumption, fueled by both technological awareness and environmental urgency. Often referred to as the "sustainability generation," Gen Z consumers are rejecting the wastefulness of fast fashion in favor of more mindful practices, such as thrifting, upcycling, and investing in quality over quantity. Platforms like Depop and Poshmark have gained massive traction, making secondhand shopping not just acceptable but aspirational. Social media, which once perpetuated overconsumption with endless "hauls," now features influencers advocating for capsule wardrobes, sustainable swaps, and thoughtful buying.

Technology is a double-edged sword in this transformation. While it has catalyzed the fast-paced trend cycle, it is also the key to creating systemic change.

This shift in consumption patterns is not just about rejecting the old but also embracing the new possibilities of a circular economy. Rental platforms, resale marketplaces, and repair services are reframing the idea of value in fashion, prioritizing longevity and utility over fleeting trends. Conscious consumption doesn't mean abandoning fashion—it means reimagining it in a way that aligns with both personal values and planetary limits.

The future of fashion will be less about owning for the sake of owning and more about the stories behind what we wear, the relationships we build with our clothing, and the responsibility we take for our impact. In this way, the decline of the microtrend signals not the end of style, but the beginning—I hope—of something more meaningful.

The Future Is a Return to Craft, Informed by Technology

As a kind of backlash to the "here today, gone tomorrow" trend cycle and exhausting churn of ultra-fast fashion, we're going to see a return to personal style in a way that's more authentic than just trying on trends like costumes. With this, we'll see a reconnection to our clothing and a return to tailoring and craftsmanship.

I just bought a new pair of pants, and if they're the only ones I buy all year I'll be okay with that. They're black and barrel legged, giving that effortlessly cool, slouchy look while still being elevated. I call them my David Bowie pants because their shape reminds me of David Bowie's striped bodysuit by Kansai Yamamoto. They make me feel like a rockstar, despite the fact that the fashion influencers on Instagram are now wearing skinny jeans again (to this I say, no thank you).

My Bowie trousers weren't inexpensive, but they also aren't cheap. They're made with care, consideration, and attention to detail by a local designer who has a small shop on Queen Street West in Toronto. What makes these pants special for me is not just the quality but my connection to the designer and her connection to my neighborhood.

I am not the only one taking this buy less, buy local, buy better approach. "[A] new approach is taking root," writes Erinch Sahan, chief executive of World Fair Trade Organization. "It is based on putting artisans, workers, and producer communities at the heart of the fashion industry," he says. A recent *Harper's Bazaar* article highlighted how craft was at the heart of a number of collections showed in the spring of 2024, "from the patchworked and distressed leather at Prada to the reconstructions of upcycled garments at Balenciaga, exaggerated embellishments at Loewe, and baroque lace patterns at Valentino."

The future of craft, however, will undoubtedly be informed by technology. While the emphasis on quality, connection, and authenticity will drive a return to craftsmanship, technology will play a key role in enabling these values to flourish in a modern context. Tools like 3D knitting machines and digital pattern-making software will allow designers to create intricate, bespoke pieces with a precision and efficiency that complement traditional techniques. Innovations like blockchain will offer transparency into where and how garments are made, giving consumers greater confidence in their purchases and fostering a deeper connection to the makers behind their clothing.

Technology will also help preserve and amplify traditional crafts. By digitizing patterns, techniques, and methods, designers can ensure that cultural heritage is not lost, but rather adapted for the future. Additionally, innovations in materials science will pave the way for smart, sustainable textiles that enhance the durability and functionality of garments without sacrificing their craftsmanship.

As we step into a future informed by both the slow beauty of handmade work and the efficiency of cutting-edge tools, this merging of the artisanal and the technological will redefine what it means to cherish and wear a piece of clothing. Craftsmanship will no longer be limited by what can be done solely by hand, but rather celebrated for how it can evolve with the help of modern tools, creating pieces that are not just products, but personal artifacts of innovation and care.

The Future Is Local—And Global

As I write this, the news headlines are dominated by possible tariffs imposed by President Trump during his second term in office. Already grocery stores here in Canada have started circulating newsletters highlighting products that are Canadian-owned, and encouraging us to "buy Canadian," bracing for a trade war with our neighbors to the south. President Trump's stated desire to "Make America Great Again" seems to include making things in the United States. This attempt will only reveal that no country is an island and supply chains are complex.

This moment in history underscores a tension that has always existed in fashion: its deeply local roots and its inherently global reach. While governments may impose tariffs or trade restrictions, fashion knows no borders. Supply chains crisscross continents, garments tell stories of faraway places, and technology continues to connect consumers with products and cultures worldwide.

At the same time, the push to "buy local" reflects a growing awareness of how choices impact communities and the planet. Advances in technology, like on-demand manufacturing, promise to bring production closer to home, enabling hyper-localized fashion that responds to regional tastes and needs. Meanwhile, digital platforms and global e-commerce allow even the smallest brands to reach customers around the globe.

The future of fashion is not a choice between local and global—it is both. Fashion's evolution will depend on its ability to embrace this duality, leveraging technology to create more sustainable, transparent, and interconnected systems that honor local craftsmanship while engaging with a global audience. As we look forward, it becomes clear that the future of fashion, like the world itself, is increasingly hybrid: simultaneously grounded and boundless.

If there's one thing I hope you carry forward, it's this: these points are not just about imagining the future—they're about shaping it. The future of fashion is up to all of us. Every decision we make, from the materials we choose to the technologies we adopt, influences not just what we wear but how we live. Together, we can fashion a future that's innovative, inclusive, sustainable, and reflective of the world we want.

Notes

Preface

1. Cosco, Amanda. "Interview with a Cyborg: How Machines Mesh with Mankind." *The Globe and Mail*, May 25, 2014. https://www.theglobeandmail.com/technology/tech-news/interview-with-a-cyborg-how-machines-mesh-with-mankind/article18849897/.
2. Neil Harbisson, "I Listen to Color," *TED* video, 9:33, filmed July 2012, TED Conferences, LLC. https://www.ted.com/talks/neil_harbisson_i_listen_to_color?subtitle=en.

Chapter 1

1. https://www.sciencedirect.com/science/article/abs/pii/S0264275116302244#:~:text=Street%20vending%2C%20the%20most%20prominent,misuse%20of%20the%20public%20space.
2. McKinsey & Company, "Acquiring the Advantage in a Fast-Evolving Industry," McKinsey & Company, 2023. https://www.mckinsey.com/industries/financial-services/our-insights/acquiring-the-advantage-in-a-fast-evolving-industry.
3. Author's virtual interview with Adeyemi Atanda, March 18, 2024.
4. Normcore is a unisex fashion trend characterized by simple, nondescript and ordinary clothing. It embraces the concept of "normal" as a fashion statement.
5. Statista, "Market Share of Mobile Device Vendors in Africa 2019–2023," Statista, September 22, 2023. https://www.statista.com/statistics/1167088/market-share-of-mobile-device-vendors-in-africa/.

6. McKinsey & Company, "The Future of Payments in Africa," McKinsey & Company, April 27, 2023. https://www.mckinsey.com/industries/financial-services/our-insights/the-future-of-payments-in-africa.
7. Elizabeth L. Eisenstein, *The Printing Press as an Agent of Change* (Cambridge, UK: Cambridge University Press, 1979).
8. Neil Postman, *Amusing Ourselves to Death: Public Discourse in the Age of Show Business* (New York: Penguin Books, 1985).
9. Short form of "duplicate" that is used to refer to a product made to look like a more expensive or high-quality product. See https://dictionary.cambridge.org/dictionary/english/dupe.
10. FashionTV, "Alexander McQueen's Last Show: Plato Atlantis Spring 2010 Paris Fashion Week," YouTube video, 9:49, July 1, 2010. https://www.youtube.com/watch?v=led41Il0YCg.
11. "Interview: Alexander McQueen on Plato's Atlantis," SHOWstudio, October 6, 2009, November 24, 2024. https://www.showstudio.com/projects/platos_atlantis/interview.
12. According to Forbes, Facebook overtook MySpace in terms of number of unique worldwide visitors, and in May 2009 the number of unique US visitors. Gil Press. "Why Facebook Triumphed over All Other Social Networks," *Forbes*, April 8, 2018. https://www.forbes.com/sites/gilpress/2018/04/08/why-facebook-triumphed-over-all-other-social-networks/.
13. Shirin Ghaffary and Alex Heath, "The Facebookification of Instagram," Vox, July 27, 2022. https://www.vox.com/recode/23274761/facebook-instagram-land-the-giants-mark-zuckerberg-kevin-systrom-ashley-yuki.
14. Suzy Menkes, "SuzyNYFW: 'See-Now-Buy-Now' Is New York's Hot New Reality Show," *Vogue*, September 9, 2016. https://www.vogue.co.uk/gallery/see-now-buy-now-at-new-york-fashion-week-thakoon.
15. IGI Global, "The Appification of Literacy," accessed December 18, 2024. https://www.igi-global.com/dictionary/the-appification-of-literacy/50128.
16. Holly Stanley, "10 Mobile Commerce Trends to Watch for in 2024," *Shopify*, July 2024. https://www.shopify.com/ca/enterprise/blog/mobile-commerce-future-trends.

17. Statista, "Global: M-Commerce Revenue and Share in E-Commerce 2017–2028," Statista, April 30, 2024, accessed November 24, 2024. https://www.statista.com/statistics/1449284/retail-mobile-commerce-revenue-worldwide/.
18. Rickey E. Richardson, Laura Gordey, and Reggie Hall, "Amazon's Fast Delivery: The Human Cost," *Journal of Business Ethics Education* 17 (2020): 251–254. https://www.neilsonjournals.com/JBEE/JBEEpromos/Amazon17P.pdf.
19. Katie Tarasov, "Amazon Returns: What Really Happens to Them?" CNBC, January 28, 2022. https://www.cnbc.com/2022/01/28/amazon-returns-what-really-happens-to-them.html.
20. Richard Pallot, "Amazon Destroying Millions of Items of Unsold Stock in One of Its UK Warehouses Every Year, ITV News Investigation Finds," ITV News, June 21, 2021. https://www.itv.com/news/2021-06-21/amazon-destroying-millions-of-items-of-unsold-stock-in-one-of-its-uk-warehouses-every-year-itv-news-investigation-finds.
21. Aditi Bharade, "The App Data Has Spoken, and Gen Z's Love for Temu Is Real," Business Insider, November 2024. https://www.businessinsider.com/temu-hottest-gen-z-app-amazon-downloads-popularity-appfigures-2024-11.
22. Marc Bain, "How Nike's SNKRS App Community Inspired Its Digital Strategy," Quartz, November 7, 2019. https://qz.com/quartzy/1747382/how-nikes-snkrs-app-community-inspired-its-digital-strategy.
23. Shopify, "Social Commerce Trends: 10 Ways to Sell on Social Media in 2023." *Shopify*, 2023. https://www.shopify.com/ca/enterprise/blog/social-commerce-trends.
24. Capital One Shopping, "Facebook Marketplace Statistics," *Capital One Shopping*, 2024. https://capitaloneshopping.com/research/facebook-marketplace-statistics/.
25. David Curry, "Depop Revenue and Usage Statistics (2024)," *Business of Apps*, November 4, 2024. https://www.businessofapps.com/data/depop-statistics/.
26. ThredUp, "2024 Resale Market and Consumer Trend Report," accessed November 16, 2024. https://www.thredup.com/resale.

27. Joan Kennedy, "The Life Cycle of a Viral Fashion Tren,." *Business of Fashion*, July 5, 2023. https://www.businessoffashion.com/articles/marketing-pr/the-life-cycle-of-a-viral-fashion-trend/.
28. Vanessa Friedman, "Smartphones Are Killing Off the Runway Show," *The New York Times*, February 11, 2016. https://www.nytimes.com/2016/02/11/fashion/new-york-fashion-week-smartphones-killing-off-runway-show.html.
29. Joan Kennedy, "The Life Cycle of a Viral Fashion Trend," *Business of Fashion*, July 5, 2023. https://www.businessoffashion.com/articles/marketing-pr/the-life-cycle-of-a-viral-fashion-trend/.
30. Vivien Lee, Jasmine Cubillan, and Victoria Montalti, "The Nap Dress: Best Styles and How to Wear Them," *Refinery29*, accessed November 13, 2024. https://www.refinery29.com/en-us/the-nap-dress-best-styles.
31. JD Shadel, "What Is Ultra Fast Fashion? Investigating Why It's Ultra Bad," *Good On You*, October 4, 2024. https://goodonyou.eco/ultra-fast-fashion/.
32. "Half of fast fashion clothes made of new plastics," BBC News, June 10, 2021. https://www.bbc.com/news/business-57433221.
33. Jenny Cowley, Stephanie Matteis, and Charlsie Agro, "Experts Warn of High Levels of Chemicals in Clothes by Some Fast-Fashion Retailers," CBC News, October 1, 2021. https://www.cbc.ca/news/business/marketplace-fast-fashion-chemicals-1.6193385.
34. *The Economist,* "The People Formerly Known as the Audience," *The Economist*, July 9, 2011. https://www.economist.com/special-report/2011/07/09/the-people-formerly-known-as-the-audience.
35. TED, "*Why Your Self-Worth Shouldn't Be Based on Your Productivity* | Alain de Botton," YouTube video, 13:19. June 23, 2020. https://www.youtube.com/watch?v=eO7wHh2J4aA.
36. Dean Talbot, "Magazine Publishing Statistics," *WordsRated*, April 4, 2023. https://wordsrated.com/magazine-publishing-statistics/.
37. Chris Michaud, "The Decline of Newspapers in Four Charts," *Brookings*, November 29, 2022. https://www.brookings.edu/articles/the-decline-of-newspapers-in-four-charts/.

38. Statista, "Social Media Advertising - Worldwide," *Statista*, accessed November 11, 2024. https://www.statista.com/outlook/dmo/digital-advertising/social-media-advertising/worldwide.
39. Pauline De Leon, "Kim Kardashian's SKIMS Shapewear Has Sold Out on the First Day, Earning $2 Million USD," *Hypebae*, September 12, 2019. https://hypebae.com/2019/9/kim-kardashian-skims-shapewear-sold-out-restock-earnings.
40. Sapna Maheshwari, "Kim Kardashian's Skims Loungewear Gets a Lift from Pandemic Demand," *The New York Times*, April 9, 2021. https://www.nytimes.com/2021/04/09/business/dealbook/kardashian-skims.html.
41. Benjamin Mullin, "Kim Kardashian's Skims Doubles Valuation to $3.2 Billion," *Bloomberg*, January 27, 2022. https://www.bloomberg.com/news/articles/2022-01-27/kim-kardashian-s-skim-underwear-brand-doubles-valuation-to-3-2-billion.
42. FashionUnited, "Most Valuable Fashion Brands," *FashionUnited*. Accessed November 11, 2024. https://fashionunited.com/i/most-valuable-fashion-brands.
43. Jenna Caldwell, "SKIMS," *Time*, March 30, 2022. https://time.com/collection/time100-companies-2022/6159502/skims/.
44. Natalie Robehmed, "At 21, Kylie Jenner Becomes the Youngest Self-Made Billionaire Ever," *Forbes*, March 5, 2019. https://www.forbes.com/sites/natalierobehmed/2019/03/05/at-21-kylie-jenner-becomes-the-youngest-self-made-billionaire-ever/.
45. BBC News, "Kylie Jenner: Forbes Drops Celebrity from Billionaire List," *BBC News*, May 29, 2020. https://www.bbc.com/news/business-52854345.
46. The Guardian, "Kylie Jenner Makes $600M from Selling Majority Share in Her Beauty Company." *The Guardian*, November 19, 2019. https://www.theguardian.com/lifeandstyle/2019/nov/19/kylie-jenner-makes-600m-from-selling-majority-share-in-her-beauty-company.
47. *Business of Fashion*, "Aimee Song," *Business of Fashion*, accessed November 11, 2024. https://www.businessoffashion.com/people/aimee-song/.
48. Erin Griffith, "The Creator Economy Is Booming and Transforming Business." *The New York Times*, December 6, 2023. https://www.nytimes.com/2023/12/06/business/dealbook/content-creator-economy.html.

49. Goldman Sachs, "The Creator Economy Could Approach Half a Trillion Dollars by 2027," *Goldman Sachs*, September 2023. https://www.goldmansachs.com/insights/articles/the-creator-economy-could-approach-half-a-trillion-dollars-by-2027.
50. Erin Griffith, "The Creator Economy Is Booming and Transforming Business," *The New York Times*, December 6, 2023. https://www.nytimes.com/2023/12/06/business/dealbook/content-creator-economy.html.
51. Kimberly A. Whitler, "When It Comes to Influencers, Smaller Can Be Better," *Harvard Business Review*, September 2024. https://hbr.org/2024/09/when-it-comes-to-influencers-smaller-can-be-better.
52. Ellen Nguyen, "Are Influencer Partnerships the Inevitable Future of Business?" *BBC Worklife*, October 13, 2023, https://www.bbc.com/worklife/article/20231013-are-influencer-partnerships-the-inevitable-future-of-business.
53. Amy de Klerk, "Luke Meagher, aka HauteLeMode, Is a New Kind of Fashion Critic," *Vogue*, August 17, 2023. https://www.vogue.com/article/luke-meagher-aka-hautelemode-is-a-new-kind-of-fashion-critic.
54. Nathalie Atkinson, "Meet the New Crop of Fashion Critics Who All Have One Thing in Common: An Honest Opinion," *The Globe and Mail*, July 29, 2024. https://www.theglobeandmail.com/life/style-advisor/article-the-best-part-of-modern-fashion-criticism-an-honest-opinion/.
55. Grazia Magazine, "Gucci Fest 2020: Everything You Need to Know," *Grazia Magazine*, November 2020. https://graziamagazine.com/us/articles/gucci-fest-2020-details/.
56. Highsnobiety, "How Fashion Brands Became Media Companies," *Highsnobiety*, June 14, 2022. https://www.highsnobiety.com/p/special-report-fashion-brands-become-media-content-social/.
57. Highsnobiety, "How Fashion Brands Became Media Companies," *Highsnobiety*, June 14, 2022. https://www.highsnobiety.com/p/special-report-fashion-brands-become-media-content-social/.
58. Kristen Bateman Weiss, "How Beauty Editors Are Making the Transition to Brand Jobs: Part 2," *Fashionista*, May 24, 2019. https://fashionista.com/2019/05/beauty-editors-brands-career-transition-part-2.

59. Reuters, "Guidance on Sustainable Claims after Dismissal of H&M Greenwashing Class Action," *Reuters*, June 2, 2023. https://www.reuters.com/legal/legalindustry/guidance-sustainable-claims-after-dismissal-hm-greenwashing-class-action-2023-06-02/#:~:text=June%202%2C%202023%20%2D%20On%20May,violated%20California%20and%20Missouri%20consumer.
60. Amy Farley, "How the Diet Prada Cofounders Became the Fashion Industry's Most Influential Watchdogs," *Fast Company*, May 22, 2019. https://www.fastcompany.com/90345174/most-creative-people-2019-diet-prada-tony-liu-lindsey-schuyler.
61. Elizabeth Paton, Vanessa Friedman, and Jessica Testa, "What to Know About Balenciaga's Campaign Controversy," *The New York Times*, November 28, 2022. https://www.nytimes.com/2022/11/28/style/balenciaga-campaign-controversy.html.
62. https://www.glossy.co/pop/glossy-pop-newsletter-rhodes-lip-case-offers-tiktok-a-marketing-masterclass/.
63. Capital One Shopping, "Instagram Shopping Statistics (2024): User & Revenue Growth," last updated September 13, 2024, accessed November 24, 2024. https://capitaloneshopping.com/research/instagram-shopping-statistics/.
64. TikTok, "Introducing TikTok Shop," *TikTok Newsroom*, September 12, 2023. https://newsroom.tiktok.com/en-us/introducing-tiktok-shop.
65. Dan Frommer, "TikTok Shop Is Huge. Will It Last?" *The New Consumer*, January 2024. https://newconsumer.com/2024/01/tiktok-shop-is-huge-will-it-last/.
66. Vogue Business, "Live Streaming Ushers in a New Era for E-Commerce," June 28, 2024. https://www.voguebusiness.com/story/technology/live-streaming-ushers-in-a-new-era-for-e-commerce.
67. Nikki Baird, "Livestream Shopping Is Not Going to Take Over E-Commerce," *Forbes*, March 5, 2023. https://www.forbes.com/sites/nikkibaird/2023/03/05/livestream-shopping-is-not-going-to-take-over-e-commerce/.

Chapter 2

1. Ami Sedghi, Diane von Furstenberg and Net-a-Porter Team Up to Sell Google Glass," *The Guardian*, June 9, 2014. https://www.theguardian.com/technology/2014/jun/09/diane-von-furstenberg-google-glass-net-a-porter.
2. Amanda Cosco, "Fashion and Technology Collide on the Runway at Fashion Art Toronto," *Toronto Star*, April 26, 2015. https://www.amandacosco.com/content/fashion-and-technology-collide.
3. Amanda Cosco, "Fashion and Technology Collide on the Runway at Fashion Art Toronto," *Toronto Star*, April 26, 2015. https://www.amandacosco.com/content/fashion-and-technology-collide.
4. Google. "Made with Code Zac Posen," *Google Blog*, September 11, 2015. https://blog.google/outreach-initiatives/arts-culture/made-with-code-zac-posen/.
5. Brittany Talarico, Zac Posen and Google Partner to Create an LED-Coded Gown–and You Have to See It on Coco Rocha," *People*, May 3, 2016. https://people.com/style/zac-posen-and-google-partner-to-create-a-led-coded-gown-and-you-have-to-see-it-on-coco-rocha/.
6. Amanda Cosco, "Why Toronto Is a Hotbed of Pioneering Wearable Technology," *The Globe and Mail*, January 15, 2015. https://www.amandacosco.com/content/why-toronto-is-a-hotbed-of-pioneering-wearable-technology.
7. Amanda Cosco, Why Toronto Is a Hotbed of Pioneering Wearable Technology," *The Globe and Mail*, January 15, 2015. https://www.theglobeandmail.com/technology/why-toronto-is-a-hotbed-of-pioneering-wearable-technology/article22447906/.
8. Amanda Cosco, Why Toronto Is a Hotbed of Pioneering Wearable Technology," *The Globe and Mail*, January 15, 2015. https://www.theglobeandmail.com/technology/why-toronto-is-a-hotbed-of-pioneering-wearable-technology/article22447906/.
9. Glogger, "MannGlassEye1999crop," *Wikimedia Commons*, June 29, 2012. https://commons.wikimedia.org/wiki/File:MannGlassEye1999crop.jpg.
10. Amanda Cosco, Why Toronto Is a Hotbed of Pioneering Wearable Technology," *The Globe and Mail*, January 15, 2015. https://www.theglobe

andmail.com/technology/why-toronto-is-a-hotbed-of-pioneering-wearable-technology/article22447906/.

11. Gregory Ferenstein, Hands-on with the Muse Brain-Sensing Headband: The Most Important Wearable of 2014 (Exclusive)," *VentureBeat*, December 8, 2014. https://venturebeat.com/business/hands-on-with-the-muse-brain-sensing-headband-the-most-important-wearable-of-2014-exclusive/.
12. Rebecca Cringean. "Silicon Valley Fashion Week Finishes Up Its Second Season and Gears Up for Growth," *The Spin-Off*, November 4, 2016. https://www.the-spin-off.com/news/portrait/Interview-Silicon-Valley-Fashion-Week-Finishes-Up-Its-Second-Season-and-Gears-Up-For-Growth-12660.
13. Amanda Cosco, "The Brave New Future of High-Tech Fashion," *Toronto Star*, October 31, 2015. https://www.thestar.com/life/beauty-and-fashion/the-brave-new-future-of-high-tech-fashion/article_e8296e1a-e519-5c6e-9fc4-a61d75c925ae.html.
14. Amanda Cosco, "Canadian-Made Wearable Tech Monitoring Astronauts' Health in Space," *Toronto Star*, February 27, 2020. https://www.thestar.com/life/canadian-made-wearable-tech-monitoring-astronauts-health-in-space/article_8c731929-90cb-5db7-97a2-a3d93995656e.html.
15. Electric Runway, "Electric Runway Covers MakeFashion 2016," YouTube video, 4:47, April 10, 2016. https://www.youtube.com/watch?v=0LcEdSFvYE0.
16. Paul Chi, "Met Gala 2016: See Every Star on the Red Carpet," *Vanity Fair*, May 3, 2016. https://www.vanityfair.com/style/2016/05/met-gala-2016-red-carpet.
17. Amanda Cosco, "The Social Age of Wearable Tech: Beyond the Quantified Self," *Wareable*, March 7, 2016. https://www.wareable.com/wearable-tech/the-social-age-of-wearable-tech-beyond-the-quantified-self.
18. Amanda Cosco, "Billie Whitehouse—'Design Is Emotional,'" *Electric Runway Podcast*, episode 1, November 19, 2015. https://electricrunwayreport.substack.com/p/electric-runway-episode-1-billie-514.

19. Amanda Cosco, "Behnaz Farahi: Fashion Is Architecture," *Electric Runway Podcast*, episode 11, February 11, 2016. Buzzsprout. https://www.buzzsprout.com/admin/629959/episodes/1778875-electric-runway-episode-11-behnaz-farahi-fashion-is-architecture.
20. Deena Robinson, "10 Companies Called Out for Greenwashing," Earth.org, July 17, 2022. https://earth.org/greenwashing-companies-corporations/#:~:text=For%20example%2C%20in%202019%2C%20H%26M,themselves%20appear%20more%20environmentally%20friendly.

Chapter 3

1. World Bank, "How Dialogue Is Shifting Bangladesh's Textile Industry from Pollution Problem to Pollution Solution," *World Bank*, February 15,2017. https://www.worldbank.org/en/news/feature/2017/02/15/how-dialogue-is-shifting-bangladeshs-textile-industry-from-pollution-problem-to-pollution-solution.
2. Nazra Mahjabeen Sabet and Ayman Anika, "Bangladesh's Fashion Pollution: A Wake-Up Call," *Asia News Network*, June 6, 2024. Accessed November 26, 2024. https://asianews.network/bangladeshs-fashion-pollution-a-wake-up-call/.
3. IPEN, "Study Finds Textile Industry in Bangladesh a Significant Source of PFAS Water Pollution," accessed November 14, 2024. https://ipen.org/news/study-finds-textile-industry-bangladesh-significant-source-pfas-water-pollution.
4. Md. Kamruzzaman and SM Najmus Sakib, "Chemicals, Industrial Waste Contamination Turn 6 Bangladesh Rivers Untreatable," Anadolu Agency, March 14, 2022. https://www.aa.com.tr/en/asia-pacific/chemicals-industrial-waste-contamination-turn-6-bangladesh-rivers-untreatable/2534527.
5. Energy Policy Institute at the University of Chicago (EPIC), "Air Quality Life Index (AQLI) Annual Update 2023: The Global Burden of Particulate Air Pollution," August 2023. https://aqli.epic.uchicago.edu/wp-content/uploads/2023/08/AQLI_2023_Report-Global.pdf.

6. https://www.eco-business.com/news/bangladesh-is-losing-its-battle-with-air-pollution/.
7. Uddin, M. (2022). *Bangladesh Stories*. Dhaka, ULAB Press.
8. "What Is Automation?" IBM, accessed December 22, 2024. https://www.ibm.com/topics/automation.
9. Rohit Panikkar, Leon Xiao, Anand Sahu, and Rohit Sood, "Your Questions About Automation, Answered," McKinsey & Company, July 8, 2022. https://www.mckinsey.com/capabilities/operations/our-insights/your-questions-about-automation-answered.
10. James Manyika et al., "A Future That Works: Automation, Employment, and Productivity," McKinsey Global Institute, January 2017. https://www.mckinsey.com/~/media/mckinsey/featured%20insights/Digital%20Disruption/Harnessing%20automation%20for%20a%20future%20that%20works/MGI-A-future-that-works-Executive-summary.ashx.
11. Jon Emont, "The Robots Are Coming for Garment Workers. That's Good for the U.S., Bad for Poor Countries," *Wall Street Journal*, February 16, 2018, https://www.wsj.com/articles/the-robots-are-coming-for-garment-workers-thats-good-for-the-u-s-bad-for-poor-countries-1518797631.
12. Beckert, S. (2014). *Empire of Cotton: A Global History*. New York: Alfred A. Knopf.
13. Green, N.L. (1999). Sweatshop Migrations: The Garment Industry Between Home and Shop. *American Behavioral Scientist* 42 (6): 987–1000.
14. Jordyn Holman, "Textile Mills in the Carolinas Are Closing. Tariffs and Trade Policy Are to Blame," *New York Times*, January 21, 2024. https://www.nytimes.com/2024/01/21/business/economy/textile-mills-carolina-trade-de-minimis.html.
15. Friedrichs, A. (2018). Sewing Modernity: How the Sewing Machine Allowed for a Distinctively Feminine Experience of Modernity. *aspeers* 11: 51–75. https://www.aspeers.com/sites/default/files/pdf/friedrichs.pdf.
16. Gordon, S. (2009). *Make It Yourself: Home Sewing, Gender, and Culture, 1890–1930*. New York: Columbia University Press. http://www.gutenberg-e.org/gordon/.

17. Tansy Hoskins, "'They Left Us Starving': How the Fashion Industry Abandoned Its Workers." *openDemocracy*, January 18, 2021. https://www.opendemocracy.net/en/oureconomy/they-left-us-starving-how-fashion-industry-abandoned-its-workers/.
18. Jordyn Holman, "Textile Mills in the Carolinas Are Closing. Tariffs and Trade Policy Are to Blame," *New York Times*, January 21, 2024, https://www.nytimes.com/2024/01/21/business/economy/textile-mills-carolina-trade-de-minimis.html
19. Anne-Marie Schiro, "Fashion: Two New Stores That Cruise Fashion's Fast Lane," *New York Times*, December 31, 1989. https://www.nytimes.com/1989/12/31/style/fashion-two-new-stores-that-cruise-fashion-s-fast-lane.html.
20. Anne-Marie Schiro, "Fashion: Two New Stores That Cruise Fashion's Fast Lane," *New York Times*, December 31, 1989. https://www.nytimes.com/1989/12/31/style/fashion-two-new-stores-that-cruise-fashion-s-fast-lane.html.
21. Anne-Marie Schiro, "Fashion: Two New Stores That Cruise Fashion's Fast Lane," *New York Times*, December 31, 1989. https://www.nytimes.com/1989/12/31/style/fashion-two-new-stores-that-cruise-fashion-s-fast-lane.html
22. Retailisation, "How Vertical Integration Helps Fashion Leaders Grow," accessed December 22, 2024. https://www.retailisation.com/insights/how-vertical-integration-helps-fashion-leaders-grow#:~:text=How%20does%20Zara%20use%20vertical,sold%20annually%20in%20their%20stores.
23. "How Zara's Supply Chain Is Driving Its Success," ThomasNet Insights, accessed December 22, 2024. https://www.thomasnet.com/insights/zara-supply-chain/.
24. "The Zara Phenomenon: How Fast Fashion Redefined the Global Retail Industry," *Retail Times*, accessed December 22, 2024. https://retailtimes.co.uk/the-zara-phenomenon-how-fast-fashion-redefined-the-global-retail-industry/#:~:text=Ortega's%20vision%20was%20simple%20yet,the%20cornerstone%20of%20its%20success.

25. Channing Hargrove, "Balenciaga's Latest Sneakers Look an Awful Lot Like Zara's," Refinery29, September 27, 2017. https://www.refinery29.com/en-us/2017/09/174102/balenciaga-sneakers-zara-knock-off.
26. Gabby Bess, "How Fashion Brands like Zara Can Get Away with Stealing Artists' Designs," Vice, July 22, 2016. https://www.vice.com/en/article/how-fashion-brands-like-zara-can-get-away-with-stealing-artists-designs-tuesday-bassen/.
27. Eric Wilson, "Dress for Less and Less," *New York Times*, May 29, 2008. https://www.nytimes.com/2008/05/29/fashion/29PRICE.html.
28. More Perfect Union, "It's Not Just Shein: Why Are ALL Your Clothes Worse Now?" YouTube video, 14:53, July 20, 2023. https://www.youtube.com/watch?v=jCwbU41Icfw.
29. Clean Clothes Campaign, "Climate Change," accessed November 26, 2024. https://cleanclothes.org/climate-change.
30. "Fashion Waste Facts and Statistics," *Business Waste*, accessed November 27, 2024. https://www.businesswaste.co.uk/your-waste/textile-recycling/fashion-waste-facts-and-statistics/.
31. @e.cxhi, TikTok video, People Don't Love Their Clothing Anymore, February 3, 2024. https://www.tiktok.com/@e.cxhi/video/7331556829383626015.
32. Elizabeth Paton, "H&M, a Fashion Giant, Has a Problem: $4.3 Billion in Unsold Clothes," *New York Times*, March 27, 2018. https://www.nytimes.com/2018/03/27/business/hm-clothes-stock-sales.html.
33. Elizabeth Paton, "H&M, a Fashion Giant, Has a Problem: $4.3 Billion in Unsold Clothes," *New York Times*, March 27, 2018. https://www.nytimes.com/2018/03/27/business/hm-clothes-stock-sales.html.
34. World Bank, "El Costo de la Moda Para el Medio Ambiente," *World Bank*, September 23, 2019. https://www.worldbank.org/en/news/feature/2019/09/23/costo-moda-medio-ambiente.
35. United Nations Environment Programme (UNEP), "Fashion's Tiny Hidden Secret," *UNEP*, accessed November 26, 2024. https://www.unep.org/news-and-stories/story/fashions-tiny-hidden-secret#:~:text=Laundry%20alone%20causes%20around%20half,clear%20humans%20consume%20plastic%20regularly.

36. Don-Alvin Adegeest, "Garment Workers Among the Lowest-Paid Industrial Workers Globally," *FashionUnited*, January 5, 2024. https://fashionunited.uk/news/fashion/garment-workers-among-the-lowest-paid-industrial-workers-globally/2024010573416.
37. Jon Emont, "Big Fashion Still Hasn't Figured Out How to Pay a Living Wage," *Wall Street Journal*, December 30, 2023. https://www.wsj.com/business/big-fashion-still-hasnt-figured-out-how-to-pay-a-living-wage-3675153f.
38. Clean Clothes Campaign, "Unsafe Workplaces," accessed November 29, 2024. https://cleanclothes.org/unsafe-workplaces.
39. Tansy Hoskins, "'They Left Us Starving': How the Fashion Industry Abandoned Its Workers," openDemocracy, January 18, 2021. https://www.opendemocracy.net/en/oureconomy/they-left-us-starving-how-fashion-industry-abandoned-its-workers/.
40. CityNews, "The Reasons Clothing Sucks Now | The Big Story," November 15, 2004 https://www.youtube.com/watch?v=DkCLF3mZIF8
41. u/crown_wonderland, "Aritzia Has Become Sooo Tacky Now," Reddit, March 23, 2022, https://www.reddit.com/r/Aritzia/comments/tjg9rr/aritzia_has_become_sooo_tacky_now/?rdt=35395.
42. __kamikaze__, comment on u/crown_wonderland, "Aritzia Has Become Sooo Tacky Now," Reddit, March 23, 2022. https://www.reddit.com/r/Aritzia/comments/tjg9rr/aritzia_has_become_sooo_tacky_now/?rdt=35395.
43. Izzie Ramirez, "Your Stuff Is Actually Worse Now," *Vox*, January 4, 2023. https://www.vox.com/the-goods/23529587/consumer-goods-quality-fast-fashion-technology.
44. Author interview with David Birnbaum, August 27, 2024.
45. Sophie Benson, "Are Microfactories the Answer to Making Fashion On-Demand?" *Vogue Business*, May 27, 2024. https://www.voguebusiness.com/story/companies/are-microfactories-the-answer-to-making-fashion-on-demand.
46. Adrián Hernández, "Learning from Adidas' Speedfactory Blunder," *Supply Chain Dive*, February 4, 2020. https://www.supplychaindive

.com/news/adidas-speedfactory-blunder-distributed-operations/571678/.

47. Adrián Hernández, "Learning from Adidas' Speedfactory Blunder," *Supply Chain Dive*, February 4, 2020. https://www.supplychaindive.com/news/adidas-speedfactory-blunder-distributed-operations/571678/.
48. Uddin, M. (2022). *Bangladesh Stories*. Dhaka: ULAB Press.
49. Author interview with Jonathan Zornow.
50. Elizabeth Segran, "Unspun's Weaving Machine Could Help Solve the Fast-Fashion Crisis," *Fast Company*, August 12, 2024. https://www.fastcompany.com/91147669/unspun-weaving-machine-fast-fashion.
51. "What Is 3D Printing? An Overview," 3DPrinting.com, accessed December 22, 2024. https://3dprinting.com/what-is-3d-printing/.
52. Kristen, P. (2017). *Printed to the Nines*. New Degree Press.
53. SLS is a type of 3D printing.
54. Dan Howarth, "3D-Printed Dress Worn by Dita Von Teese Unveiled," Dezeen, March 7, 2013. https://www.dezeen.com/2013/03/07/3d-printed-dress-dita-von-teese-michael-schmidt-francis-bitonti/.
55. Danit Peleg, "3D Printing Fashion: How I 3D-Printed Clothes at Home," YouTube video, 11:07, July 22, 2015. https://www.youtube.com/watch?v=3s94mIhCyt4.

Chapter 4

1. Simon Greenwold, "Spatial Computing," master's thesis, Massachusetts Institute of Technology, 2003. https://acg.media.mit.edu/people/simong/thesis/SpatialComputing.pdf.
2. Tom Emrich, "Mixed Reality, Wearable Tech, and AI: 2024, the Year Spatial Computing Takes Off," *The Drum*, January 22, 2024. https://www.thedrum.com/opinion/2024/01/22/mixed-reality-wearable-tech-and-ai-2024-the-year-spatial-computing-takes.

3. Dan Howarth, "Immersive Virtual World by Gareth Pugh and Inition Installed at Selfridges," *Dezeen*, January 11, 2014. https://www.dezeen.com/2014/01/11/immersive-virtual-world-by-gareth-pugh-and-inition-installed-at-selfridges/.
4. "Live 360 Degree Virtual Reality Catwalk Experience for Topshop," YouTube video, 1:31, posted by "Topshop," February 22, 2014. https://www.youtube.com/watch?v=c8jSlq8Tqlc.
5. Erika Adams and Adele Chapin, "Rebecca Minkoff Is the First Designer to Let You Watch a Show in Virtual Reality," *Racked*, September 3, 2015. https://www.racked.com/2015/9/3/9247771/rebecca-minkoff-virtual-reality-headset-google-cardboard.
6. Hiroko Tabuchi, "Tommy Hilfiger Introduces Virtual Reality Headsets for Shoppers," *New York Times*, October 20, 2015. https://www.nytimes.com/2015/10/21/business/tommy-hilfiger-introduces-virtual-reality-headsets-for-shoppers.html.
7. HTC Vive, "HTC VIVE Partners with GQ to Ignite Shanghai Fashion Week with First-Ever VR Runway Show Featuring Fashion Designed in VR," *HTC Vive Newsroom*, March 29, 2018. https://www.vive.com/us/newsroom/2018-03-29-2/.
8. M. Marko, "29 Virtual Reality Statistics to Know in 2023," *Leftronic*, March 7, 2023. https://leftronic.com/blog/virtual-reality-statistics.
9. Statista, "Reported Price of Leading Consumer VR Headsets Worldwide as of 2023, by Device," accessed December 26, 2024. https://www.statista.com/statistics/1096886/reported-price-of-leading-consumer-vr-headsets-by-device/.
10. Cheon, E.-J. and Pyo, J.-H. (2021). Clinical Predictors of Cybersickness in Virtual Reality (VR) Among Highly Immersive Users. *Scientific Reports* 11 (1): 12190. https://doi.org/10.1038/s41598-021-91573-w.
11. Meta announced in the fall of 2024 it would shut down Spark AR Studio in a move that surprised many.
12. "Swipe Right to Meet Your Perfect Lipstick Match," *Toronto Star*, accessed December 2, 2024. https://www.thestar.com/life/swipe-right-to-meet-your-perfect-lipstick-match/article_666eccf5-08b5-51b6-a713-9510069e31ba.html.

13. Hilary Milnes, "How Rebecca Minkoff's Digital Store Rewrites the Rules of Retail," *Digiday*, October 8, 2015. https://digiday.com/marketing/rebecca-minkoff-digital-store/.
14. Hilary Milnes, "How Rebecca Minkoff's Digital Store Rewrites the Rules of Retail," *Digiday*, October 8, 2015. https://digiday.com/marketing/rebecca-minkoff-digital-store/.
15. Clayton O'Toole, Jeremy Schneider, Kate Smaje, and Laura LaBerge, "How COVID-19 Has Pushed Companies over the Technology Tipping Point—and Transformed Business Forever," *McKinsey & Company*, October 5, 2020. https://www.mckinsey.com/capabilities/strategy-and-corporate-finance/our-insights/how-covid-19-has-pushed-companies-over-the-technology-tipping-point-and-transformed-business-forever.
16. Helen Papagiannis, "How AR Is Redefining Retail in the Pandemic," *Harvard Business Review*, October 2020. https://hbr.org/2020/10/how-ar-is-redefining-retail-in-the-pandemic.
17. Sapna Maheshwari, "Lululemon to Buy Mirror, a Fitness Start-Up, for $500 Million," *New York Times*, June 29, 2020. https://www.nytimes.com/2020/06/29/business/lululemon-buys-mirror.html.
18. Brooke DiPalma, "Lululemon's Ill-Timed Mirror Acquisition Is Now Almost Worthless," *Yahoo Finance*, December 21, 2024. https://finance.yahoo.com/news/lululemons-ill-timed-mirror-acquisition-is-now-almost-worthless-124822875.html.
19. Graham Bowley and Yuliya Parshina-Kottas, "David Bowie's Costumes in Augmented Reality," *New York Times*, March 20, 2018. https://www.nytimes.com/interactive/2018/03/20/arts/design/bowie-costumes-ar-3d-ul.html.
20. Elle Hunt, "Faking It: How Selfie Dysmorphia Is Driving People to Seek Surgery," *The Guardian*, January 23, 2019. https://www.theguardian.com/lifeandstyle/2019/jan/23/faking-it-how-selfie-dysmorphia-is-driving-people-to-seek-surgery.
21. Technality, "Bold Glamour: The Real Cost of Generative AI," YouTube video, 4:55, March 10, 2023. https://www.youtube.com/watch?v=y3-rpEYajXA&t=.

22. Lindsay Kornick, "New Bold Glamour TikTok Filter Blasted as 'Psychological Warfare' and 'Pure Evil,'" *Fox News*, February 28, 2023. https://www.foxnews.com/media/new-bold-glamour-tiktok-filter-blasted-psychological-warfare-pure-evil.
23. Björn Wallenberg, "Ikea on the Collaboration with Apple: 'Super Interesting for Us,'" *DI Digital*, June 17, 2017. https://www.di.se/digital/ikea-om-samarbetet-med-apple-superintressant-for-oss/.
24. Aircards, "What Is WebAR? A Complete Guide to Browser-Based Augmented Reality," *Aircards Blog*, accessed December 26, 2024. https://www.aircards.co/blog/what-is-webar?utm_source=chatgpt.com.
25. Shopify, "The Complete Guide to Ecommerce Returns," *Shopify Enterprise Blog*, accessed December 10, 2024. https://www.shopify.com/enterprise/blog/ecommerce-returns.
26. National Retail Federation, "Customer Returns in the Retail Industry," 2024. https://nrf.com/research/customer-returns-retail-industry.
27. Electric Runway, "This Rihanna-Backed Startup Is Using Machine Learning to Innovate Fit," *Electric Runway Podcast*, episode 113, April 21, 2022. https://www.buzzsprout.com/629959/episodes/10518667-this-rihanna-backed-startup-is-using-machine-learning-to-innovate-fit.
28. Reed Tucker, "Is Google Glass Cool or Just Plain Creepy?" *New York Post*, July 14, 2014. https://nypost.com/2014/07/14/is-google-glass-cool-or-just-plain-creepy/.
29. KRON, "Woman Attacks Journalist, Destroys His Google Glass," YouTube video, 1:43, April 14, 2014. https://www.youtube.com/watch?v=Sigtu1m9N3I Woman Attacks Journalist, Destroys His Google Glass.
30. Stephanie Condon, "Why GE's Use of Google Glass Marks a Turning Point for AR," *ZDNet*, August 14, 2017. https://www.zdnet.com/article/why-ges-use-of-google-glass-marks-a-turning-point-for-ar/.
31. Obsess, "Obsess Launches the First-Ever Shopping Apps for Apple Vision Pro," *Obsess* (blog). February 2, 2024. https://obsessar.com/blog-obsess-launches-the-first-ever-shopping-apps-for-apple-vision-pro/.
32. Casey Neistat, "The Thing No One Will Say About Apple Vision Pro," YouTube video, 12:34, February 3, 2024. https://www.youtube.com/watch?v=UvkgmyfMPks.

Chapter 5

1. Natashah Hitti, "Hanifa Presents Pink Label Congo Fashion Collection Using 3D Models," *Dezeen*, June 5, 2020. https://www.dezeen.com/2020/06/05/hanifa-pink-label-congo-fashion-collection-3d-models/.
2. Natashah Hitti, "Hanifa Presents Pink Label Congo Fashion Collection Using 3D Models," *Dezeen*, June 5, 2020. https://www.dezeen.com/2020/06/05/hanifa-pink-label-congo-fashion-collection-3d-models/.
3. Teddy Tinson, "A Virtual Fashion Show, Without the Hiccups," *The New York Times*, July 8, 2020. https://www.nytimes.com/2020/07/08/style/hanifa-pink-congo-avatar.html.
4. Thomas Stackpole, "What Is Web3?" *Harvard Business Review*, May 2022. https://hbr.org/2022/05/what-is-web3.
5. Thomas Stackpole, "What Is Web3?" *Harvard Business Review*, May 2022. https://hbr.org/2022/05/what-is-web3.
6. Luca Solca, "Prada Needs More Than a Tune-Up." *Business of Fashion*, accessed January 3, 2025. https://www.businessoffashion.com/opinions/luxury/prada-needs-more-than-a-tune-up/.
7. Ruonan Zheng, "Prada Quietly Launched on Chinese E-Commerce Platforms. Can It Keep Up?" *Jing Daily*, January 10, 2018. https://jingdaily.com/posts/prada-china-e-commerce/.
8. "Social Media Case Study: Burberry Encourages Customer Participation with Art of the Trench," *Digital Training Academy*, July 2013. http://www.digitaltrainingacademy.com/casestudies/2013/07/social_media_case_study_burberry_encourages_customer_participation_with_art_of_trench.php.
9. Cody Godwin, "The £7,500 Dress That Does Not Exist," BBC News, November 14, 2019. https://www.bbc.com/news/business-49794403.
10. This Outfit Does Not Exist, Instagram page, accessed December 15, 2024. https://www.instagram.com/thisoutfitdoesnotexist.
11. Philip Maughan, "Inside RTFKT: The Virtual Sneaker Brand Merging Fashion & Tech." Highsnobiety, accessed January 3, 2025. https://www.highsnobiety.com/p/rtfkt-interview/.

12. Neer Varshney, "Someone Paid $170,000 for the Most Expensive CryptoKitty Ever," The Next Web, January 2, 2019. https://thenextweb.com/news/most-expensive-cryptokitty#:~:text=Someone%20purchased%20Dragon%2C%20a%20CryptoKitty,sale)%20in%20December%20last%20year.
13. Mary Monson Solicitors. "Cryptocurrency and NFT Pump and Dump Scheme Fraud." Mary Monson Solicitors. Accessed December 15, 2024. https://marymonson.co.uk/free-legal-advice/cryptocurrency-and-nft-pump-and-dump-scheme-fraud/.
14. Walter Loeb, "Gucci Leads in Crypto Transactions," *Forbes*, August 4, 2022. https://www.forbes.com/sites/walterloeb/2022/08/04/gucci-leads-in-crypto-transactions/.
15. Dana Thomas, "Dolce & Gabbana Just Set a $6 Million Record for Fashion NFTs." *The New York Times*, October 4, 2021. https://www.nytimes.com/2021/10/04/style/dolce-gabbana-nft.html.
16. Meghan Hall, "Dolce & Gabbana Under Fire with Class Action Lawsuit Surrounding NFT Project." Yahoo Finance, December 28, 2024. https://finance.yahoo.com/news/dolce-gabbana-under-fire-class-164500548.html.
17. Paul Tassi, "Epic Reveals It Made $50 Million from One Set of 'Fortnite' Skins," *Forbes*, May 11, 2021. https://www.forbes.com/sites/paultassi/2021/05/11/epic-reveals-it-made-50-million-from-one-set-of-fortnite-skins/.
18. SuperJoost, "Eyes Wide Shut," Substack, June 8, 2023. https://superjoost.substack.com/p/eyes-wide-shut.
19. "Coach Introduces 'Find Your Courage'." *PR Newswire*, February 7, 2024. https://www.prnewswire.com/news-releases/coach-introduces-find-your-courage-302063081.html.
20. "Bitstrips," Wikipedia, last modified November 22, 2023. https://en.wikipedia.org/wiki/Bitstrips.
21. Alice Finney, "Metaverse Fashion Week to Take Place in Decentraland," *Dezeen*, March 21, 2022. https://www.dezeen.com/2022/03/21/decentraland-metaverse-fashion-week-2022/.
22. "TOMMY HILFIGER Joins the First-Ever Decentraland Metaverse Fashion Week," PVH, March 24, 2022. https://www.pvh.com/news/tommy-hilfiger-metaverse-fashion-week-2022.

23. "Buuut... Fashion Week in the Metaverse Turned Out to Be a Flop," Ypulse, April 6, 2023. https://www.ypulse.com/newsfeed/2023/04/06/buuut-fashion-week-in-the-metaverse-turned-out-to-be-a-flop/.
24. Jay Peters, "Decentraland's Metaverse Fashion Week Shows How Much Work Virtual Runways Have Left to Do," *The Verge*, March 28, 2023. https://www.theverge.com/23668846/decentraland-metaverse-fashion-week-2023.
25. James Clayton, "Metaverse: What Happened to Mark Zuckerberg's Next Big Thing?" BBC News, September 25, 2023. https://www.bbc.com/news/technology-66913551.
26. Google Trends, "Interest over Time for 'Metaverse,'" accessed December 14, 2024. https://trends.google.com/trends/explore?date=all&q=metaverse&hl=en.
27. Scott Stein, "The Metaverse Isn't a Destination. It's a Metaphor'," CNET, March 21, 2022. https://www.cnet.com/tech/computing/features/the-metaverse-isnt-a-destination-its-a-metaphor/.
28. Baconandmeggs, "Chat Do You Think I'll Ever Get My Money Back #Scammed #TikTokMadeMeBuyIt," TikTok, October 14, 2024. https://vm.tiktok.com/ZMkYJTEx2/.
29. Dominique Muret, "Louis Vuitton Launches New NFT: A Virtual Trunk Costing 6,000 Euros." *Fashion Network*, accessed January 3, 2025. https://ww.fashionnetwork.com/news/Louis-vuitton-launches-new-nft-a-virtual-trunk-costing-6-000-euros,1581431.html.
30. Marc Bain, "Roblox to Sell Physical Goods Through Shopify Integration," *The Business of Fashion*, September 6, 2024. businessoffashion.com.

Chapter 6

1. The Tonight Show Starring Jimmy Fallon, "Tonight Showbotics: Jimmy Meets Sophia the Human-Like Robot," YouTube video, 8:03, April 25, 2017. https://www.youtube.com/watch?v=Bg_tJvCA8zw.
2. Euronews, "OpenAI Halts Using ChatGPT's Sky Voice after Complaints It Sounded 'Eerily' like Scarlett Johansson," last modified May 21, 2024. https://www.euronews.com/next/2024/05/21/openai-removes-ai-

assistant-voice-that-resembles-scarlett-johansson#:~:text=OpenAI%20halts%20using%20ChatGPT's%20Sky,'eerily'%20like%20hers%20%7C%20Euronews.

3. TED, "The Disappearing Computer — and a World Where You Can Take AI Everywhere | Imran Chaudhri | TED," YouTube video, May 9, 2023, accessed January 6, 2025. https://www.youtube.com/watch?v=gMsQO5u7-NQ.
4. Marques Brownlee, "The Worst Product I've Ever Reviewed... For Now." *YouTube video*, 20:11. Published April 14, 2024. https://www.youtube.com/watch?v=TitZV6k8zfA.
5. David Pierce, "Rabbit R1 Review: Nothing to See Here." *The Verge*, May 2, 2024. https://www.theverge.com/2024/5/2/24147159/rabbit-r1-review-ai-gadget.
6. Eric Schmidt, "The Tinkerer's Apprentice." *Project Syndicate*, January 19, 2015. https://www.project-syndicate.org/magazine/google-european-commission-and-disruptive-technological-change-by-eric-schmidt-2015-01#:~:text=They%20started%20with%20images.,well%2C%20caught%20the%20world's%20attention.
7. Google. "Ooh Ahh . . . Google Images Presents a Nicer Way to Surf the Visual Web." *Google Blog*, July 20, 2010. https://googleblog.blogspot.com/2010/07/ooh-ahh-google-images-presents-nicer.html.
8. MG Siegler, "Google Image Search: Over 10 Billion Images, 1 Billion Pageviews a Day," *TechCrunch*, July 20, 2010. https://techcrunch.com/2010/07/20/google-image-search/?utm_source=chatgpt.com.
9. February 8, 2017. https://www.theverge.com/2017/2/8/14549798/pinterest-lens-visual-discovery-shazam.
10. Luke Leitch, 2023. "Edward Crutchley Spring 2024 Ready-to-Wear Collection." *Vogue*. October 2, 2023. https://www.vogue.com/fashion-shows/spring-2024-ready-to-wear/edward-crutchley.
11. Nyima Jobe, "How AI Is Amplifying Creativity in the Fashion World," *The Guardian*, February 8, 2024. https://www.theguardian.com/fashion/2024/feb/08/ai-london-fashion-week.

12. Marc Bain, "H&M Group's New AI Tool Lets Anyone Play Designer," *The Business of Fashion*, October 24, 2023. https://www.businessoffashion.com/articles/technology/hm-group-is-using-ai/.
13. "Levi's Faces Backlash for Plan to Use AI-Generated Models to Increase Diversity," *Brainz Magazine*, March 29, 2023. https://www.brainzmagazine.com/post/levi-s-faces-backlash-for-plan-to-use-ai-generated-models-to-increase-diversity.
14. Levi Strauss & Co. 2023. "LS&Co. Partners with Lalaland.ai to Test AI-Generated Models." *Unzipped*. March 22, 2023. https://www.levistrauss.com/2023/03/22/lsco-partners-with-lalaland-ai/.
15. Meredith Clark, 2023. "Levi's Faces Backlash over Plans to Use AI Models to Increase Diversity." *The Independent*. March 25, 2023. https://www.independent.co.uk/life-style/fashion/levis-ai-models-diversity-backlash-b2310280.html.
16. Tarrant Glynn, 2023. "Levi's Decision to Use AI Models Instead of Real Models to Promote Diversity Misses the Point. Representation Matters, and This Feels Like a Step Backward." *X* (formerly Twitter), March 26, 2023. https://x.com/GlynnTarrant/status/1639907035763417090.
17. Ashley Carman. https://www.theverge.com/authors/ashley-carman.
18. Amanda Cosco, 2016. "Chatbots Go Chic—Epytom on AI for Fashion." *Electric Runway* (podcast). Episode 42, November 2016. https://electricrunway.com.
19. u/MyBallsBern4Bernie. "AI Fashion Stylist." *r/fashionwomens35*. March 15, 2023. https://www.reddit.com/r/fashionwomens35/comments/1btea1y/ai_fashion_stylist/.
20. Madeleine Schulz, "Personal Style Is Trapped in the Algorithm's Echo Chamber," *Vogue Business*, October 18, 2023. https://www.voguebusiness.com/story/fashion/personal-style-is-trapped-in-the-algorithms-echo-chamber.
21. Madeleine Schulz, "Personal Style Is Trapped in the Algorithm's Echo Chamber," *Vogue Business*, October 18, 2023. https://www.voguebusiness.com/story/fashion/personal-style-is-trapped-in-the-algorithms-echo-chamber.

22. Madeleine Schulz, "Personal Style Is Trapped in the Algorithm's Echo Chamber," *Vogue Business*, October 18, 2023. https://www.voguebusiness.com/story/fashion/personal-style-is-trapped-in-the-algorithms-echo-chamber.
23. Samantha West, "H&M Faced Backlash over Its Monkey Sweatshirt Ad. It Isn't the Company's Only Controversy," *The Washington Post*, January 19, 2018. https://www.washingtonpost.com/news/arts-and-entertainment/wp/2018/01/19/hm-faced-backlash-over-its-monkey-sweatshirt-ad-it-isnt-the-companys-only-controversy/.
24. Jenni Reid, "H&M Shares Jump 13% as Profit Smashes Expectations." *CNBC*, March 27, 2024, accessed January 6, 2025. https://www.cnbc.com/2024/03/27/hm-shares-jump-13percent-as-profit-smashes-expectations-.html.
25. BBC News, "Fashion Giants Like H&M and Burberry Burning New Clothes." July 19, 2018, accessed January 6, 2025. https://www.bbc.com/news/business-44885983.
26. Helene Moo, "I ordered a dupe of my own sweater." TikTok, July 2023. https://www.tiktok.com/@helenemoo/video/7424117586801036577?_t=8qSfPLb0GxB&_r=1.
27. The Fashion Law, "A New Lawsuit Lifts the Lid on Shein's AI-Powered Ultra-Fast Fashion Model." *The Fashion Law*, April 12, 2024. https://www.thefashionlaw.com/a-new-lawsuit-lifts-the-lid-on-sheins-ai-powered-ultra-fast-fashion-model/.
28. Laurel Deppen, "Shein RICO, Copyright Infringement Lawsuit." *Fashion Dive*, November 13, 2024. https://www.fashiondive.com/news/shein-rico-copyright-infringement-lawsuit/732787/.
29. Astha Rajvanshi, "How Shein's Use of AI is Reshaping Fast Fashion," *Time*, September 20, 2024. https://time.com/7022660/shein-ai-fast-fashion/.
30. Renan Botelho, "Legal Questions Arise as Walmart Sells 'Birkin Bag' Lookalike for $50," *Yahoo News*. December 31, 2023. https://www.yahoo.com/news/legal-questions-arise-walmart-birkin-175535502.html.
31. PYMNTS, "Walmart Expands Omnichannel Experiences and Fulfillment Solutions for Third-Party Sellers," August 2024. https://www.pymnts

.com/walmart/2024/walmart-expands-omnichannel-experiences-and-fulfillment-solutions-for-third-party-sellers/.

32. Joy Buolamwini, "How I'm Fighting Bias in Algorithms." TED, filmed November 2016, posted November 2016. https://www.ted.com/talks/joy_buolamwini_how_i_m_fighting_bias_in_algorithms.
33. R. Daneshjou et al., Disparities in dermatology AI performance on a diverse, curated clinical image set. *Science Advances*, August 12, 2022, 8(32):eabq6147. doi: 10.1126/sciadv.abq6147. Epub 2022 Aug 12. PMID: 35960806; PMCID: PMC9374341.
34. Maghan McDowell, "As Fashion Resets, Its Algorithms Should Too," *Vogue Business*, June 23, 2020. https://www.voguebusiness.com/technology/as-fashion-resets-its-algorithms-should-too?status=verified.
35. Katharine Miller, "Privacy in the AI Era: How Do We Protect Our Personal Information?" *Stanford Institute for Human-Centered Artificial Intelligence (HAI)*, March 18, 2024. https://hai.stanford.edu/news/privacy-ai-era-how-do-we-protect-our-personal-information.

Chapter 7

1. Amanda Cosco, "Episode 19: Aaron Rowley – A Textile Factory in a Box," *Electric Runway Podcast*, April 16, 2016. https://open.spotify.com/episode/1O51ocNRnQ3oNNpeiLooSr?si=d1df93cb17d447c2.
2. Daniel Cooper, "How Electroloom's Clothes-Printing Revolution Died," *Engadget*, September 14, 2017. https://www.engadget.com/2017-09-14-electroloom-clothes-printing-startup-death-aaron-rowley.html.
3. Fashion for Good, "Understanding Bio-Material Innovations: A Primer on the Science, Challenges, and Future Opportunities," December 2020, accessed December 16, 2024. https://fashionforgood.com/wp-content/uploads/2020/12/Understanding-Bio-Material-Innovations-Report.pdf.
4. "Biomaterials Market: Industry Analysis, Trends, and Forecast," Polaris Market Research, accessed June 28, 2024. https://www.polarismarketresearch.com/industry-analysis/biomaterials-market.

5. "Biomaterials Market: Global Forecast to 2027," MarketsandMarkets, accessed June 28, 2024. https://www.marketsandmarkets.com/Market-Reports/biomaterials-393.html.
6. Suzanne Lee, "Grow Your Own Clothes," TED Conferences video, 8:40, 2011. https://www.ted.com/talks/suzanne_lee_grow_your_own_clothes.
7. Amanda Cosco, "How Biotechnology Will Bring Our Clothes to Life," *Electric Runway Podcast*, November 20, 2017. https://open.spotify.com/episode/480Q1vtcOzQ9KKGF3W19du?si=e16a0eeaab284cc8.
8. Bolt Threads, *"Bringing Fashion into the Future: Microsilk™ Dress by Bolt Threads and Stella McCartney,"* YouTube video, 2:15, October 24, 2017. https://www.youtube.com/watch?v=u8fS6aR2_6g.
9. Stella McCartney, "Frayme Mylo™ Mycelium Bag," *Stella's World*, accessed June 28, 2024. https://www.stellamccartney.com/ca/en/stellas-world/frayme-mylo-mycelium-bag.
10. Ellen Rosen, "Are Mushrooms the Future of Alternative Leather?" *The New York Times*, December 14, 2022. https://www.nytimes.com/2022/12/14/business/leather-fake-mycelium-mushrooms-fashion.html.
11. Amanda Cosco, "EP 149: Biotechnology is the New Design Tool," *Electric Runway Podcast*, February 22, 2024. https://open.spotify.com/episode/6U0cpxiWYtqugK53w5Bamp.
12. Amanda Cosco, "In a World of Greenwashing, Modern Meadow Is the Real Deal," *Electric Runway Podcast*, May 2, 2023. https://open.spotify.com/episode/61QifGptM8gdJbPl5Y4PAF.
13. Electric Runway. "Coperni Bag Made of 99% Air." YouTube video, 7:22. Posted November 20, 2023. https://www.youtube.com/watch?v=JwI42xRv-Vk&t=567s.
14. de Monchaux, N. (2011). *Spacesuit: Fashioning Apollo*. Cambridge, MA: MIT Press.
15. "Hazel Fellows and the Women Who Made Apollo Spacesuits." *Smithsonian Voices: National Air and Space Museum Blog*, July 16, 2019. https://womenshistory.si.edu/blog/hazel-fellows-and-women-

who-made-apollo-spacesuits#:~:text=Smithsonian%20National%20Air%20and%20Space,Apollo%20program%20from%201962%2D1974.

16. Isabelle Dumé, "Supramolecular Biomass Foam Removes Microplastics from Water," *Physics World*, December 15, 2023. https://physicsworld.com/a/supramolecular-biomass-foam-removes-microplastics-from-water/.

About the Author

Amanda Cosco is a freelance creative strategist and multimedia journalist with over a decade of experience exploring the intersection of creativity and innovation. As the founder of Electric Runway, a leading platform covering how emerging technologies are transforming the global fashion industry, Amanda has built a reputation as a thought leader in the space where fashion and beauty meet the future.

Through Electric Runway, Amanda has reported from every stage of the fashion supply chain—from garment factories in Bangladesh to the front row at New York Fashion Week. She has interviewed more than 100 CEOs, designers, technologists, and change-makers in fashion innovation and has presented her research and reporting all over the world, including the United States, Nigeria, the Philippines, Estonia, Hong Kong, Spain, Finland, and Germany. Her work unpacks the transformative power of technology across retail, manufacturing, and consumer experiences.

On the business-to-business side, Amanda works with the most innovative brands on their runway to success through strategic brand development services.

Index

3D printing, 72–73, 88–92, 188
3D weaving technology, 87

A

Aarabi, Parham, 104
Aboah, Adwoa (3D model: London Fashion Week), 110
ACloset (digital wardrobe), 171
Adidas (micro-factory efforts), 86
Afterworld: The Age of Tomorrow (Balenciaga), 144
AirPods (Apple), launch, 61–62
Alexander McQueen
  Plato's Atlantis, 8–10
  robots/camera, usage, 37
  Spring/Summer 1999 show, 203–205
Alexander Wang and Vivo (designer phone), 31
Algorithmic bias, 181–183
Algorithmic Justice League, 183
Algorithmic monoculture, 172–174
AliExpress (online-only retailer), 22
Alphabots (Walmart), 92
AltspaceVR, 95–96
Amazon, impact, 14–15
Amoruso, Sophia, 17–18
Amusing Ourselves to Death (Postman), 5
Andersen, Hans Christian, 134–135
Apple Vision Pro, usage, 97, 123
Apple Watch, 50, 61–62
Apps, number (increase), 17
App store (Apple), launch, 14
Aritzia, 81–82
ARKit (Apple), usage, 106
Armani x Samsung (designer phone), 31
Artificial intelligence (AI), 157, 177–178
  personal stylist function, 168–173
  software, 159–161
Artificial Intelligence for Fashion (Luce), 161
ARworks, Vodafone launch, 110
ASOS, 14, 93, 163
Aspire Mirror, 182
Astroskin (Hexoskin), 52
Atanda, Adeyemi, 3
Atkinson, Nathalie, 27
Augmented apparel, 114–115
Augmented reality (AR), 97, 103–105, 150
  in-store AR, 106–109
  mirrors, usage, 106–107
Aura Blockchain Consortium, initiative/collaboration, 152
Automation, 67, 92–94
  fashion technology, equivalence, 72–74
  impact, 83
  threat, 73
Avatars, 146–148
Ayesu, Joseph, 206
Ayoung-Chee, Anya, 141

B

"Bad Romance" (Lady Gaga), 9
Balenciaga, 77
  Afterworld: The Age of Tomorrow, 144–145
  crypto payments, 139
  Gift Shop, 30
Bangladesh
  apparel exports, 68
  knit workers, employment, 74
Bangladesh Stories (Uddin), 71
Bankman-Fried, Sam (FTX crash), 141–143
Barbie Fashion Designer (Mattel online game), 83–84
Beckert, Sven, 73
Bellabeat, 46
Bertelli, Patrizio, 130
Betabrand, 44–45
Biddell, Evan, 36–37

Bieber, Hailey, 31
Biggs, Taylen (fashion host), 27
Bio-Alloy, creation, 196
BioLogic (bio-skin), 192–193
Biomaterials, 187, 189–190, 192–198
Biotechnology, 187, 189–190, 195–198
    challenges/future, 200–202
Bird, Matthew, 82–83
Birkin, Jane (Birkin bag), 180
Birnbaum, David, 83
Bitcoin, 138–139
Bitmoji (Bitstrips), 146–147
Bitonti, Francis, 57, 88
Bleasdale, Cecilia, 12–13
Blockchain technology, usage, 131
BODS (Marzano), 153
Bodycon dress (photo), 12
Bold Glamour Filter, examination, 113–114
Bolt Threads, 193–194
Boohoo (online-only retailer), 21
Bored Apes Yacht Club, 147–148
Bottega Veneta, offering, 30–31
Bowie, David (costumes, 3D examination), 111
Branded filters, usage, 111–114
Brands, media companies (equivalence), 28–29
Brown, Haniff, 120
Buolamwini, Joy, 182–183
Burberry, 116
    "Art of the Trench" campaign, 130–131
    Black (launch), limited-time lens (usage), 112
    inventory, destruction, 176
    see-now, buy-now approach, 19
Burch, Tory, 195
Burning Man, 38, 46–48, 50

C

Camera, impact, 23–24
"Caress of the Gaze" (3D-printed cape), 57
Celebrities, impact, 22–27
Chamberlain, Emma (YouTuber), 27
Chanel, physical pop-up, 112–113
ChatGPT, 160–161
Circular Fashion Summit, 95
Clean Girl, 18–20
Cline, Ernest, 148
Clustered Regularly Interspaced Short Palindromic Repeats (CRISPR), 190
Coelho, Camila (social media figure), 25
Commerce, application, 13–16
Computer vision, impact, 163–164
Connected clothing, 62–64, 71
Conscious Collection (H&M), 29
Conscious consumption, future, 205–210
Consumer Electronics Show (CES), 54–57, 108
Cook, Tim, 31, 123
Coperni
    Air Swipe bag, 198–200
    Spring/Summer 2023 presentation, 203–205
Cosco, Amanda, 41f, 49f, 56f, 133f
COVID-19 pandemic, impact, 4–5
Craft, return (future), 207—209
Creators, impact, 22–27
Crutchley, Edward (ready-to-wear collection, generative AI usage), 165
Crypto crash, 141–143
Cryptocurrencies, impact, 138, 155
CryptoKitties (Dapper Labs), development, 138–139
CryptoPunks (Larva Labs), launch, 140–141
Cutlan, Alison (CUTLAN Lab), 195
Cybersickness, 102–103

D

Danes, Claire (illuminated dress), 54
Darriba, Aduen, 58
DASH (clothing boutique), 24
Data
    privacy, 183–184
    scraping, 178–179
Decentraland (3D virtual-world platform), 149–150
Decentralization, advantages, 154
Dempsey, Laura, 49
Depop, 17, 207
Design-make-sell system, 85
Design-sell-make system, 85
Devil Wears Prada (comedy-drama), 20
Dierck, Christine, 65
Digital Product Passports (DPPs) digital record, 63, 65, 155
Digital thrifting, 16–18
Digital tools (adoption), COVID-19 (impact), 108–109
Digital wearables, creation, 153
Dijkstra, Maartje, 88–90
Dior
    Dior Eyes (head-mounted display), 100–101
    lenses, usage, 112

sunglasses (testing), AR (usage), 97
Direct-to-consumer content, 28
Disney Princess Magic Mirror, 106
DIY ethos, impact, 50
Dolce & Gabbana, NFT strategy (reconsideration), 142
Dolce & Gabbana x Motorola (designer phone), 31
Dorsey, Jack, 2–3
DressX (digital-only fashion marketplace), 135–136
Drinkwater, Matthew, 166
DrumPants, 59–60
Duffy, Patrick, 95

E

Ecofab Limited (sustainable label), 69–70
Electric Runway, launch, 48–50
Electroloom, 187–189
Electron-beam melting technology (GE Additive), 91
Embedded environments, usage, 111–112
Emotiv EPOC x Brainwave headset, 53
Emperor's New Clothes (Andersen), 134–136, 138
Empire of Cotton: A Global History (Beckert), 73
Emrich, Tom, 96
Epytom (chatbot), 170, 173
Esho, Tijion, 113

F

Fabric of Reality, The (Fashion Innovation Agency/HTC Vive curation), 101
Facebook Marketplace, launch, 16–17
Factory jobs (loss), automation (threat), 73
False narratives, challenge, 135
Farahi, Behnaz, 56–57, 59
Fashion
    AI, usage/opportunity, 157–158, 161–162, 184–185
    Aritzia, private equity involvement (impact), 82
    biotechnology, challenges, 200
    data, problem, 174–177
    fourth wall, smartphone camera (impact), 6–11
    future, 124–126
    industry, brands (relationship), 29
    local/global emphasis, 209–210
    materials, problem, 190–191
    technology, collision, 35–38
Fashion Art Toronto (FAT) event, 35, 37
Fashion Revolution, leverage, 29–30
Fashion Tech Berlin, 88–89
Fashion Week (New York), 7, 35
Fashion Week, transformation, 11
Fast fashion, 21–22, 76–78
    plastic, usage, 21–22
    problems, 80–83, 180
    social media, impact/blame, 79
Ferragni, Chiara (social media figure), 25
Fiber-optic dress, creation (Mann), 45f
Finch, FFFACE.ME (collaboration), 115
Fit
    assessment, spatial computing (usage), 117–120
    problems, automation (impact), 83
Fit-finding, 117–120
Focals (Kitchener AR glasses), 122
Forte VFX1, release, 98
Fortnite earnings, 143
Fournier, Pierre-Alexandre, 52
Friedman, Vanessa, 19
Friedrichs, Annabel, 75
Fulfillment, automation (relationship), 92–93
Fundawear project (Whitehouse), 55–56
Furstenberg, Diane von, 26, 35

G

Galloway, Scott, 19
Gaming, influence/integration/culture, 143–144, 153, 155
Garments, AI generation, 164–167
Garment workers, safety (absence), 81
Garten, Ariel, 43
Generative AI, usage/controversy, 165–172
Gerber (micro-factory setup), 85–86
GER Mood Sweater, 56–57, 56f
Gevinson, Tavi, 129
Giana, Alan (lawsuit), 179
Global carbon emissions, fashion industry (impact), 80
Global e-commerce startups, 4
Good on You blog, 21
Google Glass, 42, 121
Google Images (Google Image Search), 162–163
Google Lens, 164
Google, Levis (partnership), 50
Gorbould, Hilary (influencer), 26–27
Gordon, Sarah A., 75
Green, Nancy L., 74

Greenwashing, 63
Greenwold, Simon, 96
Grider, Daniel, 100–101
GTCO Fashion Weekend, 1, 3–4
Gucci
shows/film, 19–20, 97, 123–124, 140
virtual Gucci bag, sale, 145
GucciFest, launch, 28

H
Hadid, Bella (liquid polymer dress creation), 204–205
Hadid, Gigi (runway walk), 8
Hall, Matt, 141
Hanifa, show, 127–128, 131, 132, 155
Hanne, Leonie (social media figure), 25
Hartman, Kate, 40–41
Haul (Amazon release), 21
Haul culture, 79
Hennes & Mauritz (H&M), 14, 175, 180
AI usage, 176
Conscious Collection, 29, 63
Creator Studio, 166–167
unsold inventory, 80
workers, living wage (nonattainment), 80–81
Herpen, Iris van, 89–90
Hexoskin, founding, 52
Hildreth, Alexandra, 173–174
Hill, Brian, 82
Hinton, Geoffrey, 158
Hoover, Shannon/Maria Elena, 52
Horizon Worlds (Meta), 151
House of Alexander McQueen, Dijkstra (involvement), 88–89
HTC (Vive), Valve Corporation (partnership), 101
Humane AI, 195–196

I
IKEA, 14
IKEA Place, 116
Industrial Revolution, sewing maching (introduction), 75
Industry watchdogs, 29–30
Influencers, impact, 22–27
Influencing, career choice, 23
Instagram, images focus, 10–11
Instagram Shopping, introduction, 31–32
In-store AR, 106–109
Intellectual property (challenges), AI (impact), 181
InteraXon (wearable tech startup), 43
International Latex Corporation (ILC), 200
Internet (interpretation), AI (usage), 177–178
Internet-connected devices, 49
Internet of Things (IoT), 32, 35, 39, 66, 121, 155
hallmarks, 47
usage, 39–40
iPhone (Apple), 6
True Depth technology, 106
Iridescence, digital-only dress (sale), 131–133, 134
It girls, 23, 37

J
Jacquemus (see-now, buy-now approach), 19
Jaskowska, Johanna, 131–132
Jenner, Kris (interview), 27
Jenner, Kylie, 24–25
Jonze, Spike, 159
Just-in-time (JIT) production, Zara usage, 77

K
Kardashian, Kim, 23–24
Kate Spade, offering, 30–31
Keel Labs (Kelsun, usage), 197–198
Keeping Up with the Kardashians (TV series), 24–25
Kennedy, Joan, 18
Khaite, AR technology demonstration, 110
Kim, Jaesuk, 102
Kintematics Dress (Nervous System design/printing), 91
Kiva Systems (robot development), 92
KKW Beauty, founding, 24
Klukas, Chelsea, 52
Knight, Nick, 10
Kornit Digital (direct-to-fabric printing), 86
Kurtz, Adam, 78
Kylie Cosmetics, 25
Kyocera Visual Phone VP-210, introduction, 6–7

L
Lablaco, 95
Laser EyeTap, 42, 42f
Leaf (Bellabeat), 46
LED lights, usage, 53
Lenses (Snapchat introduction), 111–112
LeSavage, Halie, 81

Levi Strauss & Co, AI backlash, 167
Li, Fei-Fei, 184
Light Detection and Ranging (LiDAR) technology, usage, 117–120
Lim, Chriselle (social media figure), 25
Lindlad, Chris, 44
Lipner, Heather, 114
Literacy rates, increase, 5
Livestream shopping, e-commerce sales percentage, 32
Loftus, Daniella, 134
London Fashion Week, 110
Loomia (Maxey), 37
Lopez, Juan, 76
Louis Vuitton, 30–31
  Riot Games, partnership, 144
  VIA Tile Trunk, 155
Luce, Leanne, 161–162
Luckey, Palmer, 98
Lundstrüm, Mosha, 27

M

Machine learning, usage, 179
Made with Code (Google), 37
Magnetic Motion collections (Dijkstra), 90
Mainstream fashion, expense (reduction), 78–79
Maison Meta, AI Fashion Week, 166
MakeFashion, 52–55
Make It Yourself: Home Sewing, Gender, and Culture (Gordon), 75
Maker Festival Toronto, 48
Mann, Jenn, 46
Mann, Steve, 41–43, 41f
  Laser EyeTap, 42, 42f
Ma, Richard, 132
Market Movement, Burning Man (impact), 47
Marketplace setups, 4
Marks & Spencer
  AR T-shirts, 114
  Ecofab Limited client, 69–70
Marzano, Christine, 153
Mass customization, 83–87
Materials, problem, 190–191
Mattel Media (Mattel Interactive), launch, 83–84
Maxey, Madison, 37
McCartney, Stella (Bolt Threads collaboration), 194
McLuhan, Marshal, 6
Meagher, Luke, 27
Memento (lifelogging camera), 42
Memojis (Apple), 146
Meta, Essilor-Luxottica (collaboration), 122
Metamaterials, 187
Meta materials, 198–200
Metaverse (Zuckerberg), 148–151
Metaverse Fashion Week (Decentraland), 149–150
Met Gala, 91
  "Fashion in an Age of Technology," 54
  red-carpet event, 13
Meyer, Sébastien, 205
Micro-factories, 72–73, 83–87
Microsilk, usage, 193–194
Migicovsky, Eric, 46
Milan Fashion Week, 115
Milkis-Edwards, Marianna, 170
Millns, Andy, 99
Minimum order quantities (MOQs), absence, 85
Minkoff, Rebecca, 11, 19
  interactive mirrors, 107
  VR experience, Google Cardboard usage, 99–100
Mirror Mirror AI, generative AI (usage), 171–172
Misguided (online-only retailer), 21
Mobile commerce (m-commerce), 13–14
Mobile money transfers, acceptance, 2
Mob Wife, 18–20
Modenova, Natalia, 135
Modern Meadow, 196, 198
ModiFace, 104–105
Monchau, Nicholas de, 200
Moore, Tobin, 15
Moschino, offering, 30–31
Motorola V2288e, purchase, 30
Mugler (see-now, buy-now approach), 19
Muhkle, Christine, 26
Muse (InteraXon), 43
Mvuemba, Anifa, 127
MycoWorks, 194–195
Myhre, Helene, 178–179
Mylo (Bolt Threads), 194

N

Nadi X, Whitehouse launch, 55
Nanomaterials, 198–200
Nasty Gal, 17–18
Nayar, Dinesh, 167
Near-field communication (NFC) tags, online digital identity, 62–64
Neidlinger, Kristin, 56–57, 59

Nest (Google) thermostat, 39
Newton, Casey, 164
Nigeria
electronic payments, increase, 4–5
street vending, urban employment, 2
visiting/revisiting, 4
Non-fungible tokens (NFTs), 137–141, 153
North American Free Trade Agreement, garment production (location shift), 75–76
Nymi wristband, usage, 40

O

Obama, Barack (automation warning), 93
Ocean Medallion (Princess Cruises launch), 54–55
Oculus Quest, usage, 96
Oculus Rift campaign/usage, 98, 99, 101
O'Mahony, Marie, 51
OMSignal, Ralph Lauren (collaboration), 51–52
Online activism, 29–30
On-shore robotic manufacturing, 86
Ororo, 51
Oscars (red-carpet events), 13
Overconsumption, problem, 206

P

Pacific Jeans conference (Bangladesh), 69
Paris Fashion Week, 194
PDD Holdings, revenue report, 15
Pebble (smartwatch), Fitbit purchase, 46
Peer-to-peer marketplaces, 16–18
Peleg, Danit, 90
Pernot-Day, Peter, 180
Philipp Plein, crypto payments, 139
Philips, Peeter, 9
Phygital fashion future, 155–156
Pink Label Congo Collection, 127–128, 131, 155
Pinterest Lens, 164
Plate, Kristen, 88
Platforms (image-sharing capabilities), invention, 11
Plato's Atlantis (McQueen show), 9–10
Point-of-sale (POS) system, 2
Posen, Zac, 37
illuminated dress, creation, 54
Protolabs, collaboration, 91
Poshmark, 17, 207
Postman, Neil, 5
Prada, offering, 30–31
Prada x Samsung (designer phone), 31
Pretty Little Thing (online-only retailer), 21
Priestley, Miranda, 20
Printed to the Nines (Plate), 88
Project B, bra shopping technology, 120
Project Jacquard (Levis/Google partnership), 50
Project Primrose (Max Conference unveiling), 64–66
Project Runway Canada (Biddell), 36
PRONOUNCE, HTC Vive (collaboration), 101
Proxima dress (Dempsey), 49f
Pseudomorphs, 58
Public School, Autumn/Winter 2016 presentation, 35
Pugh, Gareth, 98

Q

Qiu, Elena, 79
QR codes, usage, 62–64, 110

R

Rabkin, Eugene, 27
Radio-frequency identification (RFID), 38–39
Ralph Lauren
OMSignal, collaboration, 51–52
see-now, buy-now approach, 19
virtual wardrobe, 147
Rana Plaza collapse (2013), 70–71
Ready Player One (Cline), 148, 149
Rebecca Minkoff
brand, 11
see-now, buy-now approach, 19
Redgert Comms, 26–27
Reishi, 194–195
Retail exhibitions, browsing, 4
Revenue opportunities, social media (impact), 4
Rhode Lip Case (iPhone case), 31
Roblox
branded experiences, collaborations, 144
physical goods sale, Shopify collaboration, 155
Robot-mounted cameras, usage, 9
Rocha, Coco, 37
Rodinia Generation (micro-factory example), 85
Roggero-Lovisi-Catherine, 196
Rosen, Jay, 22
Rowley, Aaron, 187–189
RTFKT, founding, 136–137
Runways

AR, impact, 109–111
digital design, usage, 127–128
iconic moments, 203–205

S
Sahan, Erinch, 208
Samsung Gear VR, usage, 100
Sartan, Anastasia, 170
Scam culture, 153–154
Schmidt, Eric, 162
Schmidt, Michael (3D-printed gown), 88
Scott, Kendra, 108–109
"Search by Image" (Google), 163–164
Selective laser sintering (SLS), usage, 88
Self-fashioning, 25
Sephora, 14
Virtual Artist launch, 103–104
Sewing machines, impact, 74–76
Shadel, JD, 21
Shapeways (3D-printed clothing), 90–91
Shapovalova, Daria, 135
Shein (SHEIN) (online retailer), 21, 22, 179–180
Shima Seiki (WHOLEGARMENT introduction), 74
Shipley, Emma J, 106
Shoppable content, 16, 32
Silicon Valley Fashion Week, 38, 44–46, 45f, 48
Singer, Isaac Merritt, 73
Singularity, concept, 158
Smart apparel production, requirements, 61
Smart fabrics, 51–52
Smart glasses, usage, 120–122
Smart Mirror (LG), examination, 108
Smartphones
democratization ability, 23
fashion, impact, 30–31
IBM invention, 6
impact, 6–11, 18–20
Smoke Dress, creation, 58
Snapchat, 146
dysmorphia, 113
Snapdragon Wear 1200 process (Qualcomm release), 121–122
SNKRS (Nike) app, 15–16
Snow Crash (*Stephenson*), 148
Social commerce, 16–19
Social media, 1
"Dress, the," 11–13
fashion, impact, 31–33
impact, 4, 28, 31–33
Social Web, read-write characteristic, 130
Song, Aimee (blogging), 25–26
Sophia the Robot (Hanson Robotics), 157–158
Sovo Gear (light-up hoodies), 49
Spark AR Studio, 103
Spatial computing, usage, 95, 117–120, 124–126
Speedfactories, abandonment, 86–87
Spider Dress (embedded protection system), 58
Stand-alone apps, suage, 116–117
Stein, Scott, 150
Stephenson, Neal, 148
Stitch Fix, launch, 170–171
StockX app, 123
Storytelling, 25, 62–63
Street vending (Nigeria urban employment), 2
Style Rookie (Gevinson), 129
Sweatshop Migrations: The Garment Industry Between Home and Shop (Green), 74

T
Taymour, Hillary, 165
Technology
application, 72
impact, 5–6
Teese, Dita Von, 88–90
Televisions, introduction, 5–6
Temu (mobile commerce domination), 15
Texprocess Americas (micro-factory), 85–86
Thom Browne X Samsung (designer phone), 31
ThredUp, computer vision (usage), 184–185
Thrift online shopping, downsides, 17
TikTok Shop, impact, 32
Tom Ford (see-now, buy-now approach), 19
Tomlinson, Lydia, 173
Tommy Hilfiger
brand, 8, 11
Ecofab Limited client, 69–70
Fall 2015 collection runway show (observation), Samsung Gear VR (usage), 100
see-now, buy-now approach, 19
Tommy Play (Roblox event), 144
Topshop (Fall/Winter fashion show), observation (Oculus Rift usage), 99
TranSwarm Entitites (3D printed dress), 89

Trends, smartphone (impact), 18–20
Trufelman, Avery, 27
Try-before-you-buy, 105, 108
Try-on experience, augmentation, 105–106
Turner, Chandra, 29
Tu, Robert, 48–49

U
Uddin, Mostafiz, 71
UGG, Snapchat lens (usage), 112
Ultra-fast fashion, 21–22
Uniqlo, 14
  magic mirror, 107
Unspun (3D weaving technology), 87, 185

V
Vaillant, Arnaud, 205
Valdsgaard, Michael, 116
Vega (Unspun weaving machine), 87
Versace x Nokia flip phone (designer phone), 31
Vinted (app), 17
Viral fashion, 11–13
Virtual Artist (ModiFace development), 104
Virtual reality (VR), 150
  experience, Google Cardboard (usage), 99–100
  usage, 97–103
Virtual try-on (VTO), 105, 133
  limitations, 108
Vloggers, attendees (interaction), 3–4
Voyeurism, 97–103

W
Walmart, 14
  Birkin (Wirkin) (Walmès), 180–181
Walsh, Natalie, 46, 47–48
Walton, Jennifer, 36–37, 36f
Wang, Wen (Tangible Media Group), 192
Warby Parker, Home Try-On Program/AR try-ons, 105–106
Warzecha, Monika, 81
Watkinson, John, 141
Wearable light, 37–38, 47
Wearables, 55–59, 64–66
Wearable technology, 39–40, 60–62
Wearable Wireless Webcam, 42
WearComp project, 42
We Are Wearables, 38, 40–43, 48, 59
Wear It Smart (conference), 51
Web 3.0, 128–131, 140, 151–152, 155
WebAR, usage, 116–117
Westfield, AR try-on experience, 106–107
West, Kayne, 24, 77
Whitehouse, Bilie, 55, 59
WHOLEGARMENT technology (Shima Seiki introduction), 74
Winkelmann, Mike (Beeple) (NFT sale), 137
Wintour, Anna, 35–36, 129
Wipprecht, Anouk, 57–59, 63
World Maker Faire, 57
Wristables, term (usage), 55

Y
Yamamoto, Kansai, 208

Z
Zaful (online-only retailer), 22
Zara, 14, 163, 180
  just-in-time (JIT) production usage, 77
  knockoffs, 77–78
  operations, expansion, 76–77, 175
  popularity, increase, 8
Zendaya, outfit (change), 13
Zornow, Jonathan, 87
Zuckerberg, Mark, 10, 148–151